The Complete Sybase ASE Quick Reference Guide

ASE versions 12.0, 12.5.4 & 15.0.1
4th edition

Rob Verschoor

Sypron Publications

The Complete Sybase ASE Quick Reference Guide

ASE versions 12.0, 12.5.4 & 15.0.1
4th edition

by Rob Verschoor

ISBN 90-806117-1-9

Published by:
Sypron B.V.
P.O. Box 10695
2501 HR Den Haag
The Netherlands
Internet **www.sypron.nl**
Email **sypron@sypron.nl**

Printed in The Netherlands

First edition	:	January 2001	(ASE 11.9 & 12.0)
Second edition	:	March 2002	(ASE 11.9, 12.0 & 12.5)
Third edition	:	July 2004	(ASE 12.0, 12.5, 12.5.1 & 12.5.2)
Fourth edition	:	August 2006	(ASE 12.0, 12.5.4 & 15.0.1)

Contents

Introduction 5

About this Quick Reference Guide 5
ASE versions covered in this edition 5
ASE server page size 5
How complete is 'Complete' ? 6
How dynamic is 'Dynamic' ? 6
How to use this Quick Reference Guide 6
Syntax conventions 6
Acronyms 7
Errata 7
Electronic version of code samples 7
Undocumented commands: warning & disclaimer 7

Developer Topics 8
1. Datatypes 8
2. Identifiers 9
3. Quotes & Comments 9
4. Operators 9
5. Datatype conversion functions 10
6. Date & Time 10
7. String functions 12
8. System functions 14
9. Mathematical functions 18
10. Trigonometric functions 18
11. Login/user/role functions 19
12. Miscellaneous functions 20
13. Text & Image data 20
14. Aggregate functions 21
15. DML statements 21
16. Joins 24
17. Tables 25
18. Encrypted Columns (12.5.3a) 28
19. Indexes 30
20. Referential Integrity Constraints 31
21. Object storage properties 32
22. Views 33
23. Rules & Defaults 33
24. Stored Procedures 34
25. Triggers 35
26. Identity columns 37
27. Programming & flow control 38
28. Cursors 40
29. Example of cursor programming 42
30. Transactions 42
31. Example of transaction programming 43
32. Locking 44
33. Java in ASE (SQLJ) 46
34. XML (XPath/XQuery/SQLX) in ASE (12.5.1) 47
35. Web Services (15.0) 49
36. Miscellaneous stored procedures 51
37. Settings affecting query results 52
38. Settings affecting query plans 53
39. Settings for displaying query plan information 55
40. Miscellaneous settings 56

DBA Topics 57
41. Database devices & dump devices 57
42. Device mirroring 58
43. Creating & maintaining databases 58
44. Temporary databases (12.5.0.3) 60
45. Dumping & loading databases 61
46. Segments 63
47. Thresholds 64
48. Logins 64
49. Database users 67
50. Roles 68

51. Permissions ... 69
52. Row-level access control (12.5) ... 71
53. Managing server configuration options ... 72
54. Memory allocation in ASE 12.0 ... 74
55. Memory allocation in ASE 12.5+ ... 74
56. Named caches & buffer pools ... 74
57. Update statistics ... 76
58. sp_sysmon ... 77
59. Reorg ... 78
60. Languages & messages ... 78
61. Character set & sort order ... 80
62. Setting up sybsyntax, pubs3 & sybsystemprocs ... 80
63. Configuring parallel processing ... 81
64. Miscellaneous DBA commands ... 82

Advanced DBA Topics ... 84
65. Setting up the 'dbccdb' database ... 84
66. 'dbccdb' stored procedures ... 84
67. Supported DBCC commands ... 86
68. Unsupported DBCC commands ... 88
69. ASE Traceflags ... 93
70. Configuring remote access with RPCs ... 94
71. Configuring remote access with CIS ... 95
72. Component Integration Services (CIS) features ... 95
73. XP Server ... 99
74. Lock promotion ... 99
75. Auditing ... 100
76. Database recovery ... 102
77. Resource limits ('Resource Governor') ... 103
78. Logical Process Manager ('Execution Classes') ... 104
79. Abstract Query Plans ... 105
80. Query metrics capture (15.0) ... 106
81. MDA tables / monitoring tables (12.5.0.3) ... 107
82. Advanced configuration parameters ... 107
83. Replication Server ... 108
84. ASE Replicator (12.5) ... 108
85. Job Scheduler (12.5.1) ... 108
86. Enterprise Java Beans (12.5 only) ... 108
87. Shared memory dumps ... 109

Miscellaneous Topics ... 110
88. The interfaces file ... 110
89. Server programs ... 110
90. Client programs ... 112
91. ASE environment variables ... 115
92. Running servers as Windows NT services ... 116
93. Global variables: Session-specific ... 117
94. Global variables: Server-wide, non-static ... 118
95. Global variables: Server-wide, static ... 119
96. Logical keys ... 120
97. Catalog stored procedures ... 120
98. Issues with BCP-in ... 121
99. Minimally logged operations ... 121
100. Monitor Server & Historical Server ... 121
101. ASE limits ... 122
102. ASE licensing ... 122
103. Essential DBA tasks ... 124
104. ASE resources on the Internet ... 124

Index ... 125

Introduction

My first experience with Sybase was in 1989, when I worked on a project using version 3 of Sybase SQL Server running on Stratus hardware. At the time, I thought this client-server database thing was pretty complicated stuff, but the enormous number of features in today's Adaptive Server Enterprise (ASE) make that old software look nostalgically simple. In fact, when ASE 11.5 was released a few years ago, I found out there was an upper limit to the amount of brain cells I could allocate for remembering the details of all those ASE commands, functions and procedures. As a survival strategy, I started writing down the things I forgot most often, and this evolved into the ASE Quick Reference Guide you are reading right now.
This book will provide you with the information you need most often when working with ASE: it contains all documented ASE commands, functions and system stored procedures you might need in practice; it also contains some useful undocumented commands. A detailed index is included, so you can find your information quickly. Whether you are a DBA or a developer, this book has the answers you're looking for.

First edition (January 2001)
My special thanks go to David Owen, for sending the email message that started it all off; to Anthony Mandic and Joop Bruggink, for reviewing and commenting draft versions; and to Simone, for her endless support and countless cups of tea.

Second edition (March 2002)
The second edition has been updated for ASE 12.5.0.1, and contains numerous improvements and additions. As a result, the number of pages has increased, but it still fits in your pocket! I'd like to thank everyone who bought a copy of the first edition, provided feedback, or stimulated the continuation of this book in other ways.

Third edition (July 2004)
The third edition has been updated for ASE 12.5.2, and is even more complete than before. To keep the size of the book unchanged while adding many new and existing commands, some less common topics, like 'Logical keys' and 'Catalog stored procedures', had to be compressed. Since there is now a separate quick reference guide for Replication Server (see **www.sypron.nl/repqr**), most of that section is gone, too.
I hope this edition will be even more useful than the previous ones.

Fourth edition (August 2005)
The fourth edition has been updated for ASE 12.5.4 ESD#1 and 15.0.1, and is getting ever more complete: new sections have been added to cover XML processing and web services, and the sections about session-specific settings have been restructured. Also, improvements were made in many sections. As a result, 20 pages had to be added. I'm sure this book is still small enough though, and I hope it continues to be a great DBA companion.

Rob Verschoor
Rotterdam, August 2005

About this Quick Reference Guide

ASE versions covered in this edition
The information in this ASE Quick Reference Guide applies to ASE version 12.0 or later, and to a Unix/Linux environment, except where indicated otherwise. Much of the information is still valid for older ASE versions, although this is not indicated explicitly.
In this Quick Reference Guide, notations like '**(15.0)**' indicate new or changed functionality as of the corresponding ASE version (obviously, 15.0 in this example); likewise, '**(pre-12.5)**' indicates functionality existing until version 12.0, but not in 12.5.
This fourth edition is updated for ASE 12.5.4 ESD#1 and ASE 15.0.1. Note that '15.0' should be read as 'up to and including 15.0 ESD#2'. Also note that some new functionality in 12.5.4 was not yet available in 15.0.1 as this book went to press.

ASE server page size
Starting with ASE 12.5, an ASE server can have a page size of 2Kb, 4Kb, 8Kb or 16Kb. In this book, the words 'server page size' refer to this feature. This page size is specified when the server is created. In pre-12.5, the server page size is always 2Kb.

How complete is 'Complete' ?

I have called this ASE Quick Reference Guide 'Complete', because it covers almost all ASE issues you may need in daily practice. However, it is obvious that a 140-page booklet simply cannot contain the same amount of information as a bookshelf filled with full-size ASE manuals -- no matter how small you print. For practical reasons, the following information has therefore been omitted:

- The exact permissions required to execute a command are not included; in any case, the server will tell you when you don't have the right permissions by raising an error message.
- Many (but not all) server configuration options are included. For those, it is indicated whether the option is 'static', 'dynamic' or 'semi-dynamic' (see below).
- Details about the language for describing abstract query plans are not included.
- Some features are covered only partly or not at all, such as High Availability, DTM, Unicode, Full Text Search, Advanced Security Mechanisms, LDAP, PAM, Job Scheduler, SNMP, and the Real-Time Database messaging features.
- Sybase Replication Server is covered only minimally; please refer to my other book, *'The Complete Sybase Replication Server Quick Reference Guide'* (**www.sypron.nl/repqr**) instead.
- Installation of ASE is not covered (see the platform-specific installation guide that is included with your ASE deliverables).

Also, note that this Quick Reference Guide is not a tutorial: the reader is expected to be familiar with the basic concepts of ASE.

How dynamic is 'Dynamic' ?

In ASE 12.5, ASE server configuration has been significantly improved: many configuration options related to memory allocation have become 'dynamic' instead of 'static' as in 12.0 and earlier versions. However, DBAs should be aware of the following behaviour: some of these new dynamic configuration options are not fully dynamic when their configured value is decreased: any memory that was already allocated for the configuration option, but would be redundant for the new, lower configured value, is not released until the next ASE restart (and until this restart, this memory can therefore not be used for increasing other config options); in this Quick Reference Guide, such configuration options are indicated as 'semi-dynamic' (but **sp_configure** and **sp_helpconfig** will display 'dynamic'), while fully dynamic configuration options are indicated as 'dynamic'.

How to use this Quick Reference Guide

All information in this ASE Quick Reference Guide is grouped by topic, such as 'Triggers' or 'Locking' (see the table of contents). Information that is relevant to more than one topic is repeated; for example, **sp_rename** can be used on different types of objects and is therefore included in the sections 'Tables', 'Triggers' and 'Stored Procedures', among others.

The index contains all commands, functions, stored procedures and global variables in alphabetical order. Many references are included in the index more than once; for example, **sp_extendsegment** is also included as **extendsegment, sp_**.

Each command description includes the things you need most: the syntax, a short description of the functionality and parameters, and often an example. This will usually be sufficient; when you need more details or background information, see the *ASE Reference Manual* (which is part of the standard ASE documentation). The section 'ASE Resources on the Internet' on page 124 contains some further suggestions for finding ASE-related information.

Syntax conventions

The syntax notation follows commonly used conventions, and will usually be self-explanatory. Still, here are some guidelines:

- Literal text, such as keywords or specific strings, is printed in **bold**. Placeholders for variables or parameters are printed in *italic* - you should replace this with something. For example: **drop table** *table_name*.
- Parentheses - '**(**' and '**)**' - and commas are part of the command itself. Square brackets - '**[**' and '**]**' -, curly brackets - '**{**' and '**}**' - and pipes - '**|**' - are never part of a command, but indicate optional parts of the command.
- In some cases, the syntax has been simplified for practical reasons. For example, the **alter table** command, which has a rather complex syntax, has been split up into smaller commands relevant to a specific topic, such as **alter table**...**lock** and **alter table**...**partition**. Also, non-essential bits of syntax have sometimes been omitted for better readability; for example [**NULL** | *table_name*] is used, though [{**NULL** | *table_name*}] would have been more formally correct.
- ASE often allows object names to be qualified with an owner name and/or a database name. However, these optional qualifiers have been omitted from the command syntax for better readability. When using a qualified object name as a

parameter for a stored procedure, note that this must be enclosed in quotes (e.g. **sp_help 'dbo.my_table'**).

- For stored procedures, the parameter names have been chosen for maximum clarity, and may therefore be different from the actual parameter names in the procedure source code. When you want to specify a parameter 'by name', (i.e. **sp_helprotect @role_name = 'employee_role'**), use **sp_help** to determine the parameter's actual name.

Acronyms

The following acronyms are used in this Quick Reference Guide:

ASE	Adaptive Server Enterprise
APL	**allpages** lock scheme
DOL	Data-Only Lock scheme(s) (i.e. **datapages** and/or **datarows**)
DDL	SQL 'Data Definition Language' statements (**create table**, **create database**, etc.)
DML	SQL 'Data Manipulation Language' statements (**select**, **insert**, **update**, **delete**, etc.)
DTM	Distributed Transaction Management
JAR	Java Archive file format, containing compiled Java bytecode
HA	High Availability
OS	Operating System
RI	Referential Integrity
T-SQL	Transact-SQL, the (trademarked) SQL implementation by Sybase
db_id	a database ID as stored in **master..sysdatabases**
db_name	a database name
ptn_id	**(15.0)** a partition ID as stored in **master..syspartitions**
ptn_name	**(15.0)** a partition name
spid	a session ID (as displayed by **sp_who**, for example)
suid	a login ID as stored in **master..syslogins**
uid	a database user ID as stored in **sysusers**
a.k.a.	also known as
➢p.28	see page 28

Errata

Errata will be available on-line at **www.sypron.nl/qr/errata.html**. Please email any errors or comments to **qr@sypron.nl**.

Electronic version of code samples

The code samples and the more complex queries described in this book are available electronically at **www.sypron.nl/qr/examples.html**.

Undocumented commands: warning & disclaimer

Most information in this ASE Quick Reference Guide concerns documented and supported functionality. However, some useful undocumented or unsupported commands are included as well. Please note that using undocumented or unsupported commands may constitute a risk: such commands may have unexpected side effects, may cause irreversible damage to your databases and/or lead to loss of data. Use such commands entirely at your own risk, and do not contact Sybase Technical Support for assistance. When a command is not documented (and therefore not supported), this is indicated in the description.

In any case, neither the author, nor the publisher, nor Sybase Inc. (nor its subsidiaries), assume any responsibility for errors or omissions, nor do they accept any liabilities for damages resulting from the use of the information in this book.

Developer Topics

1. Datatypes

System datatype	Minimum, maximum	Bytes of storage
tinyint	0 , 255	1
smallint	-32768 , 32767	2
(15.0) unsigned smallint	0 , 65535	2
int[eger]	-2147483648 , 2147483647	4
(15.0) unsigned int[eger]	0 , 4294967295	4
(15.0) bigint	-2^{63}, 2^{63} - 1 (19 digits)	8
(15.0) unsigned bigint	0 , 2^{64} - 1 (20 digits)	8
bit	0 , 1 (cannot be **NULL**)	1 (for max. 8 cols)
numeric [(*precision* [, *scale*])] **decimal** [(*precision* [, *scale*])] (*precision* + *scale* ≤ 38)	-10^{38}, 10^{38} -1	2 - 17
money	-922337203685477.5808, +922337203685477.5807	8
smallmoney	-214748.3648, 214748.3647	4
float [(*precision*)] *precision* ≤ 48 **real** **double precision**	these datatypes are floating point numbers; their range and the amount of required storage is platform-dependent	
datetime precision=3 millisec	01-Jan-1753 , 31-Dec-9999	8
smalldatetime precision=1 minute	01-Jan-1900 , 06-Jun-2079	4
(12.5.1) date	01-Jan-0001 , 31-Dec-9999	4
(12.5.1) time precision=3 millisec	12:00AM , 11:59:59.999PM	4
char(*n*) **(pre-12.5)** *n* ≤ 255	any character value	*n*
varchar(*n*) **(12.5)** *n* ≤ 16296	any character value	1..*n*
nchar(*n*)	any character value	*n**@@ncharsize**
nvarchar(*n*)	any character value	1..*n**@@ncharsize**
binary(*n*) **(pre-12.5)** *n* ≤ 255	any binary value	*n*
varbinary(*n*) **(12.5)** *n* ≤ 16296	any binary value	1..*n*
timestamp	unique, assigned by ASE	8
(12.5) unichar(*n*) *n* ≤ 8148	any Unicode value	*n**@@unicharsize**
(12.5) univarchar(*n*)	any Unicode value	1..*n**@@unicharsize**
(15.0) unitext	any Unicode value	max. 2Gb
text	any character value	max. 2Gb
image	any binary value	max. 2Gb

Note 1: For date & time values (**[small]datetime; time**), ASE does not store time zone information; if needed, applications must handle this themselves (also ➢p.11).
Note 2: In 12.5, the maximum length of (**var**)**char** and (**var**)**binary** columns depends on the server page size and the table's lock scheme (see **dbcc serverlimits** on page 92); for string expressions, local variables and stored procedure parameters, the max. length is 16384 bytes, independent of the server page size.
Note 3: Java classes can also be used as datatypes; ➢p.46.
Note 4: a **timestamp** column always has a unique value within a database. Note that this value is essentially an internal counter and is unrelated to real-life clock time.
Note 5: **identity** columns are a special case of numeric/integer datatypes; ➢p.37.
Note 6: in 15.0, **unsigned tinyint** can be used, though this is identical to **tinyint**.

sp_addtype *type_name*, **'***datatype* [(*length*) | (*precision* [, *scale*])] **'** [, **'identity'** | **'null'** | **'not null'**]
In the current database, creates a user-defined datatype named *type_name*, based on a system datatype. A user-defined datatype can be used for columns, local variables and procedure parameters. Also, rules and defaults can be bound to it.
Examples:

```
sp_addtype my_type, 'numeric(5,2)', 'not null'
sp_bindrule rule_gt_zero, my_type
declare @var1 my_type
create table my_table (a my_type, b int)
```

sp_droptype *type_name*
Drops the specified user-defined datatype, which must not be in use.

sp_help *type_name*
Displays the specified user-defined datatype. To display a list of all user-defined datatypes, use this query: **select name from systypes where usertype > 99**

2. *Identifiers*

Identifiers can be up to 30 characters long (30 bytes in multi-byte character sets). ASE is case-sensitive for identifiers by default; for case-insensitive identifiers, install a case-insensitive sort order with the **charset** utility (➢p.112).
With **set quoted_identifier on**, identifiers may contain spaces, special characters etc., if the identifier is enclosed in double quotes (up to 28 characters). In 12.5.1, identifiers can be enclosed in square brackets (up to 28 characters).
Examples: **set quoted_identifier on**
create table "This is my table!" ("My Column!" int, YourColumn int)

(12.5.1) select [name] from [sysobjects] where [type] = 'U'

3. *Quotes & Comments*

/ ...comment... */*
Comment delimiters, which can extend over multiple lines; they may also be nested.

-- *a comment until the end of the line*
Single-line comment delimiter. All text after **--** until the end of the line, is a comment.

Quotes as string delimiters
Character constants (often referred to as 'strings') must be enclosed in either single or double quotes; the opening and closing quote must be identical. When the delimiter quote appears twice, it evaluates to a single character in the string.
Examples: **'abc'** or **"abc"** -- these strings are identical
"'" -- a string consisting of a single quote, enclosed in double quotes
'He said: "How are you ?" ' -- a string containing double quotes
"He said: ""How are you ?"" " -- the same string, but in double quotes

Line continuation character
Strings in T-SQL statements can span multiple lines when using the line continuation character '\'. This character will not be part of the actual string.
Example: **exec(' print "This is a pretty long string, but fortunately, \
we can use two lines for it !" ')**
Without '\', this example is still valid T-SQL, but the string contains a newline.

4. *Operators*

Numeric operators
For all numeric datatypes, the operators **+**, **-**, *****, **/** are available. In pre-12.5.4, **%** (modulo) is available for **tinyint**, **smallint** and **int** only; in 12.5.4, also for **numeric**, **float**, etc. Additional mathematical functions exist, such as **abs()** and **power()**;➢p.18.

String operators
The only string operator is **+**, which concatenates two strings (**||** is identical to **+**, but is undocumented). For string functions (like **substring()**),➢p.12.

Logical operators
Logical operators are used in logical expressions, which evaluate to true or false (except for some cases involving **NULL** values, where the result can be unknown).

- **=, <> , != , > , >= , <, =<, !>** (not greater than), **!<** (not less than) - comparisons
- **and**, **or** - combines two logical expressions: **if (@a > @b) and (@x != @y)**
- **not** - negates a logical expression: **if not (@a > @b)**
- [**not**] **like** - a pattern matching operator; see next paragraph.
- [**not**] **in** - matches a list of values: **where a in (3,4,5)** - this is equivalent to **where a=3 or a=4 or a=5**
- [**not**] **between** - matches an interval (incl. boundaries): **where a between @x and @y** - this is equivalent to **where a >= @x and a <= @y**
- ***=, =*** - outer join operators; ➢p.25.
- **exists**, **any**, **all**, **in** - subquery operators; ➢p.23.
- **is** [**not**] **NULL** - matches (or not) a **NULL** value

Pattern matching operators
The **like** operator allows pattern matching on [**var**]**char** and [**uni**]**text** data. It uses the wildcards **%** (matches any string of zero or more characters), **_** (underscore; matches a single character), **[** and **]** (to specify a range or series of characters to match) and **^** (specifies character(s) not to match). To match a wildcard character itself, use the **escape** clause to make a subsequent wildcard a normal character instead.
Examples: **select name from my_table where name like '%[Ss]mith%'**
select name from my_table where name like '_mith%'

select name from my_table where name not like '%~_%' escape '~'
if @var like '[^a-zA-Z0-9]' print '@var contains non-letters/digits'

The **patindex()** function on page 13 also provides pattern matching functionality.

Bit operators

The following bit operators are available (for **int/smallint/tinyint** operands only):

Operator	Logical operation	Example
&	bitwise AND	**select 5 & 3** returns **1 (0101 & 0011 = 0001)**
|	bitwise OR	**select 5 | 2** returns **7 (0101 | 0010 = 0111)**
^	bitwise EXOR	**select 5 ^ 3** returns **6 (0101 ^ 0011 = 0110)**
~	bitwise NOT	**select ~1** returns **-2 (~0001 = 1110)**

5. Datatype conversion functions

convert (*datatype* **[(** *length* **)|(** *precision* [, *scale*]**)]** [*nullability*], *expression* [, *style*]**)**
Converts *expression* to the specified *datatype*, provided the value of *expression* is compatible with *datatype*. *datatype* can be any datatype, except a user-defined datatype. When a target datatype of **varchar** is specified without a length, the result will be just as long as necessary (but at most 30 characters). The *nullability* of the result datatype can be specified explicitly as **null** or **not null**. *style* is only used for formatting of date/time data (➢p.10) and **[small]money** data (see below).
Examples: **select convert(numeric(10, 2), @float_value)**
select convert(varchar, 123) returns **'123'**
select col1 = convert(int null, 123) into t1

For **[small]money** data, specifying **1** for *style* formats a value with commas as 1000's separators (undocumented). By default, no such separators are included.
Example: **declare @v money select @v = 98765432**
select convert(varchar, @v, 1) returns **98,765,432.00**

In 15.0, **isdate()** / **isnumeric()** can validate some datatypes before conversion;➢p.12.

(12.5.1) cast (*expression* **as** *datatype* [**(** *length* **)|(** *precision* [, *scale*]**)**] **)**
Identical to **convert()**, but without the *style* and *nullability* options.
Example: **select cast(123 as varchar)** returns **'123'**

hextoint (*hex_string* **)**
Returns the platform-independent integer equivalent of a hexadecimal string, which must be either a character expression or a valid hexadecimal string, with or without a '0x' prefix, enclosed in quotes. Example: **select hextoint('0x1F')** returns **31**

(15.0) hextobigint (*hex_string* **)**
Same as **hextoint()**, but converts to a **bigint** datatype.

inttohex (*integer_expression* **)**
Returns the platform-independent hexadecimal equivalent of the *integer_expression*, without a leading '0x'. Example: **select inttohex(31)** returns **0000001F**

(15.0) biginttohex (*integer_expression* **)**
Same as **inttohex()**, but converts from a **bigint** datatype.

bintostr (*binary_value* **)**
Converts a **(var)binary** value to a **varchar(255)** string (undocumented).
Example: **select bintostr(0x1A0F)** returns **'1a0f'**

strtobin (*hex_string* **)**
Converts a hexadecimal string to a **varbinary(255)** value (undocumented).
Example: **select strtobin('1A0F')** returns **0x1a0f**

6. Date & Time

Date/time formatting

Expressions of datatypes **datetime**, **smalldatetime**, **date** and **time** can be formatted as a character expression with the **convert()** function:
convert (*char-or-varchar-datatype*, *datetime_expression*, *style* **)**
style specifies the formatting, as in the table below. When *style* < 100, the digits for 'century' are suppressed (except for styles **0** and **16**). The default *style* is **0**.

style	**Date/time formatting**
0, 100	Apr 15 2006 5:41PM
1, 101	04/15/2006
2, 102	2006.04.15
3, 103	15/04/2006
4, 104	15.04.2006
5, 105	15-04-2006
6, 106	15 Apr 2006
7, 107	Apr 15, 2006
8, 108	17:41:52
9, 109	Apr 15 2006 5:41:52:283PM
10, 110	04-15-2006
11, 111	2006/04/15

style	**Date/time formatting**
12, 112	20060415
13, **(12.5.1)** 113	2006/15/04
14, **(12.5.1)** 114	04/2006/15
15, **(12.5.1)** 115	15/2006/04
(12.5.1) 16, 116	Apr 15 2006 17:41:52
(12.5.1) 17	5:41PM
(12.5.1) 18	17:41
(12.5.1) 19	5:41:52:283PM
(12.5.1) 20	17:41:52:283
(12.5.3) 21, 22	06/04/15
(15.0) 23	2006-04-15T17:41:52

Example: some time ago, **select convert (char(11), getdate(), 106)** returned the string **'15 Apr 2006'**.

getdate()
Returns the current date and time on the system where this ASE server is running. Note that this time may be different from the date/time on the client system. Also note that ASE does not store or show time zone information (also see **getutcdate()** below).

(12.5.3) getutcdate()
Returns the current UTC (aka. GMT) date and time on the system where this ASE server is running. The UTC adjustment depends on the time zone setting on the ASE host. ASE does not show or store the time zone, but the ASE host's time zone offset (in minutes) can be calculate with **select datediff (mi, getdate(), getutcdate())**

(12.5.1) current_date()
Returns the current date on the system where this ASE server is running.

(12.5.1) current_time()
Returns the current time on the system where this ASE server is running.

(12.5.0.3) day(*date_time_value* **)**
Returns the day number for the specified date. Equivalent to **datepart(dd, ...)**.

(12.5.0.3) month(*date_time_value* **)**
Returns the month number for the specified date. Equivalent to **datepart(mm, ...)**.

(12.5.0.3) year(*date_time_value* **)**
Returns the year for the specified date. Equivalent to **datepart(yy, ...)**.

datename (*datepart*, *date_time_value***)**
Returns the *datepart* (see below table) of a date/time value as an ASCII string.
Example: **select datename(dw, '15-Apr-2006')** returns **'Saturday'**.

datepart (*datepart*, *date_time_value***)**
Returns the *datepart* (see below table) of a date/time value as an integer.
Example: **select datepart(dw, '15-Apr-2006')** returns **7**.

datediff (*datepart*, *date_time_1*, *date_time_2***)**
Returns the difference between two date/time values (*date_time_2* - *date_time_1*), expressed in the specified *datepart* unit (see below table).
Example: **select datediff(dd, '15-Apr-2003', '15-Apr-2004')** returns **366**.

dateadd (*datepart*, *nr_units*, *date_time_value***)**
Returns the date/time value produced by adding *nr_units datepart* units (see below table) to the date/time value specified. To subtract, specify a negative number.
Example: **select dateadd(dd, 21,'15-Apr-2006')** returns **'May 6, 2006 12:00 AM'**.

Possible values for *datepart* in the above functions are as follows:

Full name	**Abbrev.**	**Values returned by datepart() & datename()**
year	yy	1 - 9999 for **date**; 1753-9999 for **datetime**; 1900-2079 for **smalldatetime**
quarter	qq	1 - 4
month	mm	1 - 12
week	wk	1 - 54
day	dd	1 - 31
dayofyear	dy	1 - 366
weekday	dw	1 - 7 (Sunday - Saturday by default)

hour	hh	0 - 23
minute	mi	0 - 59
second	ss	0 - 59
millisecond	ms	0 - 999
calweekofyear	cwk	1 - 53
calyearofweek	cyr	see 'year/yy' above
caldayofweek	cdw	1 - 7 (Monday-Sunday)

set datefirst *day_nr*
Sets the first day of the week (1..7, 1=Sunday) for the current session. In 12.5.0.3, **@@datefirst** contains the current setting.

set dateformat *fmt_string*
Sets the day-month-year order to be used when converting date values in the current session. *fmt_string* can be **'mdy'**, **'myd'**, **'dmy'**, **'dym'**, **'ydm'** or **'ymd'.** In 12.5, the current setting can be found with **get_appcontext ('SYS_SESSION', 'dateformat')**.

(15.0.1) isdate *(character_expression* **)**
Returns **1** if the expression is a valid **datetime** value, and **0** if not. ➢p.12.

7. String functions

In ASE 12.5, the maximum length of a string expression is 16384 bytes, irrespective of the server page size. In pre-12.5, this maximum is 255 bytes.

ascii (*character_expression* **)**
Returns the ASCII code (in decimal; 0..255) for the first character in the expression. Example: **select ascii('ABC')** returns **65** (= hex 41).

char (*integer_expression* **)**
Converts a single-byte integer value to a single character. **char()** is the inverse of **ascii()**. *integer_expression* must be between 0 and 255.
Examples: **char(65)** = **'A'**; **char(10)** = newline; **char(9)** = tab.

charindex (*character_expression_1*, *character_expression_2* **)**
Searches the 2nd expression for the first occurrence of the 1st expression and returns an integer representing its starting position, or 0 if it is not found. If the 1st expression contains wildcards, these are interpreted literally (also see **patindex()** below).
Example: **select charindex('b', 'abc')** returns **2**.

char_length (*character_expression* **)**
Returns the number of characters in a character expression or **text** column. For variable-length data in a table column, **char_length()** strips the expression of trailing blanks before counting the number of characters. For multibyte character sets, use the system function **datalength()** to determine the number of bytes.
Example: **select char_length('abcd')** returns **4**.

compare (*char_expr_1*, *char_expr_2*, [*collation_name* | *collation_nr*] **)**
Compares the two character expressions using the specified collation (default is binary collation). Returns 1 if *char_expr_1* > *char_expr_2*; -1 if *char_expr_2* > *char_expr_1*; 0 if *char_expr_1* = *char_expr_2*.

difference (*character_expression_1*, *character_expression_2* **)**
Calculates the soundex values (see **soundex()** below) for each of the character expressions, and returns the integer difference between the values. Note: this is not the same as the difference between the two character expressions themselves !.

(15.0.1) isdate (*character_expression* **)**
Returns **1** if the expression is a valid **datetime** value, and **0** if not. The current **set dateformat** setting is taken into account if needed.
Examples: **select isdate('29-Feb-2006')** returns **0**
select isdate('29/02/08') returns **1** (with **set dateformat dmy**)

(15.0.1) isnumeric (*character_expression* **)**
Returns **1** if the expression is a valid integer, numeric, float or money value; **0** if not.
Example: **select isnumeric('123'), isnumeric('0.5'), isnumeric('$987.65')** returns 3***1**
select case isnumeric(col_a) when 1 then convert(int, col_a) else NULL end from my_table

(12.5.0.3) left (*expression*, *integer_expression* **)**
Returns the *integer_expression* left-most characters of the specified character or

binary *expression*. Equivalent to **substring(** *expression*, **1**, *integer_expression* **)**.

(12.5.0.3) len (*expression* **)**
Returns the number of characters in *expression*. Equivalent to **char_length(**...**)**.

lower (*character_expression* **)**
Converts the expression to lowercase. Example: **select lower('aB1')** returns **'ab1'**.

ltrim (*character_expression* **)**
Removes leading blanks from the character expression.
Example: **select '[' + ltrim('   abc') + ']'** returns **'[abc]'**.

patindex ('%*pattern*%', *char_expression* [**using** { **bytes** | **chars** | **characters** }] **)**
Returns an integer representing the starting position of the first occurrence of *pattern* in *char_expression*; returns 0 if *pattern* is not found. By default, **patindex()** returns the offset in characters. To return the offset in bytes (for multibyte character sets) specify **using bytes**. The **%** wildcard character must precede and follow *pattern*, except when searching for first or last characters. **patindex()** can also be used on **text** data.
Example: **select patindex('%c%', 'abcde')** returns **3**.

replicate (*char_expression*, *integer_expression* **)**
Returns a string containing *char_expression* repeated the *integer_expression* number of times or as many times as will fit in the maximum string length, whichever is less.
Example: **select replicate('xyz', 3)** returns **'xyzxyzxyz'**

reverse (*expression* **)**
Returns the reversed character or binary *expression*.
Example: **select reverse('abcd')** returns **'dcba'**

right (*expression*, *integer_expression* **)**
Returns the *integer_expression* right-most characters of the specified character or binary *expression*. Example: **select right('abcdefg', 3)** returns **'efg'**

rtrim (*character_expression* **)**
Removes trailing blanks from the character expression.
Example: **select '[' + rtrim('abc   ') + ']'** returns **'[abc]'**.

soundex (*character_expression* **)**
Returns a 4-character soundex code for character strings. Note: this is a rather rudimentary implementation of a soundex algorithm, which should not be mistaken for a full-fledged soundex-based retrieval system.

sortkey (*character_expression*, [*collation_name* | *collation_nr*] **)**
Returns a **varbinary** hex string representing the character expression according to the specified collation (default is binary collation).

space (*integer_expression* **)**
Returns a string containing *integer_expression* spaces. **space(0)** returns **NULL**.

str (*numeric_expression* [, *length* [,*nr_decimals*]] **)**
Returns a right-adjusted character representation of the floating point number. *length* (default=10) sets the number of characters to be returned (including the decimal point, all decimal digits, and blanks); *nr_decimals* (default=0) sets the number of decimal digits to be returned. **str()** rounds the decimal portion of the number so that the results fit within the specified length.
Example: **select str(123.45, 6, 2)** returns **'123.45'**.

(12.5.0.3) str_replace (*character_expr_1*, *character_expr_2*, *character_expr_3* **)**
Replaces all occurrences of *character_expr_2* in *character_expr_1* with *character_expr_3*. Note that **NULL** for the 3rd parameter works differently (better) in 12.5.1.
Examples: **select str_replace('abcbd', 'b', 'XYZ')** returns **'aXYZcXYZd'**
(12.5.0.3) select str_replace('abcbd', 'b', NULL) returns **NULL**
(12.5.1) select str_replace('abcbd', 'b', NULL) returns **'acd'**

stuff (*character_expression_1*, *start*, *length*, *character_expression_2* **)**
Deletes *length* characters from the 1st expression, starting at position *start*, and then inserts *character_expression_2* at *start*. To delete characters without inserting other characters, *character_expression_2* must be **NULL** (not **''**, which will insert a single space). To only insert characters, *length* must be 0.
Example: **select stuff(stuff('ORACLE', 4, 2, 'S'), 1, 2, NULL)** returns **'ASE'**.

substring (*character_expression*, *start*, *length* **)**
Returns part of a character or binary string, starting at position *start* for *length* characters. Note that *length* may be specified longer than the remaining string length. Also note that by specifying 0 for either *start* or *length*, a **NULL** value results.
Example: **select substring('abcdef',3,2)** returns **'cd'**.
(12.5) to_unichar (*integer_expression* **)**
Returns the Unicode expression for the specified integer expression.

(12.5) uhighsurr (*unicode_expression*, *start* **)**
Tests the Unicode value at position *start* in the Unicode expression: if this is the high half of a surrogate pair, returns **1**; otherwise returns **0**.

(12.5) ulowsurr (*unicode_expression*, *start* **)**
Tests the Unicode value at position *start* in the Unicode expression: if this is the low half of a surrogate pair, returns **1**; otherwise returns **0**.

upper (*character_expression* **)**
Converts the expression to uppercase. Example: **select upper('aB1')** returns **'AB1'**.

(12.5) uscalar (*unicode_expression* **)**
Return the Unicode scalar value for the first character in the Unicode expression.

(12.5.1) xmlextract (...), **xmlparse(**...**)**, **xmlrepresentation(**...**)**, **xmltest**
(15.0) xmlvalidate(...**)**
XML functions; see p.47.

Left-padding a number with zeroes
To convert a number to an **n**-character string with leading zeroes, use this query:
select right(replicate('0', n) + convert(varchar, 123), n) returns **'000123'** for **n** = 6

The not-so-empty string
In a character expression, an empty string (i.e., '') evaluates to a single space.
Examples: **select 'a' + '' + 'b'** results in **'a b'** (3 characters)
select 'a' + NULL + 'b' results in **'ab'** (2 characters)
select 'a' + space(0) + 'b' results in **'ab'** (2 characters)
select 'a' + substring('xyz',0,3) + 'b' results in **'ab'** (2 characters)

8. System functions

(12.5.1) audit_event_name (*audit_event_id* **)**
Returns the description of an audit event ID; ➢p.102.

col_name (*object_id*, *column_id* [, *db_id*] **)**
Returns the column name for specified column for the specified object.
Example: **select col_name(1, 4)** returns **'type'**.

col_length (*object_name*, *column_name* **)**
Returns the defined length of column. Use **datalength()** to see the actual data size.

curunreservedpgs (*db_id*, *lstart*, *default_value* **)**
Returns the number of free pages on the device fragment starting at logical page number *lstart* (as stored in **master..sysusages**). *default_value* will be returned in case the information cannot currently be retrieved.

(pre-15) data_pgs ([**(12.5)** *db_id*,] *object_id*, { *doampg* | *ioampg* } **)**
Returns the number of pages used by the table (*doampg*) or index (*ioampg*), excluding pages used for internal structures. Use in a query against **sysindexes**; see **rowcnt()** for an example. Replaced by **data_pages()** in 15.0.

(15.0) data_pages (*db_id*, *object_id* [, *index_id* [, *ptn_id*]] **)**
Replaces **data_pgs()** and **ptn_data_pgs()** in 15.0.

(15.0) datachange (*table_name*, *partition_name*, *column_name* **)**
Returns the amount of modified rows (as a percentage of the table's total #rows) for the particular table (in the current database), partition, or column since the last time **update statistics** was run. This is supported for normal (non-proxy) user tables in user databases only. **NULL** can be specified for *partition_name* and *column_name*.
Example: **select datachange('my_table', NULL, NULL)**

datalength (*expression* **)**
Returns the length of *expression* in bytes. *expression* is usually a column name. If

expression is a character constant, it must be enclosed in quotes.

db_id ([*db_name* **])**
Returns the ID of the specified database. Without *db_name*, of the current database.

db_name ([*db_id* **])**
Returns the database name for *db_id*. Without *db_id*, for the current database.

(12.5.0.3) derived_stat ({ *object_name* | *object_id* **}, {** *index_name* | *index_id* **}**
[(15.0) , *ptn_name* | *ptn_id* **] , '***statistic***')**
Returns a statistic for the specified table or index, and optionally, partition.
statistic can be (case-insensitive):

Full name	Abbreviated
data page cluster ratio	dpcr
index page cluster ratio	ipcr
data row cluster ratio	drcr

Full name	Abbreviated
large io efficiency	lgio
space utilization	sput

Examples: **select derived_stat ('my_table', 'ix1', 'ipcr')**
select derived_stat ('your_table', 0, 'space utilization')

(12.5) get_appcontext ('*app_context_name***', '***attribute_name***')**
Returns the value of the specified attribute in the application context; ➢p.71.

host_id ()
Returns the current session's client process ID on the host computer where the client process runs (provided the client supplied this information when connecting to ASE).

host_name ()
Returns the host computer name where the current session's client process is running (provided the client supplied this information when connecting to the server).

identity (*precision* **)**
(12.5.4) identity ([unsigned] int | smallint | tinyint)
In a **select**...**into** statement only, adds an identity column to the created table. With only a digit, the column will be **numeric** with the specified *precision*; otherwise the column will have the specified datatype.
Examples: **select *, seq=identity(6) into #t from mytable** -- creates a numeric(6)
(12.5.4) select *, seq=identity(int) into #t2 from mytable -- creates an int

(12.5.0.3) identity_burn_max (*table_name* **)**
Returns the 'burned' identity value (in varchar format!) for the specified table; ➢p.37.

index_col (*object_name*, *index_id*, *N* [, *owner_id*] **)**
Returns the name of the Nth column ($N \geq 1$) in the specified index; returns **NULL** if *object_name* is not an existing table. *owner_id* is the object owner (optional).

index_colorder (*object_name*, *index_id*, *N* [, *owner_id*] **)**
Returns the sort order of the Nth column ($N \geq 1$) in the specified index, which is either **'ASC'** or **'DESC'**. *owner_id* is the object owner (optional).

(15.0) is_quiesced (*db_id* **)**
Returns 1 if the specified database is currently quiesced and 0 if not.

is_sec_service_on (*security_service_name* **)**
Returns 1 if the specified security service is active and 0 if not.
Example: **select is_sec_service_on('unifiedlogin')**

lct_admin ('abort', *spid* [, *db_id*] **)**
lct_admin ('reserve', *nr_log_pages* **)**
lct_admin ('lastchance' | 'logfull' | 'reserved_for_rollbacks' , *db_id* **)**
lct_admin ('logsegment_freepages' | 'num_logpages', *db_id* **)**
Manages the log segment's last-chance threshold, or aborts suspended transactions:

- **'abort'** aborts the open transaction in session *spid*. If *spid* = 0, all open transactions in the specified database are aborted. Only transactions which are in 'LOG SUSPEND' mode in database *db_id* (default=current database) can be aborted.
- **'lastchance'** creates a last-chance logsegment threshold in database *db_id*.
- **'logfull'** returns 1 if the last-chance threshold has been crossed in the specified database, or 0 if it has not.
- **'reserve'** returns the number of free log pages required to successfully dump a transaction log of the size specified by *nr_log_pages*. When *nr_log_pages* = 0, returns the current setting of the last-chance threshold in the current database.

- **'reserved_for_rollbacks'** returns the number of pages currently reserved for rollback log records (CLRs) in the transaction log of the specified database.
- **'logsegment_freepages'** returns the number of currently free pages in the specified database that could be allocated to the transaction log.
- **'num_logpages'** returns the number of currently allocated log pages in the specified database (undocumented).

Example: **select lct_admin('abort', 19)** -- abort suspended transaction in session 19
select lct_admin('abort', 0, 8) -- abort suspended transactions in DB 8

license_enabled (*option* **)**
Returns **1** if the specified option is licensed, and **0** if it is not (also ➢p.122).
Example: **select license_enabled('ASE_ENCRYPTION')**

(12.5) list_appcontext ('*app_context_name*' | NULL , '*attribute_name*' | NULL)
Displays the specified attribute(s) in the specified application context(s); ➢p.71.

(12.5) lockscheme (*table_name* | *table_id* [, *db_id*] **)**
Returns the specified table's lock scheme (**allpages**, **datapages** or **datarows**); returns **'not a table'** if the specified object is not a table, or **NULL** if it doesn't exist.
Example: **select name from sysobjects where lockscheme(id) = 'datarows'**

(12.5.0.3) next_identity (*table_name* **)**
Returns the identity value (in varchar format!) to be assigned for this table (➢p.37).

object_id (*object_name* **)**
Returns the object's ID, or **NULL** if it doesn't exist.
Examples: **select object_id('your_table'), object_id('jsmith.your_table')**
select object_id('#mytable'), object_id('tempdb..my_other_table')

object_name (*object_id* [, *db_id*] **)**
Returns the object name for the specified object ID, or **NULL** if it doesn't exist.

(15.0) pageinfo (*db_id*, *page_nr*, '*attribute*' **)**
Returns an attribute of the specified database page, or **NULL** if the page or attribute doesn't exist. Specify **help** for *attribute* to see a list of supported attributes.
Examples: **select pageinfo (4, 567, 'index id')** -- index ID stored on page 567
select pageinfo (5, 876, 'allocated') -- ptn. ID if page is allocated; else 0

(12.5) pagesize ({ *table_name* [, *index_name*] | *table_id* [, *db_id* [, *index_id*]] **})**
Returns the page size (in bytes; always equal to **@@maxpagesize**) for the specified table or index; returns **0** if the specified object is not a table, or **NULL** if it doesn't exist.

(15.0) partition_id (*ptn_name* [, *db_id*] **)**
Returns the partition ID for the specified partition, or **NULL** if it doesn't exist.

(15.0) partition_name (*index_id*, *ptn_id* [, *db_id*] **)**
Returns the partition name for the specified index and partition ID, or **NULL** if it doesn't exist. Example: **select partition_name (0, 392698992)**

(15.0.1) partition_object_id (*ptn_id* [, *db_id*] **)**
Returns the object ID of the table corresponding to the specified partition ID.

pointer_size ()
Indicates a 32-bit or 64-bit ASE version; returns 4 or 8 respectively (undocumented).

(12.5.4) pssinfo (*spid*, *option* **)**
Returns attributes of session *spid* (when **0**: the current session), depending on *option*:

- **'ipaddr'** - the client IP address (for IPv6, it doesn't fit in **sysprocesses.ipaddr**)
- **'extusername'** - when using external authentication, the external user name
- **'dn'** - the distinguished name when using LDAP

(pre-15) ptn_data_pgs (*object_id*, *ptn_id* **)**
Returns the number of data pages of a partition. Replaced by **data_pages()** in 15.0.
Example: **select ptn_data_pgs(id, partitionid) '#partitions'**
from syspartitions where id = object_id('my_table')

(pre-15) reserved_pgs (*object_id*, { *doampg* | *ioampg* } **)**
Returns the number of pages allocated to table or index, including pages for internal structures. Use this in a query against **sysindexes**; see **rowcnt()** for an example. Replaced by **reserved_pages()** in 15.0.

(15.0) reserved_pages (*db_id*, *object_id* [, *index_id* [, *ptn_id*]] **)**
Replaces **reserved_pgs()** in 15.0.

(12.5) rm_appcontext ('*app_context_name***', '***attribute_name***')**
Deletes the specified attribute from the specified application context; ➢p.71.

(pre-15) rowcnt (*doampg* **)**
Returns the number of rows in a table, without scanning the entire table; instead, the rowcount is retrieved from the table's OAM page. Note that this value will usually be correct, but may be slightly off during heavy insert/delete activity on the table. Use the function in a query against the **sysindexes** table, for example:

```
select rowcnt( doampg ) from sysindexes
where indid < 2 and id = object_id( 'my_table' )
```

Replaced by **row_count()** in 15.0.

(15.0) row_count (*db_id*, *object_id* [, *ptn_id*] **)**
Replaces **rowcnt()** in 15.0.
Example: **select row_count(db_id(), object_id('my_table'))**

(12.5) set_appcontext ('*app_context_name***', '***attribute_name***', '***attribute_value***')**
Creates an attribute in the specified application context; ➢p.71.

show_sec_services ()
Lists the active security services for the current session.

(15.0) showplan_in_xml(*N***)**
Retrieves information about query optimization/execution in XML format; ➢p.55.

syb_quit ()
Causes ASE to terminate the current session. Example: **select syb_quit()**.

syb_sendmsg ('*ip_address***',** *port_nr***, '***message_string***')**
(Unix only) Sends a UDP message to the specified port; requires the config option **'allow sendmsg'** (dynamic) to be set to **1**. The config option **'syb_sendmsg port number'** (static) defines the outgoing port number used by ASE.

(12.5.0.3) tempdb_id ([*spid*] **)**
Returns the database ID of the specified session's temporary database; without *spid*, for the current session.

(15.0) tran_dumpable_status (*db_name* **)**
Returns **0** when the transaction log of the specified database can be dumped. Otherwise, returns a bitmap indicating the reasons why this is not possible:

Bit	Reason
1	the specified database does not exist
2	the transaction log is not on a separate device
4	the first log page is on a data-only fragment
8	database option **'trunc log on chkpt'** is enabled
16	non-logged writes occurred in this database
32	**dump tran**…**with truncate_only** has been performed
64	the database is newly created or upgraded;database dump is required first

(pre-15) used_pgs (*object_id*, *doampg*, *ioampg* **)**
Returns the number of pages used by a table and its clustered index. Use in a query against **sysindexes**; see **rowcnt()** for an example. Replaced by **used_pages()** in 15.0.

(15.0) used_pages (*db_id*, *object_id* [, *index_id* [, *ptn_id*]] **)**
Replaces **used_pgs()** in 15.0.

valid_name (*character_expression* **)**
Returns **0** if the *character_expression* is not a valid identifier, or a number other than **0** if it is a valid identifier.

(12.5.3) xa_bqual (*transaction_name*, **0)**
Returns the 'branch qualifier' part of a distributed transaction's name.

(12.5.3) xa_gtrid (*transaction_name*, **0)**
Returns the 'global transaction ID' part of a distributed transaction's name.

9. Mathematical functions

abs (*number* **)**
Returns the absolute value of a given expression. Example: **select abs(-3)** returns **3**.

ceiling (*number* **)**
Returns the smallest integer greater than or equal to *number.*
Example: **select ceiling(1.3)** returns **2**.

floor (*number* **)**
Returns the largest integer that is less than or equal to *number.*
Example: **select floor(1.9)** returns **1**.

exp (*number* **)**
Returns the exponential of *number.* Example: **select exp(1)** returns **2.718282** (use **convert()** to get the full precision of **2.7182818284590451**).

log (*number* **) / log10 (** *number* **)**
Returns the natural logarithm, or base 10 logarithm, of *number.*

pi ()
Returns the constant *pi.* **select pi()** returns **3.141593** (use **convert()** to get the full precision of **3.1415926535897931**).

power (*value, power* **)**
Returns *value* to the power of *power.* Example: **select power(2, 8)** returns **256**.

rand ([*integer*] **)**
Returns a random float value between 0 and 1, optionally using *integer* as a seed. For example, select **rand()** might return **0.802937** (or something else...).

(12.5.1) newid ([*flag*] **)**
Returns a unique 16-byte hexadecimal UUID/GUID value (by definition, UUIDs/GUIDs are always unique, even in different servers). *flag* specifies the result format: when **0** (=default), it's a **varchar(36)** string; when **1**: like **0**, but 4 dashes are included; when **0x0**, as a **varbinary(16)** string. Other values for *flag* are invalid are return **NULL**.
newid() is also supported in 12.5.0.3, but may return duplicate values in certain queries; it also accepts different parameters. Best upgrade to 12.5.1 when using **newid()**.
Example: **select newid(1)** returned **'519a220b-ae98-473e-be5d-fb726ecc1240'** in my ASE server - you should never see this same value returned in your server.

round (*number, integer* **)**
Rounds the *number* so that it has *integer* significant digits. A positive integer determines the number of significant digits to the right of the decimal point; a negative integer, the number of significant digits to the left of the decimal point.

sign (*number* **)**
Returns the sign of *number* : positive (+1), zero (0), or negative (-1).

(12.5.0.3) square (*number* **)**
Returns the square of the specified value. Example: **select square(-3)** returns **9**.

sqrt (*number* **)**
Returns the square root of the specified value, which must be ≥ 0.
Example: **select sqrt(36)** returns **6**.

10. Trigonometric functions

acos (*number* **) / asin (** *number* **)**
Returns the angle (in radians) having a cosine or sine of *number.*
Example: **select degrees(acos(0.5))** returns **60.000000**.

atan (*number* **)**
Returns the angle (in radians) having a tangent of *number.*
Example: **select degrees(atan(1.0))** returns **45.000000**.

atn2 (*number1, number2* **)**
Returns the angle (in radians) having a tangent of (*number1* / *number2*). *number1* typically represents the angle's sine, and *number2* its cosine.

cos (*angle* **)** / **cot (** *angle* **)** / **sin (** *angle* **)** / **tan (** *angle* **)**
Returns the cosine, cotangent, sine or tangent of the specified angle (in radians).
Example: **select cos(radians(60.0))** returns **0.500000**.

degrees (*angle-in-radians* **)**
Converts an angle from radians to degrees.
Example: **select degrees(pi()/4)** returns **45.00000**.

radians (*angle-in-degrees* **)**
Converts an angle from degrees to radians. *angle-in-degrees* should be specified as a floating-point number, otherwise the result will be truncated to an integer.
Example: **select radians(90.0)** returns **1.570796326794896600**.

11. Login/user/role functions

mut_excl_roles ('*role_1*', '*role_2*', [**'membership'** | **'activation'**] **)**
Returns 1 if the two user-defined roles (or any roles directly contained in these roles) are defined as mutually exclusive, either on **'membership'** or **'activation'** level as specified; otherwise returns 0.

proc_role ('*role_name*'**)**
Returns **1** if the current session has enabled the role directly; returns **2** if the role is contained in an enabled role; otherwise returns **0**. In 15.0, use **has_role()** instead.

(15.0) has_role ('*role_name*' [, **0**] **)**
Same as **proc_role()**, but with **0** as the second argument, the execution of this built-in function is not audited (with **1**, or with only *role_name*, it is audited); **proc_role()** is always audited. It is recommended using **has_role()** instead of **proc_role()**.

role_contain ('*role_1*', '*role_2*' **)**
Returns 1 if *role2* contains *role1*; otherwise returns 0. *role1* and *role2* are the names of system roles or user-defined roles.

role_id ('*role_name*' **)**
Returns the role ID for the specified role name as stored in **master..syssrvroles.**

role_name (*role_id* **)**
Returns the role name for the specified role ID as stored in **master..syssrvroles.**

suser_id ([*login_name*] **)**
Returns the login ID (suid) for the specified *login_name*. Without *login_name*, returns the current session's login ID.

suser_name ([*suid*] **)**
Returns the login name for the specified login ID (*suid)*, which uniquely identifies a login. Without *suid*, returns the current session's login name.

show_role ()
Displays the session's currently active system-defined roles (not user-defined roles).

user
Returns the current session's database user name, equivalent to **user_name()**. Note: this is the only built-in function that doesn't require parentheses.

user_id ([*db_user_name*] **)**
Returns the database user ID number for the specified user name, as stored in the **sysusers** table in the current database. If no *db_user_name* is supplied, it returns the ID of the current session's database user. Note: this should not be confused with server-wide login numbers as returned by the **suser_id()** function.

user_name ([*db_user_id*] **)**
Returns the database user's name for the specified user ID number. If no *db_user_id* is supplied, it returns the name of the current session's database user. Note: this should not be confused with server-wide login names as returned by the **suser_name()** function.

valid_user (*user_id* **)**
Determines whether the specified ID is a valid user or alias in at least one database in this ASE server. If valid, it returns **1**, otherwise **0**.

12. Miscellaneous functions

coalesce (*expression_1*, *expression_2* [, *expression_3*, … , *expression_n*] **)**
Returns the value of the first expression in the list which is not **NULL**; ➢p.39.

isnull (*expression_1*, *expression_2* **)**
Substitutes the value specified in *expression_2* when *expression_1* evaluates to **NULL**; otherwise returns *expression_1*. The datatypes of the expressions must convert implicitly, or you must use the convert function.

nullif (*expression_1*, *expression_2* **)**
If *expression_1* = *expression_2*, returns **NULL**; else *expression_1*; ➢p.39.

tsequal (*timestamp_1*, *timestamp_2* **)**
Compares the values of two **timestamp** columns. This function is typically used in the **where** clause of an **update** statement, to prevent updating rows that have been modified since they were first retrieved (this is also known as 'optimistic locking').
Example:
```
update mytable set mycol = mycol + 1
where primary_key = @value and tsequal(ts_column, @stored_ts_val)
```

update (*column_name* **)**
This function can only be used in a trigger; ➢p.36.

13. Text & Image data

Data of type **text** (incl. **unitext**) or **image** is stored as a separate page chain for each data row. The **text/image** column contains a 16-byte pointer to the start of this page chain. In **sysindexes** (in 15.0: **syspartitions**) all **text/image** data for a table is represented by a row with **indid** = **255**.

patindex ('%*pattern***%'**, *char_expression* [**using** { **bytes** | **chars** | **characters** }] **)**
A pattern matching function supporting **text** data. See **patindex()** (➢p.13). Note that the **like** (**%**) operator can also be used on **text** data (➢p.9).

readtext *table_name.column_name* *@text_pointer* *offset* *size* [[**no**]**holdlock**] [**readpast**] [**using** { **bytes**|**chars**|**characters** }] [**at isolation** *isolation_level*]
Reads *size* bytes of data from the specified **text** or **image** column, skipping *offset* bytes. The data read is sent to the client as a result set. For **text** columns, when **using chars** or **using characters** is specified, *size* and *offset* are measures in characters instead of in bytes. *@text_pointer* must be a **varbinary(16)** variable initialised with the **textptr()** function. For details on (**no**)**holdlock**, **readpast** and **at isolation**, see the section 'Locking' on page 44.
Example:
```
declare @ptr varbinary(16)
select @ptr = textptr(my_text_col) from my_table where key_col=123
readtext my_table.my_text_col @ptr 1024 2048
```

writetext *table_name.column_name* *@text_pointer* [**readpast**] [**with log**] *data*
Inserts or updates **text** or **image** data in the specified column. When specifying **with log**, this action is logged in the transaction log; without **with log** (=default), this is 'minimally logged' (➢p.121), requiring the **select into/bulkcopy/pllsort** database option to be set. *@text_pointer* is a **varbinary(16)** variable initialised with the **textptr()** function. When the *data* to be inserted is **text** data, it must be quoted; when it is **image** data, it must be prefixed with **0x**. The amount of data that can be accessed by **readtext** and **writetext** is limited. For more advanced functionality, use CT-Lib instead.
Example:
```
declare @ptr varbinary(16)
select @ptr = textptr(my_text_col) from my_table where key = 123
writetext my_table.my_text_col @ptr with log 'This is some text'
```

textptr (*text_column_name* **)**
Returns the text pointer (a **binary(16)** value) for the specified **text** or **image** column; this pointer is needed for subsequent use by **readtext** or **writetext**.

textvalid ('*table_name.column_name***'**, *text_pointer* **)**
Returns **1** if the given text pointer is valid, **0** if it's invalid. Note that the identifier for a **text** or **image** column must include the table name.
Example:
```
select textvalid('my_table.my_text_col', textptr(my_text_col))
from my_table where key = 123
```

set textsize *nr_bytes*
Defines the maximum number of bytes (default=**32767**) returned to the client by a

select statement for a **text** or **image** column (it does not apply to **select**...**into** or **insert**...**select**). The current setting for a session is stored in **@@textsize**.

@@textdbid / @@textobjid / @@textcolid
Contains the database ID / object ID / column ID for the object containing the column referenced by **@@textptr**.

@@textptr
Contains the text pointer (a **binary(16)** value) of the last **text** or **image** column inserted or updated by a session.

@@textts
Contains the text timestamp of the column referenced by **@@textptr**.

set textptr_parameters { **on** | **off** }
Enables (**on**) or disables (**off**=default) whether **text** or **image** data is passed 'by value' by CIS RPC calls. **@@textptr_parameters** contains the current setting for a session. See the *Component Integration Services User's Guide* for details about such RPCs.

(12.5.1) sp_chgattribute *table_name*, **'dealloc_first_txtpg'**, { **0** | **1** }
When set to **1** (default=**0**), all **text/image** pages are deallocated when a **text** or **image** column is updated to **NULL**. By default (=**0**), when a **text/image** column containing data is updated to **NULL**, one empty **text/image** page remains allocated for the row.

sp_configure 'text prefetch size', *value* (dynamic)
Defines the maximum number of **text** or **image** pages that can be prefetched (i.e. read in advance) into a buffer pool (default = **16**).

14. Aggregate functions

Aggregate functions derive a single value from zero or more rows, and are often used in select lists and **having** clauses. Aggregates ignore any **NULL** values; only **count(*)** is an exception (see below). With **distinct**, any duplicate values are removed before the aggregate is calculated; with **all** (=default), all values are used in the calculation.

avg ([**all** | **distinct**] *expression* **)**
For numeric expressions only, calculates the average value.
Example: **select avg(order_amount) from orders**

count (*)
(15.0) count_big (*)
Counts the number of rows, including rows containing **NULL** column values. **count()** returns an **int** datatype, **count_big()** returns a **bigint**.
Example: **select count(*) from my_table** returns the number of rows in **my_table**.

count ([**all** | **distinct**] *expression* **)**
(15.0) count_big ([**all** | **distinct**] *expression* **)**
Counts the number of non-**NULL** values for *expression*, returning an **int** or **bigint**.
Example: **select count(a) from my_table** returns the number of rows in **my_table** with a non-**NULL** value for column **a**.

max (*expression* **)**
Derives the highest non-**NULL** value according to the datatype of the expression.
Example: **select max(salary) from employees**

min (*expression* **)**
Derives the lowest non-**NULL** value according to the datatype of the expression.
Example: **select min(iq) from employees**

sum ([**all** | **distinct**] *expression* **)**
For numeric expressions only, calculates the sum.
Example: **select sum(order_amount) from orders**

15. DML statements

The T-SQL DML statements are **select**, **insert**, **update**, **delete** and **truncate table**. Because of the complexity of the **select** statement, the various parts of the statement are listed below in the order in which they can appear. The **from** clause and **where** clause can also be used in **update** and **delete** statements.

select [**all** | **distinct**] [**(12.5.3) top** *n*] *expression* [**,** *expression* ...] ...
Selects columns, expressions or constants. **distinct** will remove duplicate rows from the result set. The default is **all**, which includes all rows found. The result set of a **select** statement is a conceptual table, consisting of zero or more rows and one or more columns. The column names of these tables can be defined by specifying a name before or after the expression (as in the first example below).
In 12.5.3, **top** *n* is similar to doing **set rowcount** *n* first. *n* must be a constant.
Examples: **select Column_A = substring(a,1,5), b*3 'B times 3' from my_table**
select * from my_table -- selects all columns
(12.5.3) select top 5 name from employees order by birthdate desc

select *@variable = expression* [*rest-of-select-query*] [**,** *@variable* = ...]
(12.5.1) set *@variable = expression* [**,** *@variable = expression* ...] ...
Assigns a value to one or more local variables. With **select**, the expression can be part of a query; with **set** a query (i.e. **from** clause) is not allowed. Since a variable can hold only a single value, the last row in the result set is stored in the target variable(s); therefore, this should normally only be used when at most one row will be retrieved.
Examples: **select @my_var = 456, @your_var = a from my_table where key = 123**
(12.5.1) set @my_var = getdate(), @your_var = 'this is a constant'

select *select_list* **into** *table_name*
[**(12.5.3a)** *encryption_options*] [**(15.0)** *partition_options*] [*rest-of-select-query*]
Creates a new table *table_name*, and inserts the rows in the result set into this table in 'minimally logged' mode (➢p.121). For *encryption_options*, see page 29; for *partition_options*, see page 26.
Example: **select a, b, c into new_table from my_table**

(12.5) select *select_list* **into existing table** *table_name*
Inserts the rows in the result set into the existing table (➢p.97). In pre-15, this is allowed only for a proxy table. In 15.0, when inserting into a regular table, this occurs in 'minimally logged' mode (➢p.121); therefore, this same table must not occur elsewhere in the query; also, it must not have indexes.
Example: **select a, b, c into existing table my_table from your_table**

from { *table_name* | *view_name* }[*correlation_name*] [*force_options*][*lock_options*]
[**readpast**] [**,** *...more tables or views...*]
The **from** clause specifies the tables and/or views a **select** (or **update** or **delete**) statement operates on. In 12.5.1, and in **select** statements only, *table_name* can also be a nested **select** statement (a so-called 'derived table'). A *correlation_name* can be specified for each table or view, which acts as an alias for that table or view within the query. For a derived table, *correlation_name* must always be specified.
Examples: **select t1.a, t2.b from my_table t1, other_table t2**
where t1.c = t2.c and t1.a > 0

(12.5.1) select TableName from (select TableName = name from sysobjects
where type = 'U') so

force_options forces the query optimizer to use the specified query plan attributes. These options should only be used when the implications are fully understood.
force_options can be: **(** [**index** *index_name*] [**prefetch** {**2**|**4**|**8**|**16** {**(12.5)** |**32**|**64**|**128**}}] [**lru** | **mru**] [**parallel** *parallel_level*] **)**. *index_name* specifies the index to be used; specifying the table name forces a table scan. **prefetch** forces the specified I/O size, provided a corresponding buffer pool exists. **lru** / **mru** specify the buffer replacement strategy; **parallel** specifies the level of parallelism to be used for accessing this table.
lock_options specify certain locking behaviour in **select** statements. For a table, **readpast**, **holdlock** and **noholdlock** can be specified. For a view, only **readpast** is possible. See the section 'Locking' on page 44 for details.
Example: **select a, b from my_table (index ix1 parallel 5) readpast**

on *logical_expression* [{ **and** | **or** } *logical_expression* ...]
For ANSI SQL joins only, defines the join conditions. See 'Joins' on page 24.

where *logical_expression* [{ **and** | **or** } *logical_expression* ...]
When processing the query, the **where** clause is applied first (except in ANSI SQL joins, where the **on** clause applies first), determining which rows from the table(s) involved should be included in the result set. In multi-table queries, it also specifies how the different tables should be joined; see the section 'Joins' on page 24.
Example: **select t1.a, t2.b from my_table t1, other_table t2**
where t1.c = t2.c and t1.a > 0

group by [**all**] *expression* [**,** *expression* ...]
The **group by** clause is applied after the **where** clause, and organises the rows into

'groups' according to the specified list of expressions (which cannot include aggregates). The select list can contain any columns used in these expressions, as well as aggregates on any columns not used in these expressions. **group by all** will also return groups for the rows that were excluded by the **where** clause (except when a **having** clause is present, in which case **all** is ignored).

Example: **select a, b, sum(c) from my_table**
where a > 0 group by a, b

Note: in T-SQL, it is allowed to include non-aggregated columns which are not in the **group by** expressions, in the select list. However, this is normally a coding error because the results will look rather messy.

Example: **select a, b, c from my_table**
group by a, b

having *logical_expression* [{ **and** | **or** } *logical_expression* ...]

The **having** clause is applied after the **group by** clause, and determines the groups to be included in the final result set. Without a **group by** clause, **having** determines the individual rows included in the result set, just like the **where** clause. The **having** clause usually contains conditions with aggregates on the non-grouped columns.

Example: **select a, b, avg(c) from my_table**
where a > 0 group by a, b
having count(*) > 1 and min(c) > 0

Subqueries

Subqueries are **select** statements nested inside other statements. Subqueries which return a single value may occur anywhere where an expression is allowed; other subqueries are allowed in a **where** or **having** clause only.

The subquery operators **exists**, **any**, **all** and **in** can only be used on a subquery in a **where** or **having** clause; **exists** can also be used in an **if** or **while** statement:

- **all** - always combined with **>** or **<**; evaluates to true when all rows in the subquery satisfies the **>** or **<** condition.
- **any** - always combined with **>**, **<** or **=**; evaluates to true when ≥ 1 row in the subquery satisfies the **>**, **<** or **=** condition.
- [**not**] **exists** - evaluates to true when the subquery contains ≥ 1 row.
- [**not**] **in** - evaluates to true when the subquery contains ≥ 1 matching values.

Example: **select a from my_table**
where b not in (select some_value from your_table)
and exists (select * from other_table x where x.key = my_table.key)
and c > any (select yet_another_value from another_table)

if (select count(*) from my_table) = 0 print 'Table is empty!'

order by {*expression* | *seq_nr*} [**asc** | **desc**] [, {*expression* | *seq_nr*} [**asc** | **desc**]...]

The **order by** clause determines the order of the rows in the result set. The rows can be sorted according to expressions, and/or sequence numbers. A sequence number of N represents the Nth term in the select list. For each term in the **order by** clause, the sort order can be as **asc** (ascending order, default) or **desc** (descending order).

Example: **select a, b, c from my_table**
order by abs(c), 1 desc

(12.5.1) for xml [**(15.0) schema** | **all**]

Converts an SQL result set from a **select** statement to XML; ➢p.47.

Example: **select a, b, c from my_table order by b for xml**

compute *aggregate* [, *aggregate...*] [**by** *expression* [, *expression*]

The **compute** clause generates additional rows in the result set which are derived from the other rows by aggregates. Multiple **compute** clauses can be specified. For each **compute** clause without **by**, one additional 'total' row is generated. When specifying **by** and one or more expressions, an **order by** clause must be present with corresponding expressions; a 'subtotal row' will then be generated for each group of rows having different values for these expressions.

Example: **select a, b, c from my_table**
order by a,b compute sum(c) by a,b compute sum(c)

for read only | **for update** [**of (** *updated_columns_list* **)**]

Only used in cursor declarations. See the section 'Cursors' on page 40.

at isolation *isolation_level*

Specifies a transaction isolation level. See the section 'Locking' on page 44.

for browse

Only used in DB/CT-Library applications. Not for direct use in T-SQL.

plan '(*AQP-language* **)'**
Specifies an abstract query plan. See the section 'Abstract Query Plans' on page 105.

lock { **datarows** | **datapages** | **allpages** }
Only used with **select**...**into**. See the section 'Locking' on page 44.

with { **max_rows_per_page** = *nr_rows*, **exp_row_size** = *nr_bytes*, **reservepagegap** = *nr_pages*, **identity_gap** = *N* }
Only used with **select**...**into**. See the sections 'Object storage properties' on page 32 and 'Identity columns' on page 37.

union [**all**]
Merges the result sets of two separate **select** statements, while removing duplicate rows. **union all** will not remove duplicate rows.
Example: **select a from table_1 union select b from table_2**

delete [**from**] { *table_name* | *view_name* }
[**where** *clause*] [**plan '(** *AQP-language* **)'**]
Deletes rows from a table or view, without specifying join conditions.

delete { *table_name* | *view_name* } [**(12.5.3) top** *n*]
from *clause* [**where** *clause*] [**plan '(** *AQP-language* **)'**]
Deletes rows from a table or view, according to the specified join conditions.
In 12.5.3, **top** *n* is similar to doing **set rowcount** *n* first. *n* must be a constant.

update { *table_name* | *view_name* } [**(12.5.3) top** *n*]
set { *column_name* = { *expression* | **(** ***select***-*statement* **)** } [, ...] |
@*variable_name* = { *expression* | **(** ***select***-*statement* **)** } [,...] }
from *clause* [**where** *clause*] [**plan '(** *AQP-language* **)'**]
Updates columns in a table or view, or sets local variables, according to the specified join conditions. With local variables in the **set** clause, a value is assigned for every matching row (just as it would for a similar **select** statement). Note that the right-hand side of an assignment is evaluated before the update takes place; therefore, only the old value of an updated column can be assigned to a variable, not the new value.
In 12.5.3, **top** *n* is similar to doing **set rowcount** *n* first. *n* must be a constant.

insert [**into**] { *table_name* | *view_name* } [**(** *column_list* **)**] **values (** *expression_list* **)**
Inserts a single row into the specified table or view. In 12.5.1, for table columns with a default or which are nullable, the keyword **default** can be specified in the expression list to explicitly insert the default value for that column or **NULL**, respectively.
Example: **insert my_table values (123, 'test')**
(12.5.1) insert your_table (a, b) values (789, default)

insert [**into**] { *table_name* | *view_name* } [**(** *column_list* **)**] **select**-*statement*
Executes the **select** statement, and inserts the result into the specified table or view.

truncate table *table_name* [**(15.0)** *ptn_name*]
Deletes all rows from the table, or, with *ptn_name*, from the specified partition, in 'minimally logged' mode (individual row deletions are not logged, but only page deallocations are logged; ➢p.121). This is much faster than removing the rows with **delete**. Note that a delete trigger will not be activated by **truncate table**.

16. Joins

A join defines the relation between two tables in a query. Joins may be used in **select**, **update** and **delete** statements. When joining N tables, there should normally be at least (N-1) join clauses; if there are less, a Cartesian product will be generated. A maximum of 50 tables can participate in a join. Note that in a join clause, **NULL** does not match **NULL**, though in a **where** clause, it does match.
A typical join looks something like this:
select ... **from t1, t2 where t1.key = t2.key**

The following join operators are allowed: **=**, **<>** , **!=** , **>** , **>=** , **<**, **=<**, **!>**, **!<**, **like**, **not like**, **in**, **not in**, ***=**, **=***. Expressions in the join clause are also allowed.
Example: **select * from t1, t2 where substring(t1.key, 3, 5) like '%' + t2.key**

ANSI join
As of ASE 12.0, the ANSI SQL join syntax is supported, together with the classic ASE T-SQL join syntax. The two forms have differences in the **from** clause and the **where** clause. Also, ANSI SQL-style joins have a mandatory **on** clause defining the join conditions; the optional **where** clause applies after the **on** clause and filters the result

set. Note that these syntax forms cannot be mixed in a single statement. They compare as follows:

Classic T-SQL join syntax	**ANSI SQL join syntax**
from t1, t2 where t1.key = t2.key and t1.attrib > 100	from t1 inner join t2 on t1.key = t2.key and t1.attrib > 100
from t1, t2 where t1.key1 = t2.key1 and t1.key2 = t2.key2 and t1.attrib > 100	from t1 inner join t2 on (t1.key1 = t2.key1 and t1.key2 = t2.key2) and t1.attrib > 100
from t1, t2, t3 where t1.key = t2.key and t2.key = t3.key and t1.attrib > 100	from t1 inner join t2 on t1.key = t2.key inner join t3 on t2.key = t3.key and t1.attrib > 100

T-SQL outer join
In a T-SQL outer join, indicated by the join operators ***=** or **=***, the qualifying rows from the table at the side of the * are always included in the result set, even when there is no matching row in the other table.
In the following example, all rows from table t1 will be included in the result set. When there is no matching row in table t2, **NULL** will be substituted for t2.b in the result set:

select t1.a, t2.b from t1, t2 where t1.key *= t2.key

ANSI outer join
The ANSI SQL equivalent of a T-SQL outer join is the following:

***=** : **left outer join** or **left join**
=* : **right outer join** or **right join**

In an ANSI outer join, the **where** clause may affect the result set differently than in a similar T-SQL outer join, since it applies after the ANSI **on** clause (which specifies the join condition).

17. Tables

create table *table_name* **(** *one-or-more-columns* [*RI-constraints*] **)** [*lock_scheme*] [*storage_properties*] [**(15.0)** *partition_options*] [*cis_options*]
Creates a new table *table_name* with one or more columns, optionally specifying additional attributes. Multiple columns must be separated by commas. Most of the syntax is similar to **alter table** ...**add** ..., described below. For details about *partition_options*, see page 26.
Examples: **create table my_table (col_a int not NULL, col_b varchar (80) NULL, col_c datetime default getdate() not NULL, primary key (col_a))**

cis_options applies to proxy tables; syntax (see the CIS section for details; ➢p.95):
[**external table**] **at** '*server_name*.[*db_name*].[*owner*].*object_name*']

storage_properties is optional; syntax: **with** { **max_rows_per_page** = *nr_rows*, **exp_row_size** = *nr_bytes*, **reservepagegap** = *nr_pages* } [**on** *segment_name*]
See the section 'Object storage properties' on page 32 for details.

alter table *table_name* **add** *column* [...] [**with exp_row_size** = *nr_bytes*]
Adds one or more columns to the specified table, or adds single constraints; see 'Column specification' below for syntax details. Multiple clauses can be concatenated in one **alter table** statement. **exp_row_size** can only be specified when data copying is required; see the section 'Object storage properties' on page 32. The commands **alter table**...**add**, **drop**, **modify**, and **lock** can often be combined into a single **alter table** statement.
Examples: **alter table my_table add col_d int NULL , col_e int NULL**
alter table my_table add col_d int NULL add col_e int default 1
(15.0) alter table my_table add col_f as col_d * col_e materialized

Column specification
For both the **create table** and **alter table** statements above, the following syntax applies for a regular column specification:

column_name datatype [**default** { *default_expression* | **user** | **NULL** }] [{ **identity** | **NULL** | **not NULL** }] [**off row** | **in row** [**(12.5)** (*max_nr_bytes*)]] [*RI-constraint*] [**(12.5.3a)** *encryption_clause*]

In 15.0, this syntax applies to a computed column specification:

(15.0) *column_name* {**compute** | **as**} *expression* [**materialized** | **not materialized**]

For examples, see **create table** and **alter table** above. Notes:

- When adding a column with a non-**NULL** value (by specifying a default), the entire table must be copied, requiring the database option **select into/bulkcopy/pllsort**; afterwards, a database dump is recommended.
- **default** specifies the value to be used when a row is inserted but no explicit value is specified for the column. *default_expression* is an expression consisting of constant values and built-in functions, but cannot include columns or variables. A column default specified in **alter table**...**add** becomes a default constraint, bound to the column.
- **NULL** allows the column to contain **NULL** values; **not NULL** prohibits this. When neither is specified, the database-specific default setting applies (as specified by the database option **allow nulls by default**; default=**not NULL**).
- **identity** specifies that the column (which must be of datatype **numeric**) is an identity column; for details, see the section 'Identity columns' on page 37.
- **off row | in row** applies only to columns of Java datatypes. With **in row**, the column is stored on the data page; in 12.0, its size is limited to 255 bytes; in 12.5, the max. column size (in bytes) can be larger and can be specified in parentheses; default is 255. **off row** specifies that the column is stored separately as **image** data (with no size limit). If nothing is specified, **off row** is the default.
- For details about RI-constraints, see page 31.
- For details about *encryption_clause*, see page 28.
- For computed columns in 15.0, *expression* can refer only to columns from the table itself, as well as to built-in functions. Computed columns are **not materialized** by default (i.e. *expression* is re-evaluated for every matching row); when **materialized**, *expression* is stored and re-evaluated when a column changes.

alter table *table_name* **modify** *column_name datatype* [**NULL** | **not NULL**]
[**(12.5.3a)** *encryption_clause*] [, *...more columns...*] [**with exp_row_size =** *nr_bytes*]
Changes the datatype, nullability or encryption of one or more existing columns in a table. In most cases, the entire table must be copied for this, which requires the database option **select into/bulkcopy/pllsort** to be enabled; afterwards, making a database dump is recommended. Note: the commands **alter table**...**add**, **drop**, **modify**, and **lock** can be combined into a single **alter table** statement.
Example: **create table my_table (a tinyint)** -- initially, a 1-byte integer
alter table my_table modify a int -- changed to a 4-byte integer
(12.5.3a) alter table my_table modify a encrypt with my_key -- encrypt,see p.28

alter table *table_name* **drop** *column_name* [, *...more columns...*]
Removes one or more columns from the specified table. The table must be copied for this, which requires the database option **select into/bulkcopy/pllsort** to be enabled; afterwards, making a database dump is recommended. **exp_row_size** can only be specified when data copying is required; see the section 'Object storage properties' on page 32. Note: the commands **alter table**...**add**, **drop**, **modify**, and **lock** can be combined into a single **alter table** statement.
Warning: do not use this command in ASE pre-12.0; in those ASE versions, it is unsupported, undocumented, and can easily lead to data corruption.
Example: **create table my_table (a int, b int, c int)**
alter table my_table drop a, c

(15.0) alter table *table_name partition_options*
Partitions a table. Range-, list- and hash-partitioning require the configuration option **'enable semantic partitioning'** to be enabled (=**1**; dynamic; **ASE_PARTITIONS** option must be licensed). Roundrobin partitioning (see below) is identical to the pre-15 partitioning and is always enabled, independent of license options.
partition_options can be (can also be used in **create table** and **select**...**into**):

- **partition by range (** *column_list* **) (** *ptn_name* **values <= (** *max_value* **)** [**on** *seg_name*] [, *...more partitions...*] **)** - Note: *max_value* can be **MAX,** denoting the highest possible value
- **partition by list (** *column_list* **) (** *ptn_name* **values (** *list-of-values* **)** [**on** *seg_name*] [, *...more partitions...*] **)**
- **partition by hash (** *column_list* **) (** *ptn_name* [**on** *seg_name*] [, *...more partitions...*] **)**

Examples: **create table my_table (a int, b datetime) partition by hash (a) (ptn1, ptn2, ptn3)**
alter table my_table partition by range(b)(p1 values <=('01-Jan-2006'), p2 values <= ('01-Jun-2006'))

(15.0) alter table *table_name* **add partition (** *ptn_name* **values** [<=] (...) **on** *segment_name* [, *...more partitions...*] **)**
For range- and list-partitioned tables only, adds one or more partitions (hash- and

round-robin-partitioned tables must be repartitioned or unpartitioned first). For range-partitioned tables, added partitions must have a higher *max_value* than the current highest partition.
Example: **alter table my_table add partition (p3 values <= ('01-Sep-2006'))**

(15.0.1) alter table *table_name* **drop partition** *ptn_name* [, *...more partitions...*]
Drops the specified table partition(s), including corresponding local index partitions.

alter table *table_name* **partition** { *nr_partitions* | **(15.0) by roundrobin** *ptn_clause* }
Partitions an table into *nr_partitions* round-robin partitions. When using the pre-15 syntax, the table must be unpartitioned. In 15.0, *ptn_clause* can be either:

- *nr_partitions* [**on (** *seg_name*, *...more segments...* **)**]
- **(** *ptn_name* [**on** *seg_name*] [, *...more partitions...*] **)**

Note: after running this command, the first partition contains all data pages currently in the table, while the other partitions are empty. To balance the partitions, re(build) a clustered index on the table or use **bcp**.
Examples: **alter table your_table partition 3**
(15.0) alter table your_table partition by roundrobin 12

alter table *table_name* **unpartition**
Unpartitions a round-robin partitioned table; concatenating all existing partitions into 1 partition. To change the partitioning of range-, list- and hash-partitioned tables, use **alter table**...**partition by**....

alter table *table_name* { **disable** | **enable** } **trigger** [*trigger_name*]
Enables or disables the trigger, or, without *trigger_name*, all triggers for *table_name*.

alter table *table_name* **lock** { **allpages** | **datarows** | **datapages** }
Changes the lock scheme for the specified table. See page 44 for details.

drop table *table_name* [, *...more tables...*]
Drops the specified table(s).

sp_chgattribute *table_name*, *attribute*, *value*
Sets an attribute for the specified table to *value*. Possible values for *attribute* are **'concurrency_opt_threshold'**, **'max_rows_per_page'**, **'exp_row_size'**, **'fillfactor'**, **'reservepagegap'**, (all ➢p.32), **'identity_gap'** (➢p.37), **'optimistic_index_locking'** (**12.5.0.3**; ➢p.44) and **'dealloc_first_txtpg'** (**12.5.1**; ➢p.20).

sp_checksource [**NULL** [, *table_name* [, *owner_name*]]]
Checks if the T-SQL source code exists for all check constraints, defaults and triggers defined for *table_name* (➢p.51).

sp_depends *table_name* [, *column_name*]
Displays objects referring to *table_name*, and vice versa (➢p.51).

sp_estspace *table_name*, *nr_of_rows* [, *fillfactor* [, '*varcol_list*' [, *blob_len* [, *io_rate* [, **(12.5)** *page_size*]]]]
Calculates the amount of storage space required when *table_name* would contain the specified number of rows, and the time it would take to build the indexes. The table and its indexes must already exist, but can be empty. *fillfactor* specifies the **fillfactor** to be used (default = server-wide default). *varcol_list* is a comma-separated list of variable-length columns which will be completely full (default= 50% full), *blob_len* is the length of all **text** and **image** columns in a row (default=0). *io_rate* is the number of disk I/Os per second (default=30), which is used to estimate the index build times.
In 12.5, if no *page_size* is specified, the current server's page size is used.

sp_help *table_name*
Displays information about the specified table.

(15.0) sp_helpcomputedcolumn *table_name*
Displays information about the computed columns in the specified table.

sp_helppartition [*table_name*]
Displays the number of data pages in each partition for the specified table. Without *table_name*, displays the number of partitions in all tables in the current database. Uses the built-in function **ptn_data_pgs()** (➢p.16).

sp_helptext *table_name*
Displays the source text of computed columns, function indexes and partition condi-

tions for the specified table.

sp_hidetext [**NULL** [, *table_name* [, *owner_name*]]]
Hides the T-SQL source code for all check constraints, defaults, triggers, computed columns, function indexes and partition conditions defined for *table_name* (➢p.52).

sp_placeobject *segment_name*, *table_name*
Places the specified table on *segment_name*, which means that future space allocation for this table will only be performed on the database devices to which *segment_name* has been mapped.

sp_recompile *table_name*
Ensures that any stored procedure or trigger accessing table_name will have its query plan recompiled (= re-optimized) the next time it is executed (➢p.77).

sp_rename *old_name*, *new_name* [**(12.5)** , **'index'** | **'column'**]
Renames a table, column or index (➢p.52).

sp_spaceused [*table_name* [, **1**]]
Displays the current number of rows and space used for *table_name*. When **1** is specified, also display space usage for each index on this table. Without parameters, displays the cumulative space usage for all tables in the current database.

create schema authorization *current_db_user_name* [**create table** *statements*] [**create view** *statements*] [**grant** *statements*] [**revoke** *statements*]
Creates one or more tables and/or views, plus optional corresponding **grant** / **revoke** statements, in a single transaction (this can for example be used to ensure a table is only created with the proper permissions). *current_db_user_name* must be the same as the database user name in the current database (i.e. the value of **user_name()**).

18. Encrypted Columns (12.5.3a)

Column encryption was introduced in 12.5.3a, a separate release following 12.5.3. As of 12.5.4 and 15.0 ESD#2, column encryption is included in all ASE versions.

sp_configure 'enable encrypted columns', { **0** | **1** } (dynamic)
Enables (**1**) or disables (**0**) column encryption functionality. Enabling requires the **ASE_ENCRYPTION** option to be licensed.

create encryption key *key_name* [**as default**] **for** *algorithm* [**with** *options…*]
Creates an encryption key in the current database, based on the specified encryption *algorithm* (currently, only AES). The encryption password must have been set for this database with **sp_encryption system_encr_passwd**. *options* can be:

- **keylength** *length* - key length in bits; for AES: **128** (=default), **192** or **256**.
- **init_vector** [**random** | **NULL**] - with **random** (=default), uses an initialization vector during encryption, so that identical plaintext values produce different ciphertext; with **NULL**, no initialization vector is used.
- **pad** [**random** | **NULL**] - with **random**, encrypted values are padded randomly for better security; with **NULL** (=default), no padding is done.

Note: to index an encrypted column, **init_vector NULL** and **pad NULL** are required. For the **as default** clause, see **alter encryption key**.
Example: **create encryption key my_key for AES with keylength 256 init_vector null**

alter encryption key *key_name* **as** [**not**] **default**
Modifies the **as default** status of a key. When marked **as default**, this key will be used for encrypted columns where no key name was specified in the DDL statement. **sp_encryption** displays which key, if any, is the default key.

drop encryption key *key_name*
Drops the specified encryption key. No columns must be encrypted with the key.

create table *table_name*
(*column_definition* **encrypt** [**with** [*db_name*..]*key_name*], *…more columns…*)
While creating a table, defines a column for encryption with the specified key. If *db_name* is not specified, the key must be in the current database. Without the key name, the default encryption key is used, if defined. Constraints, defaults etc. must be specified before the **encrypt** clause.
Example: **create table my_table (col_a int unique encrypt with my_key)**

alter table *table_name* **add** *column_definition* **encrypt** [**with** [*db_name*..]*key_name*]
Adds a column to a table and defines it for encryption with the specified key.
Example: **alter table my_table add col_b int null encrypt with my_key2**

alter table *table_name* **modify** *column_name* **encrypt** [**with** [*db_name*..]*key_name*]
alter table *table_name* **modify** *column_name* **decrypt**
Encrypts or decrypts a column. Note that for large tables, this may take a long time.
Example: **alter table my_table modify col_c encrypt with my_key3**

select *select_list* **into** *table_name*
(*column_name* **encrypt** [**with** [*db_name*..]*key_name*][,*...more encrypted columns...*])
from ...rest of query...
While creating a table with **select...into**, defines a column for encryption with the specified key. Note that without *db_name*, *key_name* must exist in the database where the table is created.

sp_encryption [*subcommand*, *options...*]
Manages certain aspects of column encryption. Possible subcommands and options:

- **system_encr_passwd, '***new_passwd***'** [, **'***old_passwd***'**] - sets or modifies the system encryption password in the current database. This must be done before encryption keys can be created in this database.
- **help** [, *key_name*] - displays details about all encryption keys in the current database, or about the specified encryption key only.
- **help,** *key_name*, **'display_cols'** - displays all columns encrypted with the specified encryption key, including columns located in other databases.

sp_help *table_name*
Display information about the specified table, and indicates if a column is encrypted.

sp_help *key_name*
Display basic information about the specified encryption key.

To find all existing encryption keys in the current database, run this query:
```
select name, id from sysobjects where type = 'EK'
```

To find all encrypted columns for **my_table**, use **sp_help**, or run the following query:
```
select name from syscolumns where id = object_id('my_table')
and encrkeyid is not null
```

To find the encryption key for column **my_table.my_col**:
```
select key_name = object_name(encrkeyid,
                                        db_id(isnull(encrkeydb, db_name()))),
       key_db    = isnull(encrkeydb, db_name())
from syscolumns
where id = object_id('my_table') and name = 'my_col'
```

set ciphertext { **on** | **off** }
(undocumented) When set to **on** (default=**off**), for the current session, queries referring to encrypted columns will directly insert or retrieve ciphertext instead of plaintext, thus bypassing encryption/decryption. Note that this may affect existing queries since ciphertext has a **varbinary** datatype instead of the column's normal datatype.

grant create encryption key to *user_names* | *group_names* | *role_names*
revoke create encryption key from *user_names* | *group_names* | *role_names*
Grants (or revokes) permission to execute **create encryption key** to users, groups (including **public**) or roles.

grant *permission* **on** *key_name* **to** *user_names* | *group_names* | *role_names* [**with grant option**]
revoke *permission* **on** *key_name* **from** *user_names* | *group_names* | *role_names*
Grant (or revokes) permission for certain operations on a key to to users, groups (including **public**) or roles. *permission* can be:

- **alter encryption key** - allows running **alter encryption key** for the key
- **select** - allows using the key to encrypt a column.
- **all** - all of the above

NB: **with grant option** applies only when granting **select** permission.

grant decrypt on *table* [(*column_list*)] **to** *user_names* | *group_names* | *role_names* [**with grant option**]
revoke decrypt on *table* [(*column_list*)] **from** *user_names*|*group_names*|*role_names*
Grants or revokes permission to decrypt data in an encrypted column to users, groups

(including **public**) or roles (note that **select** permission is required as well). With only the table name specified, applies to all encrypted columns in that table.
Example: **grant decrypt on my_table(my_col) to manager_role, auditor_role**

19. Indexes

create [**unique**] [**clustered** | **nonclustered**] **index** *index_name* **on** *table_name* **(** { *column_name* | **(15.0)** *expression* } [**asc** | **desc**] [, *...more columns/expressions...*] **)** [**with** { [**ignore_dup_key** | **ignore_dup_row** | **allow_dup_row**], **sorted_data**, **consumers** = *nr_consumers*, **statistics using** *nr_steps* **values**, *storage_properties* }] [**(15.0) local index** [*ptn_name* [**on** *segment_name*] [, *...more partitions...*]]]
Creates an index on the specified columns of the specified table. In 15.0, an index can also be created on a computed column (which must be **materialized**), or on an expression (which can't reference computed columns): this is called a function index.
By default, an index is created as not unique and **nonclustered**, unless explicitly specified otherwise by the **unique** and **clustered** keywords. A table can have one clustered index at most, and max. 249 (APL) or 248 (DOL) nonclustered indexes.
For each index column, the column sort order within the index can be specified as **asc** (ascending, =default) or **desc** (descending) following the name of each column.
An index can contain up to 31 columns and 600 bytes (➢p.122).
In 15.0, and for range/list/hash-partitioned tables only, **local index** creates a partitioned index (=an index tree per table partition); clustered indexes (and therefore by default, **primary key** constraints) are always partitioned for these partitioning types.
Special index behaviour can be specified in the **with** clause as follows:

- **ignore_dup_key** - for unique indexes only, when a duplicate index key would result from an **insert** or **bcp**-in, that row is rejected. Other rows inserted by the statement or by **bcp** remain inserted, and the statement continues. **updates** are not affected. When creating the index, there must be no duplicate key values.
- **ignore_dup_row** - for non-unique clustered indexes only, when a duplicate data row (which is not the same as a duplicate index key !) would result from an **insert** or **update**, that row is ignored and the transaction continues (applies to APL tables only; duplicate rows are allowed for DOL tables). When creating the index, any duplicate data rows are deleted (both for APL and DOL tables).
- **allow_dup_row** - for non-unique clustered indexes only, allows duplicate data rows to be created (for APL tables only; duplicate rows are allowed for DOL tables). When creating the index, duplicate data rows are allowed and retained (both for APL and DOL tables). Note: when other, unique indexes exist on the table, their uniqueness overrides **allow_dup_row.**
- **sorted_data** - when creating an index and when the rows in the table are already in the order of the index key, index creation will usually be faster because an internal sort step can be avoided. See the *ASE Reference Manual* for details.
- **consumers =** *nr_consumers* - forces I/O parallelism during index creation.
- **statistics using** *nr_steps* **values** - uses *nr_steps* histogram steps (default=20 in pre-12.5, or the value of **'number of histogram steps'** in 12.5/12.0.0.4).

storage_properties can contain the following clauses; syntax: { **fillfactor** = *percentage*, **max_rows_per_page** = *nr_rows*, **reservepagegap** = *nr_pages* } [**on** *segment_name*]. See 'Object storage properties' on page 32 for details.
Examples: **create clustered index cix on my_table (col_a) on data_segment**
create index ix1 on my_table(col_b) with ignore_dup_key
create unique index ix2 on my_table(pkey) with reservepagegap= 8
(15.0) create index ix3 on my_table (col_a * 100, col_b) local index

drop index *table_name.index_name* [, *...more indexes...*]
Drops the specified index(es).

sp_chgattribute '*table_name.index_name***',** *attribute***,** *value*
Sets an attribute for the specified table to *value*. Possible values for *attribute* are **'max_rows_per_page'**, **'fillfactor'**, **'reservepagegap'**; see page 32 for details.

sp_helpindex *table_name*
Display information about the indexes that exist on the specified table.

sp_placeobject *segment_name***, '***table_name.index_name***'**
Places the specified index on *segment_name*, which means that future space allocation for this index will only be performed on the database devices to which *segment_name* has been mapped.

index_col (*object_name***,** *index_id***,** *N* [**,** *owner_id*] **)**
Returns the name of the Nth column ($N \geq 1$) in the specified index; ➢p.15,

index_colorder (*object_name*, *index_id*, *N* [, *owner_id*] **)**
Returns the sort order of the Nth column ($N \geq 1$) in the specified index; ➤p.15.

20. Referential Integrity Constraints

create table *table_name* **(** *...one-or-more clauses...* **)**
Creates a new table *table_name* with one or more columns and RI constraints. Each clause can be one of the following; multiple clauses can be concatenated in one **create table** statement (clauses must be separated by commas):

- *column_name datatype* [**constraint** *constraint_name*] { **unique** | **primary key** } [**clustered** | **nonclustered**] [**asc** | **desc**] [*storage_properties*]
- *column_name datatype* [**constraint** *constraint_name*] **references** [[*db_name*.]*owner_name*.]*table_name* **(** *column* **)**
- *column_name datatype* [**constraint** *constraint_name*] **check** (*check_condition*)
- *column_name datatype* **default** { *default_expression* | **user** | **NULL** }
- [**constraint** *constraint_name*] { **unique** | **primary key** } [**clustered** | **nonclustered**] **(** *list_of_columns_asc_desc* **)** [*storage_properties*]
- [**constraint** *constraint_name*] **foreign key (** *list_of_columns* **) references** [[*db_name*.]*owner*.]*table_name* **(** *list_of_columns* **)**
- [**constraint** *constraint_name*] **check (** *check_condition* **)**

The syntax for defining constraints is similar to the **alter table** statement below. See there for details, also about the *storage_properties* clause.

Example: **create table my_table (a int check (a > 0), b int constraint refcon_1 references otherdb..your_tab (key_col), c datetime default getdate(), d int unique, check (a > b), primary key (a, b))**

alter table *table_name ...one-or-more clauses...*
Adds one or more columns with an RI constraint to the specified table, or adds single constraints. Each clause can be one of the following; multiple clauses can be concatenated in one **alter table** statement:

- **add** *column_name datatype* [**constraint** *constraint_name*] **unique** [**clustered** | **nonclustered**] [**asc** | **desc**] [*storage_properties*]
- **add** *column_name datatype* [**constraint** *constraint_name*] **references** [[*db_name*.]*owner*.]*table_name* **(** *column* **)**
- **add** *column_name datatype* [**constraint** *constraint_name*] **check (** *check_condition* **)**
- **add** *column_name datatype* **default** { *default_expression* | **user** | **NULL** }
- **add** [**constraint** *constraint_name*] { **unique** | **primary key** } [**clustered** | **nonclustered**] **(** *list_of_columns_asc_desc* **)** [*storage_properties*]
- **add** [**constraint** *constraint_name*] **foreign key (** *list_of_columns* **) references** [[*db_name*.]*owner*.]*table_name* **(** *list_of_columns* **)**
- **add** [**constraint** *constraint_name*] **check (** *check_condition* **)**
- **drop constraint** *constraint_name*
- **replace** *column_name* **default** { *default_expression* | **user** | **NULL** }

Example: **alter table my_table add col_x int NULL check (col_x <= 100) add constraint c1 unique (col_y desc, col_z)**

The following applies to both the **create table** and **alter table** statements above:
default specifies the value to be used when a row is inserted but no explicit value is specified for the column. *default_expression* is an expression consisting of constant values and built-in functions, but cannot include columns or variables. When adding a constraint, a constraint name can be specified. When omitted, a unique constraint name will be generated automatically.
unique and **primary key** constraints both create a unique index; **unique** allows **NULL** values, **primary key** does not. Unless overridden with **nonclustered** or **clustered**, **unique** creates a nonclustered index, and **primary key** a clustered index (except when a clustered index already exists). In *list_of_columns_asc_desc*, the column sort order within the index can be specified as **asc** (ascending, =default) or **desc** (descending) following the name of each column.
check_condition specifies a relational expression involving one or more column names. A **references** constraint or **foreign key...references** constraint enforces that column values which are inserted or updated in the specified column(s) must exist in the table specified in the **references** clause. To drop constraints, specify the constraint name; use **sp_helpconstraint** to display the names of existing constraints. Note that constraints cannot be disabled temporarily (other than by dropping them).

storage_properties is optional; syntax: **with** { **fillfactor** = *percentage*, **max_rows_per_page** = *nr_rows*, **reservepagegap** = *nr_pages*} [**on** *segment_name*]
See the section 'Object storage properties' on page 32 for details.

sp_configure 'number of aux scan descriptors', *value* (static; 12.5:semi-dynamic)
Configuration option for allocating the number of scan descriptors. These are used by foreign key constraints, among others. With many foreign key constraints, this setting may need to be increased (as indicated by **sp_monitorconfig**; ➢p.73).

sp_help *constraint_name*
Displays information about the specified constraint.

sp_helpconstraint [*table_name* [**, 'detail'**]]
Without parameters, displays all tables in the current database with foreign key constraints or references constraints. With *table_name*, displays all constraints for this table. With **'detail'**, also displays the corresponding error message numbers.

sp_helptext *constraint_name*
Displays the T-SQL code of the specified constraint.

sp_rename *old_name***,** *new_name*
Renames a constraint from *old_name* to *new_name*.

sp_bindmsg *constraint_name***,** *error_nr*
Binds the message corresponding to *error_nr* to the specified constraint, replacing any message already bound to this constraint. When the constraint is violated, the message is printed (when the **with_log** option is enabled for *error_nr* with **sp_altermessage**, it is also written to the server errorlog), and **@@error** contains the value of *error_nr*. The message for *error_nr* must not contain formatting placeholders.

sp_unbindmsg *constraint_name*
Unbinds the message bound to the specified constraint.

21. Object storage properties

This section describes some storage properties for tables, indexes, **unique** and **primary key** constraints.

concurrency_opt_threshold
For DOL tables only, specifies the size of the table (in pages) below which the optimizer will use an index instead of a -possibly more efficient- table scan to achieve better concurrency. Possible values are -1 to 32767; the default = 15. A value of 0 disables this optimization (so a table scan will be used); -1 means the optimization is always enabled for the table. **concurrency_opt_threshold** can be specified in **sp_chgattribute** (for tables only).

exp_row_size
For DOL tables with variable length-columns only, specifies the expected average row size in bytes. This will be used to leave some free space on data pages to accommodate expanding updates. The maximum possible value is 1958. A value of 0 uses the server-wide default set by the configuration option **default exp_row_size percent**. A value of 1 fills the pages completely. **exp_row_size** can be specified in **create table**, **alter table** (when adding or modifying columns and data copying is required), **select...into** and **sp_chgattribute** (for tables and indexes).

fillfactor
Specifies the percentage to which index pages will initially be filled. Possible values are 1 to 100; a value of 0 (= default) uses the server-wide default set by the configuration option **default fill factor percent**. **fillfactor** is not maintained when rows are inserted or updated. **fillfactor** can be specified in **alter table** (for constraints), **create index** and **sp_chgattribute** (for tables and indexes).

max_rows_per_page
For APL tables only, this specifies the maximum number of rows that will be stored on a data page or an index leaf-level page. Possible values are 1 to 256; a value of 0 (= default) means that the pages will be as full as possible. **max_rows_per_page** is maintained when rows are inserted or updated. **max_rows_per_page** can be specified in **create table**, **alter table** (for constraints), **create index**, **select...into** and **sp_chgattribute** (for tables and indexes).

reservepagegap
Specifies the number of pages that will be left free when a new extent is allocated. Possible values are 0 (=default) to 255. When set to N, 1 in N pages will be left free. **reservepagegap** can be specified in **create table**, **alter table** (for constraints), **create index**, **select...into** and **sp_chgattribute** (for tables and indexes).

(12.5.1) dealloc_first_txtpg
Affects page deallocation for **text/image** columns; ➢p.20.

on *segment_name*
Specifies the segment on which the table or index will be created. **on** *segment_name* can be specified in **create table**, **alter table** (for constraints) and **create index**.

sp_configure 'default fill factor percent', *value* (static; 12.5:dynamic)
Specifies the server-wide default **fillfactor** percentage setting, which applies when **fillfactor** is not specified explicitly. Possible values are 1 to 100; a value of 0 (= default) means that the index leaf pages will be full, but some space will be left free in the intermediate-level index pages.

sp_configure 'default exp_row_size percent', *value* (dynamic)
For DOL tables only, specifies the server-wide default for **exp_row_size** which applies when **exp_row_size** is not specified explicitly for a table. *value* is the percentage (0..99) of the effective data page size that will be left free on data pages to accommodate expanding updates.

22. Views

create view *view_name* **[(** *view_column_name* **[,** *...more column names...* **])] as** *select_statement* **[with check option]**
Creates a view for the specified *select_statement*, which cannot contain **select...into**, **order by**, **compute** clauses; in pre-12.5, **union [all]** clause is also not allowed. Instead, these clauses can be applied when selecting from the view.
Each view column name may be specified in *view_column_names*. Alternatively, this can be omitted and the view column names are determined by the *select_statement*.
When using **with check option**, inserting or updating rows is allowed only when the resulting rows are still visible through the view.
Whether the view is updatable depends on the exact **select** statement specified. As a rule of thumb, when the select list contains expressions or aggregates, **group by**, **having** or **distinct** clauses, some types of joins, or (in 12.5) the **union [all]** clause, a view cannot be updated and is therefore read-only.
Examples: **create view dept_admin_view (nm, ph) as**
select name, phone_nr from personnel where dept = 'admin'

(12.5) create view sales_this_year as
select * from sales_q1 union select * from sales_q2 union
select * from sales_q3 union select * from sales_q4

drop view *view_name* **[,** *...more views...* **]**
Drops the specified view(s).

sp_checksource *view_name* **[, NULL [,** *owner_name* **]]**
Checks if the T-SQL source code for *view_name* exists (➢p.51).

sp_depends *view_name*
Displays objects referring to *view_name*, and vice versa (➢p.51).

sp_help *view_name*
Displays information about the specified view.

sp_helptext *view_name*
Displays the underlying T-SQL **select** statement which defines the specified view. Note: the **defncopy** utility (➢p.113) does the same, but formats the output better.

sp_hidetext *view_name* **[, NULL [,** *owner_name* **]]**
Hides the T-SQL source code for *view_name* (➢p.52).

sp_rename *old_name*, *new_name*
Renames a view or column from *old_name* to *new_name* (➢p.52).

create schema authorization *current_db_user_name* [**create table** *statements*] [**create view** *statements*] [**grant** *statements*] [**revoke** *statements*]
Creates tables and/or views, and sets permissions, in a transaction (➢p.28).

23. Rules & Defaults

create default *default_name* **as** *default_expression*
Creates a default. A default is the value inserted in a column when no explicit value

was specified by an **insert** statement or a **bcp**-in. *default_expression* is an expression consisting of constants and built-in functions, but cannot include columns or variables.
Examples: **create default dft1 as 99**
create default dft2 as '--Undefined-- '

create rule *rule_name* **as** *rule_expression*
Creates a domain rule. A domain rule limits the possible values in a column (rules are not enforced during **bcp**-in). *rule_expression* takes the form @*name relational_operator expression*, where *name* is an arbitrary name and *expression* consists of constants and built-in functions, but cannot include columns or variables.
Examples: **create rule r1 as @x >= 0**
create rule r2 as @d < getdate()

(12.5) create [**and** | **or**] **access rule** *rule_name* **as** *rule_expression*
Creates an access rule with the specified name. *rule_expression* will effectively (but invisibly) be part of the **where** clause of any query referring to a table to which this access rule is bound. When creating the access rule, **and** / **or** can be specified to indicate that the access rule will function as a logical **and** / **or** condition, respectively; **and** is default). Access rules are part of the 'row-level access' feature; ➢p.71.
Example: **create access rule ar1 as @owner = suser_id()**

drop default *default_name* [, *...more defaults...*]
drop rule *rule_name* [, *...more rules...*]
Drops the specified default(s) or rule(s), which must not be bound to any columns or user-defined datatypes anymore.

sp_bindefault *default_name*, **'***table_name.column_name***'**
sp_bindefault *default_name*, *user_defined_datatype* [, **'futureonly'**]
sp_bindrule *rule_name*, **'***table_name.column_name***'**
sp_bindrule *rule_name*, *user_defined_datatype* [, **'futureonly'**]
With **'***table_name.column_name***'**, binds the specified default or rule to the specified column. With *user_defined_datatype*, binds it to the specified user-defined datatype; it is also bound to existing columns of this datatype, except when **'futureonly'** is specified: in this case, existing columns are not affected.

{ **sp_unbindefault** | **sp_unbindrule** } **'***table_name.column_name***'**
{ **sp_unbindefault** | **sp_unbindrule** } *user_defined_datatype* [, **'futureonly'**]
(12.5) sp_unbindrule '*table_name.column_name***'** [, **NULL**, **'all'** | **'accessrule'**]
(12.5) sp_unbindrule *user_def_datatype* [,**NULL**|**'futureonly'**] [, **'all'** | **'accessrule'**]
With **'***table_name.column_name***'**, unbinds a default or domain rule from the specified column. With *user_defined_datatype*, unbinds a default or domain rule from the specified user-defined datatype; it is also unbound from existing columns of this datatype, except when **'futureonly'** is specified: in this case, existing columns are not affected. In 12.5, access rules are unbound only when **'accessrule'** or **'all'** is specified; with **'all'**, also domain rules are unbound.

sp_help { *rule_name* | *default_name* }
Displays information about the specified rule or default. **sp_help** *table_name* displays which rules and defaults are bound to the columns of *table_name*.

sp_helptext { *rule_name* | *default_name* }
Displays the T-SQL code of the specified rule or default.

sp_rename *old_name*, *new_name*
Renames a rule or default from *old_name* to *new_name*.

24. Stored Procedures

create proc[edure] *procedure_name*[;*number*] [[**(**] @*parameter_name datatype*] [= *default_value*] [**output**] [, *...more parameters...*] [**)**]] [**with recompile**] **as** { *T-SQL-statements* | **external name** *dll_name* }
Creates a stored procedure. With **external name**, creates an extended stored procedure (executable through XP Server; ➢p.99). To create grouped procedures, specify '*;number*' as part of the procedure name (default = '**;1**').
'=*default_value*' specifies a default value for a parameter; this value is assigned when the caller does not specify a value. **output** indicates this can be an output parameter; to actually return a value to the caller, the **output** keyword must also be specified when executing the procedure. **with recompile** forces a new query plan to be generated before every execution. For creating Java stored procedures in 12.5, ➢p.46.
Example: **create proc my_proc @p_mandatory int, @p_optional int = NULL**
as begin *... T-SQL-statements...* **end**

drop proc[edure] *procedure_name* [, *...more procedures...*]
Drops the specified stored procedure(s) or extended stored procedure. For grouped stored procedures, all procedures in the group are dropped collectively.

exec[ute] [*@return_status* =] *procedure_name* [[*@parameter_name* =] *value* | *@variable* [**output**]] [, *...more parameters...*] [**with recompile**]
Executes the stored procedure (or extended stored procedure) *procedure_name*; see the description of **exec[ute]** on page 39 for more information.

sp_configure 'allow procedure grouping', { **0** | **1** } (dynamic)
Enables (**1**, = default) or disables (**0**) procedure grouping; this allows creating multiple stored procedures with the identical names but different group numbers (i.e. **create procedure my_proc;1** and **create procedure my_proc;2**, etc.).

sp_checksource *procedure_name* [, **NULL** [, *owner_name*]]
Checks if the T-SQL source code for *procedure_name* exists (➢p.51).

sp_depends *procedure_name*
Displays objects referring to *procedure_name*, and vice versa (➢p.51).

sp_help *procedure_name*
Displays information about the specified stored procedure.

sp_helptext *procedure_name* [**(12.5)**, *group_number*]
Displays the T-SQL source code of the specified stored procedure (in 12.5, *group_number* can be specified for grouped procedures). Note: the **defncopy** utility (➢p.113) does the same, but formats the output better.

sp_hidetext *procedure_name* [, **NULL** [, *owner_name*]]
Hides the T-SQL source code for *procedure_name* (➢p.51).

(pre-12.5.1) sp_procqmode [*object_name* [, **'detail'**]]
Displays whether *object_name* (a view, stored procedure or trigger) was created in ASE version 11.0 or later, or in an earlier ASE version. With **'detail'**, displays details. If old objects still exist, consider drop and recreate them. Obsolete in 12.5.1.

sp_procxmode [*procedure_name* [, *transaction_mode*]]
Sets (with both parameters) or displays the transaction mode in which a stored procedure can be executed. *transaction_mode* can be **'unchained'**, **'chained'** or **'anymode'** (which allows both chained and unchained). By default, the mode is set to the transaction mode that was active when the procedure was created.
In 12.5.2, and only for procedures containing execute-immediate (a.k.a. 'dynamic SQL'), **'dynamic'** mode can be specified in addition to the above modes in a separate call to **sp_procxmode**. This validates permissions for such dynamic SQL against the procedure creator instead of against the procedure executor. To remove this setting, specify **'not dynamic'**.

sp_rename *old_name*, *new_name*
Renames a stored procedure from *old_name* to *new_name*.

@@nestlevel
Contains the procedure nesting level (0..16) in the current session; ➢p.117.

@@procid
In a stored procedure, contains the object ID of the currently executing procedure.

In 12.5.1, **set proc_output_params** and **set proc_return_status** determine whether messages for output parameters and return status are printed in **isql** (➢p.56).

25. Triggers

A trigger is an attribute of a user table, and is executed as a result of an **insert**, **update** or **delete** statement against that table. The trigger can perform arbitrary processing, similar to a stored procedure (but a trigger cannot have parameters). All trigger activity takes places as part of the transaction for the DML operation. Inside a trigger only, two 'virtual' tables **inserted** and **deleted** are available (constructed from the transaction log), containing the inserted and deleted rows, respectively; for an **update**, **inserted** contains the after-update values and **deleted** the before-values.

create trigger *trigger_name* **on** *table_name* **for** { **insert, update, delete** }
as *T-SQL-statements*

Creates trigger *trigger_name* for the specified DML operation(s) (**insert** and/or **update** and/or **delete**) on table *table_name*. When a trigger for the same DML operation already exists for this table, it is implicitly dropped first.

drop trigger *trigger_name* [, *...more triggers...*]
Drops the specified trigger(s).

To display the triggers defined for table **my_table**, use this query:

```
select instrig = object_name( instrig ) + case when sysstat2 & 1048676 = 0
                      then ' :enabled' else ' :disabled' end,
    updtrig = object_name( updtrig ) + case when sysstat2 & 4194304 = 0
                      then ' :enabled' else ' :disabled' end,
    deltrig = object_name( deltrig ) + case when sysstat2 & 2097152 = 0
                      then ' :enabled' else ' :disabled' end
from sysobjects where id = object_id( 'my_table' )
```

alter table *table_name* { **disable** | **enable** } **trigger** [*trigger_name*]
Enables or disables the trigger, or, without *trigger_name*, all triggers for *table_name*.

rollback trigger [**with raiserror** *error_nr*]
In a trigger, rolls back any data modifications performed in the trigger, including the DML statement that caused the trigger to be executed (➢p.42).

set triggers { **on** | **off** }
Enables (**on**) or disables (**off**) all triggers for the current session only; other sessions are not affected. Requires **replication_role**.

set self_recursion { **on** | **off** }
Within a trigger only, enables (**on**) or disables (**off**, =default) self-recursion for this trigger and for the current session only. Self-recursion occurs when the trigger executes, and it (or a nested stored procedure or another trigger) modifies a row in the same base table; with self-recursion enabled, the trigger is then executed again.

update (*column_name* **)**
This function can only be used in a trigger; it returns a logical value 'true' or 'false' depending on whether or not the originating DML statement updated the specified column. This function is typically used in an **if** statement in the trigger code. Example:
if update(prim_key) begin print 'You can't change a key!' rollback trigger end

sp_configure 'allow nested triggers', { **0** | **1** } (static)
Enables (**1**,=default) or disables (**0**) nested triggers server-wide. When enabled, a data modification in a trigger may cause another trigger to be executed; when disabled, it won't.

sp_checksource *trigger_name*
Checks if the T-SQL source code for *trigger_name* exists (➢p.51).

sp_depends *trigger_name*
Displays objects referring to *trigger_name*, and vice versa (➢p.51).

sp_hidetext *trigger_name* [, **NULL** [, *owner_name*]]
Hides the T-SQL source code for *trigger_name* (➢p.51).

sp_help *trigger_name*
Displays information about the specified trigger.

sp_helptext *trigger_name*
Displays the T-SQL source code of the specified trigger. Note: the **defncopy** utility (➢p.113) does the same, but formats the output better.

sp_rename *old_name*, *new_name*
Renames a trigger from *old_name* to *new_name*.

@@procid
In a trigger, **@@procid** contains the object ID of the stored procedure that performed the DML statement causing the trigger to fire. If the DML was not performed by a stored procedure, **@@procid** = **0** in a trigger.

@@rowcount
Before the first executable statement in a trigger, **@@rowcount** contains the number of rows that were affected by the DML statement which caused the trigger to be exe-

cuted. After the first executable statement, **@@rowcount** behaves as usual (see the section on session-specific global variables on page 115).

@@nestlevel
Contains the procedure nesting level (0..16) in the current session; ➢p.117.

26. Identity columns

An identity column is a numeric column to which the ASE server, not the application, assigns a value. This behaves as an automatically generated sequence number: the value starts at 1, and is incremented for every row inserted into the table. Note that generated identity values are not transactional: when an **insert** is rolled back, the identity value will not be re-used.
A table can have only one identity column. An identity column can be referred to by its column name, but also by the reserved column name **syb_identity** (case-insensitive).

create table *table_name* **(** *column_name datatype* [**(** *precision* **)**] **identity** [**,** *..other columns…*] **)** [**with identity_gap =** *N*]
Creates a table containing an identity column. In pre-12.5.3, *datatype* must be **numeric**; in 12.5.3, *datatype* can also be **int**, **smallint** or **tinyint**; in 15.0, also **bigint**.
precision can be specified only for **numeric** and can range from 1 to 38; default is 18.
with identity_gap specifies the maximum possible size an identity gap for this table could ever have. When this is omitted, there may be a risk of running into very large identity gaps. See **www.sypron.nl/idgaps.html** for more details on identity gaps.
Example: **create table my_table (col_a int, col_b numeric(5) identity)**
with identity_gap = 10

alter table *table_name* **add** *column_name datatype* [**(** *precision* **)**] **identity**
Adds an identity column to an existing table. Otherwise similar to **create table** above.

(12.5.0.3) identity_burn_max (*table_name* **)**
Returns the 'burned' identity value (in **varchar** format!) for the specified table. The identity column would 'jump' to this value if a **shutdown with nowait** occurred. If the table does not have an identity column, returns **NULL**.

(12.5.0.3) next_identity (*table_name* **)**
Returns the identity value (in **varchar** format!) to be assigned to the next row inserted into this table; if the table does not have an identity column, returns **NULL**. When **identity grab size** = 1, applies to the next insert by any session; when > 1, applies to the next insert by the current session.

select [*column_name* =] **identity(***precision* | **(12.5.4)** *datatype***)** [*column_name*] [**,** *…more columns…*] [**with identity_gap =** *N*] **into** *table_name* [*…other clauses…*]
Creates a new table *table_name* with a **select**…**into** statement; **identity()** adds an identity column named *column_name* to this new table (effectively adding a sequence number to the selected rows). When specifying a *precision* (1..38), the identity column will be **numeric(***precision***)**; in 12.5.4, with *datatype* (**[unsigned] int**, **smallint**, **tinyint**) it will be of that datatype. See **create table** above for details on the **identity_gap** clause.
Example: **select name, nr = identity(5) into new_tab with identity_gap = 100**
from sysobjects order by name
(12.5.4) select *, seq=identity(int) into #t2 from mytable -- creates an int

set identity_insert *table_name* { **on** | **off** }
(12.5.0.3) set identity_update *table_name* { **on** | **off** }
For the current session, **set identity_insert** allows (**on**) or disallows (**off**, default) a value for an identity column to be specified explicitly when inserting a row (by default, a value is assigned automatically). **set identity_update** allows (**on**) or disallows (**off**, default) direct updates to identity column values in existing rows. **identity_insert** and **identity_update** can each be enabled for one table at a time, or both for the same table in the current session. Note: without a unique index, there is no check against creating duplicate values in the identity column.
Examples: **create table my_table (col_a int, col_b numeric identity)**
insert my_table (col_a) values (1)
set identity_insert my_table on
insert my_table (col_a, col_b) values (2, 100)
set identity_insert my_table off

sp_chgattribute *table_name***, 'identity_gap',** *value*
Sets the maximum possible size of an identity gap for this table to *value* (must be ≥ 1;

0 removes the **identity_gap** setting for this table).
Example: **sp_chgattribute my_table, 'identity_gap', 10**

(12.5.1) sp_chgattribute *table_name*, **'identity_burn_max', 0,** '*new-identity-value*'
Sets the identity column counter for this table to the specified new value. During this operation, the table will be locked exclusively. Resetting the counter downwards is not allowed when higher column values exist in the table. For an improved version of **sp_chgattribute** (without this last restriction), see **www.sypron.nl/idgaps.html**.
Example: **sp_chgattribute my_table, 'identity_burn_max', 0, '123456'**

@@identity
Contains the last value inserted into an identity column by an **insert** or **select...into** statement in the current session. Following an insert into a table not containing an identity column, **@@identity** will be set to 0.

bcp ... **[-N] [-E] [-g** *identity_start*]
The **bcp** options **-N**, **-E** and **-g** define specific behaviour regarding identity columns. See the description of **bcp** on page 112 for details.

dbcc object_atts (*table_name*, *0*, *subcommand* [, *new_value*] **)**
Displays or patches identity values for the specified table (➢p.91).

sp_configure *config_option*, *value*
Sets configuration options related to identity columns.

- **'identity burning set factor'** (static) - Indirectly defines the maximum size of an 'identity gap' (a sudden, large jump in identity values). This maximum gap size depends on the precision of a specific identity column, and is calculated as follows: $value * 10^{-7} * 10^{(precision\ of\ the\ identity\ column)}$. *value* can be any value ≥ 1; default = 5000. For an identity column of precision **numeric(10)**, the default of 5000 allows a maximum identity gap of $5000 * 10^{-7} * 10^{10}$ = 5,000,000. When the **identity_gap** attribute is defined for a table, this overrides the maximum gap size for that table as described above. See **www.sypron.nl/idgaps.html** for more information about identity gaps.
- **'size of auto identity column'** (dynamic) - Specifies the precision (1..38; default=10) for an implicitly created identity column as a result of the database options **'auto identity'** or **'unique auto_identity index'** (see below).
- **'identity grab size'** (dynamic) - Defines the number of identity values assigned to a session when inserting into tables with an identity column (default=**1**).

sp_dboption *db_name*, *db_option*, { **true** | **false** }
Sets database options related to identity columns; in pre-12.5.1, a subsequent **checkpoint** is required (➢p.59 for details on **sp_dboption**). *db_option* can be:

- **'auto identity'** - When enabled (**true**), for each table created with **create table**, an identity column (named **'SYB_IDENTITY_COL'**, and having the precision set by **'size of auto identity column'**) will be added automatically when no identity column was specified explicitly (default = **false**).
- **'identity in nonunique index'** - When enabled (**true**), for all tables with an identity column, this column will be included in every non-unique index created on the table, thus making each index unique (default = **false**).
- **'unique auto_identity index'** - Identical to **'auto identity'**, but also creates a unique nonclustered index on the identity column automatically (default = **false**).

27. Programming & flow control

begin ... **end**
Groups one or more T-SQL statements into a block which is syntactically treated a single statement. Otherwise, the **begin** ... **end** statement has no functionality itself.

break
Exits from a **while**-loop; execution continues at the first statement after the loop.

case when *logical-expr* **then** *expr* **when** *logical-expr* **then** *expr* [...] **else** *expr-dft* **end**
case *expr* **when** *expr* **then** *expr* **when** *expr* **then** *expr* [...] **else** *expr-dft* **end**
case is not a statement, but an expression, which can occur anywhere where an expression is allowed. **case** can be used to implement if-then-else logic within a T-SQL statement: based on the value of an expression, the value of another expression is returned as the result. The datatypes of all result expressions must be compatible. At least one result expression must not be **NULL**. When the **else** clause is omitted, **else NULL** is used as a default. **case** comes in two forms:

- **select case when a > 0 then b/a when a < 0 then -1 else 0 end from my_table**

- **select case a when 1 then 'One' when 2 then 'Two' else 'Whatever' end from my_table**

coalesce (*expression_1*, *expression_2* [, *expression_3*, ... , *expression_n*] **)**
Returns the value of the first expression in the list which is not **NULL**. The list must contain at least two expressions. Because **coalesce()** is an abbreviated form of the **case** expression, the datatypes of all expressions must be compatible, and at least one result must not be **NULL**. Example: **select coalesce(3*NULL, 4, 5)** returns 4

nullif (*expression_1*, *expression_2* **)**
When *expression_1* = *expression_2*, returns **NULL**, otherwise returns *expression_1*. Because **nullif()** is an abbreviated form of the **case** expression, the datatypes of all expressions must be compatible, and at least one result must not be **NULL**.
Examples: **select nullif(1, 1)** returns **NULL**. **select nullif(1, 2)** returns **1**.
Avoid divide-by-zero: **select a/nullif(b,0)** will return **NULL** if **b** = 0.

continue
Returns to the top of a **while**-loop and re-evaluates the logical expression.

declare *@variable_name datatype* [, ...*more variables*...]
Declares a local variable of the specified name and datatype; the datatype can be a system datatype or a user-defined datatype.
Example: **declare @i int, @my_string varchar(80)**

exec[ute] [*@return_status* **=**] *procedure_name* [[*@parameter_name* **=**] *value* | *@variable* [**output**]] [, ...*more parameters*...] [**with recompile**]
Executes the stored procedure (or extended stored procedure) *procedure_name*; this name may include a server name, database name, owner name and a procedure version number. When *procedure_name* starts with '**sp_**' or '**xp_**', and it is not found in the specified database or the current database, it is searched for in the **sybsystemprocs** database, and if still not found, in the **master** database. The return status is of datatype **int**. To create an output parameter, a variable (not a value) must be specified, and the **output** keyword must be specified in both the **execute** statement and in the **create procedure** statement. Note that an expression cannot be specified as a parameter. For the first statement in a batch, the **execute** keyword is optional. **with recompile** forces a new query plan to be generated before execution.
Examples: **exec sp_helpdb**
exec my_db..my_proc 100, @result_var output
exec OTHER_SERVER...sp_who

exec @string_variable
Though not formally documented or supported, a stored procedure can be executed by specifying its name in a (**var**)**char** variable.
Examples: **declare @string_var varchar(100) select @string_var = 'sp_help'**
exec @string_var 'my_table'

select @string_var = 'SYB_BACKUP...sp_who'
exec @string_var

exec[ute] (*character_string* **)**
Executes the T-SQL statement(s) in *character_string*, which may be a concatenation of character constants and variables (but not built-in functions). This form of the **execute** statement is known as 'execute immediate' (or sometimes as 'dynamic SQL'). Example: **exec ('select * from ' + @table_name)**

NB: for executing OS commands from SQL, use **xp_cmdshell** (➢p.99).

goto *label_name*
Jumps to the specified label (note: for your comfort and safety, use **goto** reluctantly!). Example: **goto my_label --** jumps to label **my_label:**

if *logical_expression* [*AQP*] *T-SQL-statement-1* [**else** *T-SQL-statement-2*]
If *logical_expression* is true, executes *T-SQL-statement-1*. Otherwise, and only if **else** is specified, executes *T-SQL-statement-2*.
See the **while** statement for more information about the optional *AQP* clause.
Example: **if @i >= 0 print 'positive' else print 'negative'**

print { **'***format_string***'** | *@local_variable* | *@@global_variable* } [, *value_list*]
Prints the text in *format_string*, or the value of the specified local or global variable (which must be of a (**var**)**char** datatype). *@local_variable* can also contain a format string. A format can contain placeholders in the form **%n!** (**n**=1..20). The values for **n**

must be consecutive and start at 1. The placeholders are replaced by values or variables (not expressions) from the *value_list*. Errors in the placeholders or the format string result in a run-time (not a compile-time) error.
Example: **print 'My name is %1!, I'm %2! years old.', @my_name, @my_age**

raiserror *error_nr* [, *value_list*]
raiserror *error_nr* { **'***format_string***'** | **@** *variable* }] [, *value_list*] [**with errordata** *list*]
With a comma following *error_nr*, the corresponding message in the session's current language will be retrieved, formatted using values in *value_list*, and printed. For system-defined messages (in **master..sysmessages)**, *error_nr* must be between 17000 and 19999; for user-defined messages (in **sysusermessages** in the current database), *error_nr* must be ≥ 20000.
format_string or *@variable* are used to format and display a message. Without a comma following *error_nr*, no message is retrieved, but an instant message is composed from the specified format string or variable, and any values in *value_list*.
When **raiserror** completes, **@@error** will contain the value of *error_nr*. The clause **with errordata** *list* is for use with CT-Lib programs only.
Examples: **sp_addmessage 22222, 'This is a %1! message!'**
raiserror 22222, 'strange'
raiserror 33333 'This is an %1! message', instant -- note: no comma !

return [[( ] *integer_expression* [ )]] [*AQP*]
Exists from a stored procedure to the caller. If specified, *integer_expression* will be the return status value of the stored procedure. If the expression involves a query, this must evaluate to a single integer value. ASE uses negative return values to indicate certain types of errors; therefore, best don't use negative return values in your own code. When the *AQP* clause is used, the parentheses ('**(**' and '**)**') are mandatory. See the **while** statement for more information about this optional *AQP* clause.

waitfor delay '*hh:mm:ss*[*.ccc*]**'**
waitfor time '*hh:mm:ss***'**
waitfor { **errorexit** | **processexit** | **mirrorexit** }
Waits for a time or an event. **delay** waits for the specified interval (max. 24 hours); **time** waits until the specified time (max. 24 hours away); **errorexit** waits until a process terminates abnormally; **processexit** until a process terminates normally or abnormally; **mirrorexit** until a mirror (set up with **disk mirror**) terminates abnormally.

while *logical_expression* [*AQP*] *T-SQL-statement*
If *logical_expression* is true, executes *T-SQL-statement* in a loop until the expression is no longer true, or until the loop is exited via a **break**, **return** or **goto** statement.
Example: **while @i < 100 begin exec my_proc select @i = @i + 1 end**
If the expression involves a query, *AQP* can specify the abstract query plan (AQP) for this query as **plan '(** *AQP-language* **)'** ; ➢p.105 for info on abstract query plans.

use { *db_name* | *@character_variable* }
Changes the current database to *db_name*, or to the database in the character variable, effective as of the next query batch. **use** cannot be used in stored procedures or triggers. Note that the use of *@character_variable* is undocumented. Also note: system stored procedures can access other databases without actually changing the current database though the **use** command. Example: to display the layout of table **other_db..t1**, regardless of the current database: **exec other_db..sp_help t1**.

28. Cursors

Cursors can be used for implementing loop-based, sequential, non-relational algorithms like those which are common in 3GL languages. ASE has 4 types of cursors:

- **server cursor** - a cursor declared in a stored procedure.
- **language cursor** - a cursor declared in multiple command batches, outside a stored procedure.
- **client cursor** and **execute cursor** - cursors defined on the client side and implemented though OpenClient (typically in a C-program) or Embedded SQL. These cursors can not be created interactively using (for example) **isql**.

The statements in this section apply only to language cursors or server cursors.

declare *cursor_name*
[(15.0) semi_sensitive | **insensitive**] **[(15.0) scroll** | **no scroll**] **cursor**
for *select_statement* [**for** { **read only** | **update** [**of** *updated_column_names_list*] }]
Declares (creates) a cursor based on the specified **select** statement. With **no scroll** (=default), the cursor is non-scrollable (i.e. only the next row can be fetched). With **scroll**, the cursor is scrollable (i.e. any row can be fetched). With **semi_sensitive**

(=default), changes to the underlying data rows may be visible through the cursor; with **insensitive**, such changes are not visible.
It is recommended to indicate if this cursor will be updated (using **for update**, and optionally the updateable columns) or not (using **for read only**, which will disallow any update or delete operations for the cursor).
Note: for language cursors (see above), **declare**...**cursor** must be in a separate batch (i.e. not in the same batch as the **open** statement).

open *cursor_name*
Opens the specified cursor.

close *cursor_name*
Closes the specified cursor; it can be reopened with **open** *cursor_name* (the cursor query will be re-evaluated from the start).

deallocate cursor *cursor_name*
Deallocates the cursor. It must be declared again before it can be reopened.

fetch [**(15.0) next** | **prior** | **first** | **last** | **absolute** *offset* | **relative** *offset*]
[**(15.0) from**] *cursor_name* [**into** *@variable_1* [**,** *@variable_2* [**,** ...]]]
Returns a row from the specified cursor's result set. When using the **into** clause, the fetched columns are stored in the specified local variables. For a non-scrollable cursor only the next row can be fetched. For a scrollable cursor, any row can be fetched, as specified by **next** (next row), **prior** (previous row), **first** (first row in result set), **last** (last row in result set), **absolute** *offset* (row #*offset*), **relative** *offset* (offset rows forward or backwards (when *offset* < 0)).

set close on endtran { **on** | **off** }
By default, this session-specific setting is **off**. When **on**, when a transaction is committed or rolled back, all cursors opened within the transaction, and declared within the scope of the **set close on endtran** command, are automatically closed.

set cursor rows *number* **for** *cursor_name*
Defines the number of rows (default=1) that will be returned for a **fetch** from the specified cursor. Does not affect **fetch**...**into** statements.

update { *table_name* | *view_name* } **set** [*table_name*.]*column* **=** *expression* [**,** *...more column assignments...*] **where current of** *cursor_name*
Updates the row at the current position of *cursor_name* in the specified table of view.

delete [**from**] { *table_name* | *view_name* } **where current of** *cursor_name*
Deletes the row at the current position of *cursor_name* in the specified table of view.

@@sqlstatus
Contains the result status of the last cursor **fetch** statement; other statements do not alter the value of **@@sqlstatus**. Possible values are: **0** - **fetch** completed successfully; **1** - **fetch** resulted in an error; **2** - end of result set reached.

(15.0) @@fetch_status
Contains the result status of the last **fetch** statement in a scrollable cursor. Possible values are: **0**: **fetch** completed successfully; **-1**: **fetch** failed, or the fetched row is outside the result set.

(15.0) @@cursor_rows
For scrollable cursors only, contains the total number of rows in the result set of the last opened or fetched cursor. Possible values are: **0**: zero rows, or no cursor is open; **-1**: cursor is open but the total number of rows is not yet known; *N* (>**0**): the total number of rows is known: *N*.

@@rowcount
After a **fetch** statement, contains the total number of rows fetched from the cursor result set since the cursor was opened. For a scrollable cursor, this can exceed the number of rows in the result set if rows are fetched more than once.

sp_cursorinfo [*cursor_level* [**,** *cursor_name*]]
Displays information about the specified *cursor_name* or about all cursors that are active for the current session. The *cursor_level* can be:

- **N** (>0) : shows cursors inside stored procedures (server cursors) at procedure nesting level N.
- **0** : shows cursors outside stored procedures (language cursors).

- **-1** : shows language cursors and server cursors at all nesting levels.
- **NULL** : shows info on the specified *cursor_name*.

29. Example of cursor programming

This example demonstrates how T-SQL statements can be used to list all objects of a certain type in a database, ordered by their creation date, by using a cursor.

```
create procedure sp_demo_proc
   @p_objtype varchar(2) = 'U'  -- by default, list user tables
as
begin
   declare @date_fmt varchar(21), @fill varchar(30), @cnt int, @nr char(4)
   declare @obj_name varchar(30), @obj_date datetime

   declare demo_cursor cursor  -- declare the cursor
   for select name, crdate from sysobjects
       where type = @p_objtype
       order by crdate desc
   if @@error <> 0 goto err_label
   -- hmm... goto? Remember Dijkstra's 'Go To statement considered harmful'?

   open demo_cursor  -- open the cursor
   if @@error <> 0 goto err_label

   select @cnt = 0 -- initialise the result counter
   while 1 = 1     -- I'm really a C-programmer...
   begin
     fetch demo_cursor into @obj_name, @obj_date  -- fetch next row
     if @@error <> 0 or @@sqlstatus = 1 goto err_label
     if @@sqlstatus = 2 break  -- the end has been reached, exit the loop

     select @cnt = @cnt + 1  -- one more found!
     select @date_fmt = convert(char(11), @obj_date, 106) + ' ' +
                        convert(char(8), @obj_date, 8),
            @fill = space(30-char_length(@obj_name)),
            @nr = str(@cnt,4) -- assumption: no more than 9999 objects

     print '%1! Name:%2!%4!Created: %3!', @nr, @obj_name, @date_fmt, @fill
   end

   print 'Total #objects found: %1!', @cnt

   close demo_cursor  -- close cursor
   if @@error <> 0 goto err_label

   deallocate cursor demo_cursor  -- ... and clean up
   return @cnt -- return number of objects found

 err_label: -- there's been an error, wrap things up
   deallocate cursor demo_cursor
   return -1 -- return error indication
end
```

30. Transactions

When no user-defined transactions are used, each DML or DDL operation is a transaction in itself. By default, ASE uses unchained transaction mode.

begin { **tran** | **transaction** } [*transaction_name*]
Starts a user-defined transaction, with name *transaction_name*, if specified.

commit [**tran** | **transaction** | **work**] [*transaction_name*]
Commits a user-defined transaction, causing all dirty log pages for the transaction to be written to disk.

rollback [**tran** | **transaction** | **work**]
rollback [**tran** | **transaction** | **work**] { *transaction_name* | *savepoint_name* }
The first form rolls a user-defined transaction back to the outermost **begin transaction** statement. With *transaction_name*, this name must correspond to the outermost **begin transaction** or the rollback fails and the transaction remains active. With *savepoint_name*, rolls back to that savepoint. In a trigger, a **rollback** command (without a savepoint name) also aborts the batch (so subsequent statements are not executed).

rollback trigger [**with raiserror** *error_nr*]
In a trigger, rolls back any data modifications performed in the trigger, including the DML statement that caused the trigger to be executed. Any transaction this DML statement was part of remains open, and is not rolled back. Any subsequent statements in the trigger will not be executed. **@@transtate** will be 2; **@@error** will be the *error_nr* in the **raiserror** clause; if this clause is not specified, **@@error** will be 0.

save { **tran** | **transaction** } *savepoint_name*
Sets a savepoint in a transaction to allow the transaction to be partially rolled back.

prepare { **tran** | **transaction** }
Used by DB/CT-Library for two-phase commit transactions. Not for use in T-SQL.

checkpoint [**(12.5.1)** { *db_name* | **all** }]
Writes all dirty pages (both log and data pages) for the current database to disk. Also synchronises some in-memory database structures with disk. Note: if the database option **'trunc. log on chkpt'** is enabled for a database, running the **checkpoint** command will not truncate the log (this option only applies to automatic checkpoints). **(12.5.1)** With *db_name*, checkpoints that database; with **all**, all databases.

sp_procxmode [*procedure_name* [**,** *transaction_mode*]]
Sets (with both parameters) or displays the transaction mode in which a stored procedure can be executed (➢p.35).

set chained { **on** | **off** }
Enables (**on**) or disables (**off**) chained transaction mode for the current session. The current mode is indicated by **@@tranchained** (**0**=unchained;**1**=chained). The default ASE mode is unchained. In chained mode, **begin transaction** is implicitly executed for **select**, **insert**, **update**, **delete**, **fetch** and **open** statements.

set close on endtran { **on** | **off** }
Affects whether certain cursors are closed when a transaction is rolled back (➢p.41).

@@trancount
Contains the nesting level of transactions in the current session. This is incremented by each **begin transaction** statement, and decremented by each **commit**; a successful **rollback** (not to a savepoint!) resets it to **0**.

@@transtate
Contains the state of the current transaction in the current session. Possible values are: **0** - transaction in progress; **1** - transaction committed; **2** - previous statement aborted; transaction still in progress; **3** - transaction aborted and rolled back.

sp_transactions [*type*, *param1*, *param2*]
Without parameters, displays all currently active transactions, both local and distributed, in this server. Parameters may be specified to filter on distributed transactions (see the *ASE Reference Manual* for details). For local transactions, similar information is available in **master..syslogshold**.

31. Example of transaction programming

This example demonstrates how to program a nested transaction. Note that proper error handling is always essential when coding transaction logic!

```
create procedure bank_transfer_demo
   @account int, @transfer_amount money
as
begin
   begin transaction

     update accounts
     set balance = balance + @transfer_amount
     where account_no = @account
     if @@error <> 0 or @@rowcount <> 1  -- account must exist & be unique
     begin
        rollback
        print 'Error for account %1!', @account
        return -1  -- error occurred
     end

   commit    -- in a nested transaction, this is not the 'real' commit yet
   return 0  -- successful completion
end
go

-- Now, use this procedure to transfer $100 between two bank accounts
declare @s int
begin transaction
exec @s = bank_transfer_demo 123456789, 100.00
if @s = 0
begin
   exec @s = bank_transfer_demo 456789123, -100.00
   if @s = 0
   begin
```

```
      commit  -- do the 'real' (=outermost) commit here
   end
end
```

32. Locking

A lock scheme can be defined for each individual user table. Possible lock schemes are **allpages** (also known as 'page locking', the classic Sybase lock scheme), **datapages** and **datarows** (also known as 'row-level locking'). **datapages** and **datarows** are often collectively abbreviated as DOL (data-only locking), and **allpages** as APL. A table's lock scheme is stored in **sysobjects.sysstat2** as follows:

sysobjects.sysstat2 bit set	lock scheme
bit 8192	**allpages**
bit 16384	**datapages**
bit 32768	**datarows**
None of the above	**allpages**

The following query displays the lock scheme for all tables in the current database:

select name, case sysstat2 & 57344 when 32768 then 'datarows'
when 16384 then 'datapages' else 'allpages' end
from sysobjects where type in ('U', 'S')

In 12.5, this same lock scheme information can be found more easily as follows:

select name, lockscheme(id) from sysobjects where type in ('U', 'S')

sp_configure 'lock scheme', 0, { allpages | datarows | datapages } (dynamic)
Sets the default server-wide lock scheme for newly created tables; default = **allpages**.

sp_configure 'number of locks', *nr_of_locks* (static; 12.5:semi-dynamic)
Configures the maximum number of locks that can exist in the server at a time. When this limit is reached, a query requiring additional locks is aborted.

sp_configure 'read committed with lock', { 0 | 1 } (dynamic)
For DOL tables only, determines whether **select** queries on transaction level 1 and read-only cursors will hold shared row/page locks. Default= **0** =disabled; **1** =enabled.

sp_configure 'print deadlock information', { 0 | 1 } (dynamic)
Enables (**1**) or disables (**0**,=default) printing deadlock details to the server errorlog. NB: When ASE aborts a session due to a deadlock, the client receives error 1205.

sp_configure 'deadlock retries', *nr_of_retries* (dynamic)
Number of times a deadlock on an APL index page will be retried (default = 5).

(12.5.0.3) sp_chgattribute *table_name*, **'optimistic_index_lock', { 0 | 1 }**
For APL tables only, enables (**1**) or disables (**0**,=default) 'optimistic index locking' for this table, meaning no address locks are taken on index root pages to reduce lock contention. When a lock is still needed, an Exclusive-Table lock is used instead.

sp_familylock [*family_id_1* [,*family_id_2*]]
Displays the locks held by all processes in a 'family' (a number of processes executing a query in parallel). Up to two family IDs (displayed as 'fid' by **sp_who**) can be specified; without parameters, displays all locks currently held by all families.

sp_lock [*spid_1* [, *spid_2* [**(15.0),** *verbose*]]]
Displays the locks held by one or two processes with the specified *spid(s)*. Without parameters, displays all currently existing locks. When *verbose* = **1**, displays table names instead of object IDs.

sp_object_stats '*hh:mm:ss***'** [, *top_N* [, *db_name* [, *table_name* [, *option*]]]]
During the specified interval, collects lock contention statistics for all tables server-wide (without *db_name* and *object_name*), for all tables in a specific database (with *db_name*) or for a specific table only (with *table_name* and *db_name*). With *top_N* (a number), displays only the top-*N* tables with lock contention. *option* can be **'rpt_objlist'** (displays only object names) or **'rpt_locks'** (displays details; =default).

create table *table_name* **(** *column_list* **)** [**lock** { **allpages** | **datarows** | **datapages** }]
Specifies the lock scheme for a created table, overriding the server-wide default.

alter table *table_name* **lock** { **allpages** | **datarows** | **datapages** }
Changes the lock scheme for the specified table. For large tables, changing between APL and DOL schemes may take a long time, since the table is copied completely.

Changing between **datarows** and **datapages** schemes is fast, irrespective of the table size. Note: changing between APL and DOL schemes is a 'minimally logged' operation (➤p.121), and it is recommended to make a database dump afterwards. Note2: when changing between APL and DOL schemes, you should subsequently drop and recreate any triggers that exist on that table.

select *select_list* **into** *table_name* [**lock** { **allpages** | **datarows** | **datapages** }] ...
Creates a new table (with **select...into**), with the specified lock scheme. Without a lock scheme, the server-wide default is used; not the lock scheme of the source table(s).

sp_configure 'lock wait period', *nr_seconds* (dynamic)
Sets the server-wide lock wait timeout (in seconds); 0 means 'nowait'. To restore the default of 'wait forever', run **sp_configure 'lock wait period', 0, 'default'**.
When a query cannot acquire a lock within the specified time, **@@error** is set to 12205 and the transaction (if any) is aborted.

set lock wait [*nr_seconds*] / **set lock nowait**
Sets the lock wait timeout (in seconds) for the current session or in a stored procedure, overriding the server-wide setting. **set lock wait** (without *nr_seconds*) will wait forever (= default); **set lock nowait** is identical to **set lock wait 0**, and will not wait at all. When a query cannot acquire a lock within the specified time, **@@error** is set to 12205 and the transaction (if any) is aborted. Once **set lock** has been used in a session, the server-wide default will be overridden for the rest of that session.
In 12.5.0.3, **@@lock_timeout** contains the current lock wait setting for the session.
Example: **set lock wait 60** -- sets the lock wait period to 1 minute for this session

lock table *table_name* **in** { **share** | **exclusive** } **mode** [**wait** *nr_secs* | **nowait**]
Within a transaction, explicitly locks *table_name* with a Shared-Table lock or an Exclusive-Table lock. The lock wait timeout can be specified with **wait** *nr_secs* or **nowait**; if neither is specified, the current session's lock wait time, or else the server-wide default is used. If the lock cannot be acquired within the specified time, **@@error** is set to 12207, but the transaction will continue.
Example: **begin transaction**
lock table my_table in exclusive mode

{ **select** | **insert** | **update** | **delete** } ... **from** *table_name* [**readpast**] ...
{ **readtext** | **writetext** } *table_name.column_name* ... [**readpast**] ...
For DOL tables only, specifying **readpast** for *table_name* will cause the query not to be blocked by incompatible locks on that table; instead, these locks will be skipped, so that the query can continue. Note: any rows that are locked by skipped locks will be ignored by the query, so query results may be affected when using **readpast**.

set transaction isolation level *level*
{ **select** | **readtext** } ... **at isolation** *level*
Sets the specified transaction isolation level for the current session (using **set transaction**), or for a specific **select** or **readtext** query (using **at isolation**). *level* can be:

...**at isolation** *level* **set transaction isolation level** *level*	**Commonly known as:**
0 | read uncommitted	'dirty reads'
1 | read committed	'ASE default isolation level'
2 | repeatable read	'repeatable read'
3 | serializable	'holdlock' or 'avoid phantoms' (=ANSI default isolation level)

The transaction isolation level has significant effects on locking behaviour (see the *ASE Performance and Tuning Guide* for details). Note the following:

- The default isolation level in ASE is 1.
- Isolation level 0 has an effect on read operations (like **select** statements) only.
- DOL tables don't hold shared locks for level-1 **select** statements, unless **'read committed with lock'** is set to 1.
- Level 2 ('repeatable read') is supported for DOL tables only. When applied to an APL table, isolation level 3 ('serializable') will be used instead.

For **select** and **readtext** statements, **[no]holdlock** also affects the isolation level:

- **holdlock** is equivalent to isolation level 3.
- **noholdlock** is equivalent to isolation level 1.
- **shared** does not apply to an isolation level, but specifies that shared locks should be used instead of update locks.

Examples: **select col_a from my_table at isolation read uncommitted**
select col_a from my_table where key_val = 1 at isolation 3
select col_a from my_table holdlock where key_val = 1

@@isolation
Contains the session's current transaction isolation level (0, 1, 2 or 3).

For details about lock promotion, see p.99.

33. Java in ASE (SQLJ)

Java classes can be installed in an ASE database and used as datatypes, user-defined functions or stored procedures; mixed SQL/Java is known as SQLJ. Installed Java classes are local to a database, and stored in the system table **sysxtypes**; (JAR info is in **sysjars**). Use the operator **'>>'** to reference fields and methods in a class. For details on **in row** or **off row** storage of Java columns, see p.25. See the ASE manual *Java in Adaptive Server Enterprise* for more information about Java in ASE.
Examples (for Java class **MyClass**, having a field **MyField** and method **MyMethod**):

declare @my_var MyClass -- this class must have been installed; ➢p.47
select @my_var = new MyClass()
select @my_var>>MyField, @my_var>>MyMethod()
create table my_tab(col1 int, col2 MyClass, col3 MyClass in row)
insert my_tab values (123, @my_var, new MyClass())

sp_configure 'enable java', { **0** | **1** } (static)
Enables (**1**) or disables (**0**) the Java feature in ASE; in pre-15 only, enabling requires the **ASE_JAVA** option to be licensed (➢p.122).
The config options **'size of process object heap'**, **'size of shared class heap'** and **'size of global fixed heap'** (all: static; 12.5:semi-dynamic) affect Java-related memory allocation and may need to be increased when using Java in ASE.

(12.5) sp_configure 'number of java sockets', *nr_of_sockets* (semi-dynamic)
Defines the number of available Java sockets (when using the **java.net** package).

sp_helpjava [**'class'** [, *class_name* [, **'detail'** | **(12.5) 'depends'**]] | **'jar'** [, *jar_name* [, **(12.5) 'depends'**]]
Displays information about Java classes and/or JARs in the current database. For classes, specify **'detail'** to display class details. In 12.5, **'depends'** displays all database objects in the current database which depend on the class or JAR.

(12.5) sp_depends { *sqlj_function_name* | *sqlj_procedure_name* }
Displays objects referring to the specified Java function or -procedure, and vice versa.

(12.5) sp_helptext { *sqlj_function_name* | *sqlj_procedure_name* }
Displays the T-SQL statement which created the specified Java function or -procedure.

(12.5) create func[**tion**] *sqlj_function_name* **(** [*sql_parameter_name sql_datatype* [, *...more parameters...*]] **)** **returns** *sql_datatype* [**modifies sql data**]
[{ **returns NULL** | **called** } **on NULL input**] [[**not**] **deterministic**] [**exportable**]
language java parameter style java external name '*java_method_name* [**(** [*java_datatype* [, *...more java datatypes...*]] **)**] '
Creates a Java function, mapping to a static method in a Java class in the current database. When any actual function parameter is **NULL**, and with **returns NULL on NULL input** specified, the function returns **NULL** and won't invoke the Java method; with **called on NULL input** (=default), the function is executed normally. **modifies sql data** and [**not**] **deterministic** are for SQLJ compatibility and can be omitted. With **exportable**, the function resides on a remote server and will be executed via CIS.
Example: **create function my_func(par1 int) returns java.lang.String language java parameter style java external name 'MyClass.MyMethod'**

select my_func(col_1) from my_table
update my_table set col_1 = my_func(col_2)

(12.5) drop func[**tion**] *sqlj_function_name* [, *...more functions...*]
Drops the specified Java function(s) from the current database.

(12.5) create proc[**edure**] *sqlj_procedure_name* **(** [**in** | **out** | **inout**] *sql_param_name sql_datatype* [**(12.5.2)** = *default_value*] [, *...more parameters...*]] **)** [**dynamic result sets** *nr_result_sets*] [**modifies sql data**] [[**not**] **deterministic**] **language java parameter style java external name** '*java_method_name* [**(** [*java_datatype* [,*...more java datatypes...*]] **)**] '
Creates a Java stored procedure, mapping to a static method in a Java class in the current database. **in** (=default), **out** and **inout** specify an input-only, output-only and input-output parameter, respectively. **dynamic result sets** specifies the max number of SQL result sets generated; specifying **0** is identical to omitting this clause. **modifies sql data** and [**not**] **deterministic** are for SQLJ compatibility and can be omitted.

Example: **create procedure my_proc(par1 int) dynamic result sets 1 language java parameter style java external name 'MyClass.MyOtherMethod'**

(12.5) drop proc[edure] *procedure_name* [, *…more procedures…*]
Drops the specified Java procedure(s) from the current database.

(12.5) set stringsize *nr_of_characters*
Defines the maximum number of characters returned by the **toString()** Java method before truncation. **@@stringsize** contains the current setting; default=50.

To install a Java class named **MyClass** into an ASE database, follow these steps:

1. Outside ASE, create an uncompressed JAR file:
   javac MyClass.java (➔ produces file **MyClass.class**)
   jar [-]**cf0 MyJar.jar MyClass.class** (➔ produces file **MyJar.jar**)
2. (Option A): install the JAR file using the **installjava** tool (NT: **instjava**) (➤p.114):
   installjava -f MyJar.jar -S MYSERVER -U mylogin -P mypasswd -D my_db
2. (Option B, SQL): **install java [update] from file '***JAR_or_ZIP_file_pathname***'** (undocumented) Installs the Java class in the specified JAR or ZIP file into the current database. With update, overwrites an already installed class.

remove java { **class** *class_name* [, *…more classes…*] | **package** *package_name* [,*…more packages…*] | **jar** *jar_name* [,*…more jars…*] [**retain classes**] }
Drops the specified classes, packages or JARs from the current database. For JARs, the related classes are dropped as well, unless **retain classes** is specified.
To extract a JAR and its Java classes, use **extractjava** (NT:**extrjava**); ➤p.113.

A GUI debugger for Java-in-ASE is in $SYBASE/$SYBASE_ASE/debugger/Debug.jar (must be in the CLASSPATH). To start, run: **java sybase.vm.Debug** (from the command line). See the ASE manual *Java in Adaptive Server Enterprise* for details.

34. XML (XPath/XQuery/SQLX) in ASE (12.5.1)

In 12.5.1, native XML processing was introduced in ASE. Compared with the pre-12.5.1 Java-based XML features (not covered in this book), the native XML engine offers more functionality (ANSI SQLX; XPath/XQuery queries), better performance, and easier setup/configuration. In 12.5.1, ASE supports XPath queries (➤p.49).
For full details about the XML/XPath/SQLX functionality, see the manual *XML Services in Adaptive Server Enterprise*.

sp_configure 'enable xml', { **0** | **1** } (dynamic)
Enables (**1**) or disables (**0**) XML processing features. To enable, in pre-15 only, the **ASE_XML** option must be licensed.

select *…rest of statement…*
for xml [(15.0) schema | **all**] [**(15.0) returns** *datatype*] [**option '***sqlx_options…***'**] }
For a **select** statement only, specifying **for xml** converts the SQL result set to a SQLX-XML document. **returns** can only be used when the **select** is a subquery.
In 15.0, **for xml schema** generates the XML schema describing the result set generated by **for xml**, but not the result set data itself; **for xml all** generates both schema and data. For *sqlx_options*, see below.
Example: **select * from my_table where col1 > 0 order by col2 for xml option 'columnstyle=attribute statement=yes'**

xmlextract ('*xpath_query***[/text()]',** *xml_data* [**option '***options…***'**] **returns** *datatype*] **)**
Executes the XPath query against the XML data. By default, the result is returned as an XML document; when **/text()** is added to the XPath query, the outermost XML tags are removed and the result is returned as a scalar value. By default, the result datatype is **text**, unless specified otherwise (as an ASE datatype or **java.lang.String**) with **returns**. *options* can be **xmlerror** and **ncr** (see *sqlx_options* below).
Examples:

select xmlextract('//t', '<doc><t>Hello</t></doc>') returns: **'<t>Hello</t>'**

select xmlextract('//t/text()', '<doc><t>Hello</t></doc>') returns: **'Hello'**

select xmlextract('//t/text()', '<doc><t>1234</t></doc>' returns int)
returns: **1234** (as an integer)

select xmlextract('//t', xml_col option 'xmlerror=message' returns int)
from your_tab …rest of query…

xmlparse (*xml_data* [**option '***options…***'**] **)**
Parses an XML document, returning it as an **image** value. Parsed XML data can be

accessed faster than raw XML. *options* can be **xmlerror** (see *sqlx_options* below) and also **dtdvalidate={yes|no}**: with **yes** (default=**no**), the XML document is validated against an embedded DTD. Example:

```
create table my_tab (my_col int, xml_col image NULL)
insert my_tab values (123, xmlparse('<doc><t>Hello</t></doc>')) -- parsed XML
insert my_tab values (456, '<doc><t>Bonjour</t></doc>')           -- raw XML
```

xmlrepresentation (*image_column* **)**
Determines if an **image** column contains a parsed XML document; if so, returns **0**, otherwise returns >**0**; if the input is **NULL**, returns **NULL**.
Example: **select my_col, xmlrepresentation(xml_col) from my_tab**

'*xpath_query*' **xmltest** *xml_data* [**option** '*options...*']
xmltest evaluates to true or false (or **NULL**), after applying the XPath query against the XML data. This can be used like a logical expression, for example in a **where** clause, **case** expression, **if** statement etc. To negate the result, use **not**.
options can be **xmlerror** (**message** and **NULL** only); see *sqlx_options* below.
Example:

```
select my_col from my_tab
where '//t="Hello"' xmltest xml_col option 'xmlerror=NULL'
  and ...further predicates...
```

(15.0) xmlvalidate (*xml_data* [**option** '*options...*'] [**returns** *datatype*] **)**
Validate an XML document; if valid, returns the XML document itself unless **xmlvalid=message** is specified; if it is not valid, the result depends on the **xmlerror** option. *options* can contain (apart from **xmlerror**; see *sqlx_options* below):

- **xmlvalid= {document|message}**: determines the result if the document is valid: if **document** (=default), returns the raw XML document itself as a **text** value unless specified otherwise by **returns**; if **message**, returns the XML document **'<xml_valid/>'** (which can be tested for; see example below).
- **dtdvalidate={no|yes|strict}**: **no** (=default if **schemavalidate=no** or not specified): no validation is performed, only well-formedness is checked; **yes**: the document is validated against DTD specified in the document; **strict** (=default if **schemavalidate=yes**):
  - if **schemavalidate=no**, the document is validated against a DTD which must be specified in the document,
  - if **schemavalidate=yes**, every element must be declared in a DTD or schema in the document, and the document is validated against it.
- **schemavalidate= {no|yes}** (and **dtdvalidate** is not specified or **no**): **no**: no schema validation is performed, only well-formedness is checked; **yes**: schema validation is performed.
- **nonamespaceschemalocation=** '*schema_uri_list*': specifies a list of schema URIs, overriding the schema URIs specified in the **xsi:noNameSpaceSchema-Location** clause in the document (see the ASE documentation for details).
- **schemalocation=** '*namespace_schema_uri_list*': specifies a list of pairs of (namespace name, schema URI) (see the ASE documentation for details).

Examples:

```
insert your_table values (xmlvalidate(
'<!DOCTYPE msg SYSTEM "http:/www.your-site.com/your_doc.dtd">
<doc> ...data... </doc>' option 'dtdValidate=yes xmlerror=message'))

if xmlvalidate( '<doc> ...data... </doc>' option 'xmlvalid=message
                xmlerror=message' returns varchar) = '<xml_valid/>'
print 'XML is valid valid' else print 'XML is not valid'
```

In the commands above, *sqlx_options* can be (see the ASE documentation for details):

Option name	Option values	Remarks (default)
binary	**hex** | **base64**	Binary data encoding (**hex**)
columnstyle	**element** | **attribute**	Use elements (=default) or attributes for column values
entitize	**yes** | **no** | **cond**	Whether convert reserved characters to XML entities (**yes**); if **cond**, converts only if the first non-blank char is not '**<**'
format	**yes** | **no**	Format the XML (**yes**)
header	**yes** | **no** | **encoding**	Include XML header (**no**)
incremental	**yes** | **no**	Accumulate each result set row into a single (=**no**=default) text row or use multiple (=**yes**) rows
(15.0) multipleentitize	**yes** | **no**	As **entitize**, but for **for xml all**
nullstyle	**attribute** | **omit**	Formatting of **NULL** values with **columnstyle=element** (**omit**)

(15.0) ncr	**no** | **non_ascii** | **non_server**	Handling of non-ASCII data or Unicode columns (default=**non_ascii** for **for xml**); see documentation for details
prefix	any name	prefix for unnamed columns; default = **'C'**
root	**yes** | **no**	Include root element (**yes**)
rowname	any name	Name of the 'row' element (**row**)
schemaloc	URI string	**schemalocation** value
statement	**yes** | **no**	Include the SQL query (**no**)
tablename	any name	Name of the 'root' element (**resultset**)
targetns	URI string	**targetnamespace** value
xmlerror	**exception** | **NULL** | **message**	handling of XML errors: **exception** (=default) raises an error and prints a message; **NULL** returns **NULL** and sets **@@error**; message returns an error msg as an XML doc and sets **@@error**.
(15.0) xsidecl	**yes** | **no**	Specify the XML **xsi** attribute (**yes**)

XPath query language

Below is a summary of some of the main aspects of the XPath query language. For more details, see the ASE documentation. (NB: XPath is a subset of XQuery; XQL -supported in Java-based XML in pre-12.5.1- is a subset of XPath).

- One or more **/** characters match hierarchy levels in the XML document being queryied; **/***tag_name* selects the element with the specified tag; specifying ***** for *tag_name* matches all tags; **|** selects multiple tags (like an **or** condition)
- **[***n***]** identifies a node in repeating group ($n \geq 1$)
- **[***tagname***="***expression***"]** searches for nodes where the specified tags matches the expression
- **()** can be used to group elements (e.g. for use with **[…]** or **|**)
- **tolower()** and **toupper()** convert a string to lower- and uppercase, respectively
- **concat(***string* **[,** *string*]...**)** concatenates multiple strings
- **normalize-space()** compresses multiple white-space characters into one and removes leading and trailing ones.

XPath examples:
xmlextract('/', '<a><b>xyz</b></a>') returns **'<a><b>xyz</b></a>'**
xmlextract('/a', '<a><b>xyz</b></a>') returns **'<a><b>xyz</b></a>'**
xmlextract('/b', '<a><b>xyz</b></a>') returns **NULL**
xmlextract('//b', '<a><b>xyz</b></a>') returns **'<b>xyz</b>'**
xmlextract('/a/b', '<a><b>xyz</b></a>') returns **'<b>xyz</b>'**
xmlextract('/a/b/text()', '<a><b>xyz</b></a>') returns **'xyz'**
xmlextract('//b[1]', '<a><b>one</b><b>two</b></a>') returns **'<b>one</b>'**
xmlextract('//b[2]', '<a><b>one</b><b>two</b></a>') returns **'<b>two</b>'**

xmlextract('//(b|d)','<a><b>b</b><c>c</c><d>d</d></a>')
returns **'<b>b</b><d>d</d>'**

xmlextract('//b[c="two"]', '<a> <b><c>one</c><d>One!</d></b> <b><c>two</c> <d>Two!</d></b> </a>') returns **'<b><c>two</c><d>Two!</d></b>'**

xmlextract('//b[toupper(c)="TWO"]', '<a> <b><c>one</c><d>One!</d></b> <b> <c>two</c><d>Two!</d></b> </a>') returns **'<b><c>two</c><d>Two!</d></b>'**

Java-based XML functions

The used-defined Java-based functions **forxmlj**, **forxmldtdj**, **forxmlschemaj**, and **forxmlallj** map the result set of a SQL query to a SQLX-XML schema, result set document, or both (in 15.0, use **for xml schema**/**for xml all** instead).
The functions **forsqlcreatej**, **forsqlinsertj**, **forsqlscriptj** generate SQL scripts based on an SQLX-XML document.
These user-defined functions must be installed (with the **installjava** tool or **install java** command): unzip **$SYBASE/$SYBASE_ASE/sample/JavaXml/JavaXml.zip**, and follow the instructions in **JavaXml/XML/README.htm**. NB: Java must be enabled first (➢p.46).

35. Web Services (15.0)

ASE 15.0 can act both as a producer and a consumer of web services. To produce a web service, use the **create service** command to expose SQL functionality in the current ASE server as a web service. To consume a web service available from a different producer, use **sp_webservices 'add'** to create a proxy table mapping to the web service; by selecting from the proxy table, the web service is invoked. A web services engine, running outside the ASE server, must be started with **runws** (see below).

For more details, see the ASE manual *'Web Services User's Guide'*. NB: some webservices functionality is also available in pre-15, but not covered in this book.

sp_configure 'enable webservices', { **0** | **1** } (dynamic)
Enables (**1**) or disables (**0**) web services features. To enable, in pre-15 only, the **ASE_WEBSERVICES** option must be licensed.
The Web Services functionality also requires XML to be enabled (➢p.47).

To configure web services, either use Sybase Central, or follow these steps:

1. Set the config options **'enable webservices'**, **'enable cis'** and **'cis rpc handling'** to **1** (**'enable cis'** is static!)
2. Set **$SYBASE_WS** (**%SYBASE_WS%**) to **WS-15_0**
3. Set **$SYBASE_JRE** (**%SYBASE_JRE%**) to **$SYBASE/_jvm**
4. Run the script **$SYBASE/$SYBASE_WS/bin/installws** with **isql**
5. Run **grant role webservices_role** for logins that will use webservices features
6. Run **sp_addserver ws, sds,** *ws_engine_name* (typically, = ASE servername + '**_WS**'); **'ws'** is the recommended default for the first parameter.
7. Run **sp_addserver** *ws_engine_name***, sds** (with same name as previous step)
8. Add *ws_engine_name* to the **interfaces/SQL.INI** file, with the same port number as **com.sybase.ase.ws.consumer.cisport** (default: port 8183) in the properties file (default: **.../$SYBASE_WS/props/ws.properties**).
   In **$SYBASE/ $SYBASE_WS /bin**, start the web services engine with:
   runws[**.bat**] **-U** *login_name* **-P** *password* **-S** *ASE_servername* [**-f** *properties_file*]
   (Tip1: if **runws** fails, remove the redirection to **/dev/null** (NT: **NUL**) from the **runws** script to see error messages. Tip2: if the ASE login has a blank password, specify **nopasswordspecified** for *password*)
   To stop the engine, run **stopws**[**.bat**].
9. Now you can create and use web services.
   The log files for producer/consumer are in **$SYBASE/$SYBASE_WS/logs**
10. (optional) To use a web admin interface, run **configssl**[**.bat**] before starting the web service engine: **configssl -d localhost -C** *password-1* **-s** *password-2* (just choose two new passwords).
    After starting the web service engine, the admin interface can be reached at **https://localhost:8187**. See the ASE documentation for more details.

sp_webservices *subcommand* [**,** *...parameters...*]
Manages web services. *subcommand* can be:

- **'help'** [**,** '*subcommand*'] - displays usage info, optionally for *subcommand*

These subcommands apply to user-defined web services, created with **create service**:

- **'listudws'** [**,**'*service_name*'] - displays all user-defined web services, or only the specified service
- **'deploy'** [**,** **'all'** | '*service_name*'] - makes the specified user-defined web service, or all user-defined web services, accessible for consumers
- **'undeploy'** [**,** **'all'** | '*service_name*'] - makes the specified user-defined web service, or all user-defined web services, inaccessible for consumers
- **'addalias'**, '*alias_name*', '*db_name*' - specifies an alias for the specified database; *db_name* is part of the URL for user-defined web services created in this database; an alias provides an alternative
- **'listalias'** - displays all alias names for user-defined web services
- **'dropalias'**, '*alias_name*' - drops the specified alias

These subcommands apply to proxy tables mapped to external web services; in all cases, the default for *sds_name* is **'ws'** (=same as in setup step 6 above):

- **'add'**, '*wsdl_URI*' [**,** *sds_name*] [**,** '*method_name*=*proxy_table_name* [**,** ...] '] - creates a proxy table mapping to the external web service described at the specified WSDL URI. Optionally, the proxy table name can be overriden.
- **'remove'**, '*wsdl_URI*' [**,** *sds_name*] - removed the proxy table mapping for the specified WSDL URI
- **'list'** [**,** '*wsdl_URI*'] [**,** *sds_name*] - lists the proxy tables mappings, optionally for the specified WSDL URI only.
- **'modify'**, '*wsdl_URI*', **'timeout=***nr_of_seconds*' - modifies the maximum timeout value for the web service

See the ASE documentation for examples of actual webservices to map to. Note that only 'rpc/encoded' and 'document/literal' (=recommended) web services are supported.

create service *service_name* [**secure** { **clear** | **ssl** }] [**, userpath** 'path']
  [**, alias** *alias_name*] **type** { **xml** | **raw** | **soap** }
  [[**(**] @*parameter_name datatype* [**=** *default_value*] [**,**...*more parameters*...] [**)**]]
as *...T-SQL-statements...*
Creates a user-defined web service in the current database, exposing the SQL state-

ments as a web service with the specified name. With **clear** (=default), the service is accesseble through http, **ssl** requires https. **userpath** specifies a string to append to the service's URL (default=none); **alias** specifies an alias name (default=none).
type specifies how the service can be accessed:

- **xml** - accessible by a browser (via HTTP GET); output is in SQLX format
- **raw** - accessible by a browser (via HTTP GET); output is not altered
- **soap** - accessible by a SOAP client (via HTTP POST); output is in SQLX format

The web service is not accessible for consumers until **sp_webservices 'deploy'** is executed. The T-SQL text for the service can be displayed with **sp_helptext**.
Example:

```
create service my_service type xml @p1 varchar(20)
as select "echo:[" + @p1 + "]"
```

This service can be accessed in a browser at this URL:

http://localhost:8181/services/my_db?method=my_service&
username=mylogin& password=mypasswd&p1=Hello

Elements in this URL:

- **localhost** is the hostname on which the web service engine runs
- **8181** is the port number specified in the properties file for **com.sybase.ase.ws.producer.httpport** (default=8181)
- **my_db** is the database in which **my_service** is created; this can be changed by specifying the **alias** clause in **create service**.
- if **userpath** had been specified, it would have been inserted before the '**?**'
- **username**, **password** are required to log into ASE; **&p1=** specifies a value for parameter **@p1**.

Note that only services of type **xml** or **raw** can be accessed through a browser; **soap** services must be accessed through a SOAP client. For all services in database **my_db**, the WSDL is available at: **http://localhost:8181/services/my_db?wsdl**

drop service *service_name*
Drops the specified user-defined web service from the current database.

36. Miscellaneous stored procedures

(12.5.1) sp_autoformat *table_name* [, *@selectlist* [, *@whereclause* [, *@orderby* [, *@fmtspecifier* [, *@trace*]]]]]
Displays the contents of a table in the narrowest possible format. See the header comments of the source code for further information (undocumented).
Example: **sp_autoformat sysobjects, 'name, crdate', 'where type = "U" '**

sp_checkreswords [*owner_name*]
Displays all identifiers in the current database that are T-SQL reserved words. With *owner_name*, only displays identifiers in objects owned by that owner. T-SQL reserved words are case-insensitive. To display all reserved words in your ASE version, use this query: **select name from master..spt_values where type = 'W'**

sp_checksource [*object_name* [, **NULL** [, *owner_name*]]]
sp_checksource NULL [, *table_name* [, *owner_name*]]
Checks the existence (i.e. it has not manually been deleted) of the T-SQL source code for compiled objects in the **syscomments** table. When the code was hidden with **sp_hidetext**, **sp_checksource** will still consider it to exist. Without parameters, checks all compiled objects in the current database; with *object_name*, checks that object. With *table_name*, checks all check constraints, defaults, triggers, computed columns, function indexes and partition conditions on that table.

(12.5) sp_client_addr [*spid*]
Displays the TCP/IP address of the client application for the specified process. Without parameters, for all processes.

sp_depends *object_name* [, *column_name*]
Within the current database, displays objects which depend on (i.e. refer to) object *object_name*, and vice versa. Note that **sp_depends** will not show dependencies between objects in different databases. With *column_name*, displays defaults, indexes and constraints depending on this column (here, *object_name* is a table).

sp_help [*object_name*]
Displays information about the specified object. Without parameters, lists all objects in the database.

sp_hidetext [*object_name* [**, NULL** [**,** *owner_name*]]]
sp_hidetext NULL [**,** *table_name* [**,** *owner_name*]]
Hides the T-SQL source code (in the **syscomments** table) for compiled objects. Once hidden, the source code is not visible with **sp_helptext**, **defncopy** or otherwise, and cannot be 'unhidden' anymore. Without parameters, hides the code for all compiled objects in this database; with *object_name*, hides the code for that object. With *table_name*, hides the code for all check constraints, defaults, triggers, computed columns, function indexes and partition conditions on that table.

sp_rename *old_name***,** *new_name* [**(12.5) , 'index'** | **'column'**]
Renames a table, column, index, constraint, or another type of object from *old_name* to *new_name*. To rename a column or index, *old_name* must be **'***table_name.column_name***'** or **'***table_name.index_name***'**, respectively (incl. quotes). When a column and index exist with the same name, the column is renamed in pre-12.5; in 12.5, **'index'** or **'column'** must be specified to indicate which is renamed.
Examples: **sp_rename my_table, my_other_table** -- renames table **my_table**
sp_rename 'my_table.a', b -- renames column **a** of **my_table** to **b**

sp_monitor [**(12.5.2)** *options...*]
Without parameters, displays some high-level statistics about the current server. With parameters in 12.5.2, displays monitoring information from the MDA tables. Run **sp_monitor 'help'** for on-line syntax help; see the ASE documentation for more info.

sp_showplan *spid***, NULL, NULL, NULL**
sp_showplan *spid***,** *@batch* **output,** *@context* **output,** *@stmt_nr* **output**
Displays the query plan for the query currently executed by the specified process. When specified, the output parameters must be of type **int**, and can be used to retrieve query plans for other statements as well; otherwise, specify **NULL**s.

sp_syntax { **'***T-SQL-command***'** | *system_stored_procedure_name* }
Provides syntax information about T-SQL commands or system procedures; ➢p.80.

sp_who [*login_name* | **'***spid***'**]
Displays information about server processes. Without parameters, shows all existing processes; with *login_name*, shows all processes for that login; with **'***spid***'** (note the quotes!), shows only that process. Examples: **sp_who sa** and **sp_who '54'**
To display full information about one or more server processes, **select** directly from **master..sysprocesses**. For example, to display all details about your current session: **select * from master..sysprocesses where spid = @@spid**

37. Settings affecting query results

These **set** commands affect the current session only.

set ansinull { **on** | **off** }
Treats **NULL** values according to ANSI SQL (see the ASE documentation for details).

set ansi_permissions { **on** | **off** }
When **on**, requires **select** permission on all columns mentioned in an **update** or **delete** statement. When **off** (=default), these permissions are not required.

set arithabort numeric_truncation { **on** | **off** }
Defines error handling for loss-of-scale errors for implicit (not explicit) conversions involving **numeric** datatypes. When **on** (=default), the statement causing the error is aborted; when **off**, the result is truncated; in both cases, processing continues.

set arithabort arith_overflow { **on** | **off** }
Defines error handling for loss-of-precision errors during datatype conversions and divide-by-zero errors. When **on** (=default), the transaction in which the error occurs, is rolled back and any further commands in the batch are not executed. When **off**, the statement causing the error is aborted, but processing continues.

set arithignore [**arith_overflow**] { **on** | **off** }
For the errors described under **set arithabort arith_overflow**, determines whether an error message is displayed. By default, this is set to **off**, meaning a message is displayed. When **on**, no message is displayed.

set fmtonly { **on** | **off** }
When **on** (default = **off**), displays the format of query result sets from queries or stored procedures without actually executing these. Can be used in combination with **set showplan on** to compile and display the corresponding query plans.

(15.0) set nodata { **on** | **off** }
(undocumented) When **on** (default=**off**), the result set from **select** statements is not sent to the client (although the queries are executed normally).

set noexec { **on** | **off** }
When **on** (default = **off**), compiles, but does not execute queries; this is often used in combination with **set showplan on** (which must be executed first). Once set to **on**, the only command that can be executed is **set noexec off**.

set parseonly { **on** | **off** }
When **on** (default = **off**), only performs only a syntax check, but does not compile queries. This command should not be used inside a stored procedure or trigger.

set rowcount { *nr_of_rows* | *@variable* }
Limits the number of rows affected by each subsequent query to *nr_of_rows* or *@variable*. To restore the default (no limit), specify **0**. In 15.0, the current setting for a session is available in **@@setrowcount**.

set string_rtruncation { **on** | **off** }
When **off** (=default), no error is raised when a character string is truncated by an **insert** or **update** command. When **on,** an error is raised only when the truncated part contains non-space characters.

38. Settings affecting query plans

These **set** commands affect the current session only.

set forceplan { **on** | **off** }
For the current session, forces the join order for queries to be the order in which the tables appear in the **from** clause. By default, this option is disabled.

set prefetch { **on** | **off** }
When **off** (default = **on**), disables the use of large I/O pools in the current session.

(15.0) sp_configure 'optimization goal', 0, '*optimization_goal***'** (dynamic)
Defines the server-wide optimization goal, which limits possible query plans. *optimization_goal* can be: **allrows_oltp** (allows nested-loop joins only), **allrows_mix** (=default; also merge joins and parallellism), or **allrows_dss** (also hash joins).

(15.0) set plan optgoal *optimization_goal*
Overrides the server-wide optimization goal for the current session. The session's current setting is available in **@@optgoal**. Note that the optimization goal for an individual query can be overridden with an abstract query plan (➢p.105).

(15.0) set *access_method* { **0** | **1** }
(15.0.1) set *access_method* { **0** | **1** | **on** | **off** | **default** }
Allows (**1**, **on**) or disallows (**0**, **off**) a particular access method to be selected by the query optimizer, overriding the setting for the current optimization goal. Most access methods are enabled by default. With **default**, restores the default setting for the current optimization goal. Note that executing **set plan optgoal** overrides any previous settings. In 15.0.1, the current session's settings are displayed following **set option show_search_engine long** (enable traceflag 3604 first!). Multiple access methods can be combined in one **set** statement, separated by commas.
The most important access methods are:

nl_join - allows nested-loop joins (enabled in all optimization goals)
merge_join - allows merge joins (enabled in **allrows_mix**, **allrows_dss**)
hash_join - allows hash joins (enabled in **allrows_dss**)
store_index - allows reformatting (enabled in all optimization goals)
parallel_query - allows parallel queries (enabled in **allrows_mix**, **allrows_dss**)

Other access methods are (most are enabled by default for all optimization goals; see the ASE documentation for more details):

append_union_all	**group_hashing**	**merge_union_distinct**
bushy_space_search	**group_sorted**	**multi_table_store_ind**
distinct_hashing	**index_intersection**	**opportunistic_distinct_view**
distinct_sorted	**hash_union_distinct**	**(15.0.1) index_union**
distinct_sorting	**merge_union_all**	

Examples: **set nl_join 0** / **set stored_index off**

(12.5.2) sp_configure 'statement cache size', *size_in_2Kb_pages* (semi-dynamic)
Creates and enables a server-wide statement cache of the specified size (taken from **'max memory'**) for caching query plans (to save query compilation time). To disable caching, set size to 0; to disable caching for a session, use **set statement_cache off**. Also see **dbcc prsqlcache/purgesqlcache**(➢p.87).

(12.5.2) set statement_cache { **on** | **off** }
When **off** (default = **on**), disables query plan caching in the statement cache.

(15.0.1) sp_configure 'enable literal autoparam', { **0** | **1** } (dynamic)
Enables (**1**) or disables (**0**, =default) parameterization of literals in **select**, **update**, **delete** and **insert...select** statements server-wide. This applies to statements cached the statement cache (see above), and statements captured by query metrics capture (➢p.106) and abstract plan dump/load (➢p.105). This feature allows the same query plan to be used for queries with, for example, different primary key search arguments.

(15.0.1) set literal_autoparam { **on** | **off** }
Enables (**on**) or disables (**off**) literal parameterization for the current session, overriding the server-wide setting.

(15.0) sp_configure 'optimization timeout limit', *percentage* (dynamic)
Defines the server-wide optimization timeout limit (an advanced query tuning feature): the optimizer will spend at most *percentage* (**1**..**1000**; default=10% for batches, 40% for procedures) of the estimated query execution time to look for a query plan. With **0**, no timeout occurs at all.

(15.0) sp_configure 'sproc optimize timeout limit', *percentage* (dynamic)
The optimization timeout limit (see above) when optimizing stored procedures (**1**..**4000**; default=40% for procedures). With **0**, no timeout occurs at all.

(15.0) set plan opttimeoutlimit *percentage*
Overrides the server-wide optimization timeout limit for the current session. The session's current setting is available in **@@opttimeoutlimit**.

(15.0) sp_configure 'max repartition degree', *degree* (dynamic)
Defines the server-wide maximum number of partitions when dynamically partitioning intermediate data at run-time. When set to **1** (=default), this maximum is equal to the number of ASE engines. This is an advanced query tuning feature.

(15.0) set repartition_degree *degree*
Overrides the server-wide maximum repartitioning degree for the current session. The session's current setting is available in **@@repartition_degree**.

(15.0) sp_configure 'max resource granularity', *percentage* (dynamic)
Defines a server-wide optimizer hint (for advanced query tuning) about the maximum percentage (**1**..**100**; default=**10**) of resources (currently, only procedure cache) a query may use during execution. This is however not enforced during execution.

(15.0) set resource_granularity *percentage*
Overrides the server-wide maximum resource granularity for the current session. The session's current setting is available in **@@resource_granularity**.

(pre-15) set table count *value*
Sets the maximum number of tables the optimizer will consider in combination at a time when determining the optimal join order. By default, this is **4** (for joins with up to 25 tables). For any value > **8**, **8** will be used. By specifying **0**, the default is restored. This is a no-op in 15.0; use optimization timeout limits instead.

(pre-15) sp_configure 'enable sort-merge joins and JTC', { **0** |**1** } (dynamic)
Enables (**1**) or disables (**0**, =default) merge joins (a query optimization) and JTC (join transitive closure, an extra query processing step generating additional, logically implied join clauses) server-wide. By starting ASE with undocumented traceflags **334** or **384**, this config option is overridden: with **334**, JTC is enabled independent of merge joins; with **384**, merge joins are enabled independent of JTC (both server-wide). This is a no-op in 15.0; also, merge joins are enabled by default in 15.0.

(pre-15) set jtc { **on** | **off** }
Enables (**on**) or disables (**off**) JTC (join transitive closure) for the current session, overriding the server-wide setting. This is a no-op in 15.0.

(pre-15) set sort_merge { **on** | **off** }
Enables (**on**) or disables (**off**) merge joins for the current session, overriding the server-wide setting. This is a no-op in 15.0.

39. Settings for displaying query plan information

These **set** commands affect the current session only.

set showplan { **on** | **off** }
When **on** (default = **off**), displays the query plan for queries in the current session. In 15.0, with traceflag 526, also prints part of the **set statistics plancost on** output.

(15.0) set statistics plancost on
When **on** (default = **off**), displays the query plan for queries in the current session in a tree-like format, including estimated/actual numbers of rows and I/Os.

set statistics io { **on** | **off** }
When **on** (default = **off**), displays the number of I/Os per table used by queries in the current session.

set statistics time { **on** | **off** }
When **on** (default = **off**), displays the compile and elapsed time used by queries in the current session.

set statistics simulate { **on** | **off** }
When **on** (default = **off**), the optimizer uses simulated statistics (which must be created with **optdiag**; ➢p.114) for creating query plans in the current session.

set statistics subquerycache { **on** | **off** }
When **on** (default = **off**), displays statistics about internal subquery optimizations in the current session.

(15.0) set option *show_option* { **on** | **off** | **brief** | **normal** | **long** }
Displays detailed diagnostics about query optimization, replacing the pre-15 traceflags 302/310/311/317 etc. Default = **off**; the level of detail varies from **brief** to **long**. Enable traceflag 3604 to receive the output at the client. *show_option* can be:

show - enables all options collectively
show_lio_costing - displays logical I/O estimates (similar to traceflag 302 in pre-15)
show_pio_costing - displays physical I/O estimates
show_abstract_plan - displays the full abstract plan
show_missing_stats - displays a message when statistics are expected but missing
show_histograms - displays information about histograms (for joins/SARGs)
show_elimination - displays information about (semantic) partition elimination
show_pll_costing, **show_parallel** - displays information about parallel plans

The following options can also be set, but are less relevant for a DBA:

show_best_plan	**show_lop**
show_code_gen	**show_managers**
show_counters	**show_search_engine**
show_log_props	

(15.0) set plan for *option_xml* [**to** { **client** | **message** } **on** | **off**]
Displays detailed diagnostics about query optimization/execution in XML format. With **to client on**, output is sent to the client. With **to message on**, the output from the last 20 queries is buffered and must be retrieved with **showplan_in_xml** (*N*), where *N* is the query number (**0**..**19**; **-1**=last query; **0**=all buffered queries; for long XML output, use **set textsize** to avoid truncation).
option_xml can be:

show_exec_xml - displays the query plan	
show_execio_xml - displays query text, query plan, ans estimated+actual I/O counts	
show_opt_xml - displays optimizer diagnostics; roughly (but not exactly) equivalent to collectively enabling most of the options below	
show_lop_xml	**show_search_engine_xml**
show_managers_xml	**show_counters_xml**
show_log_props_xml	**show_best_plan_xml**
show_parallel_xml	**show_pio_costing_xml**
show_histograms_xml	**show_lio_costing_xml**
show_abstract_plan_xml	**show_elimination_xml**
show_final_plan_xml	

Examples: **set plan for show_exec_xml to client on**

set plan for show_exec_xml off
set plan for show_exec_xml to message on
select showplan_in_xml(1)

40. Miscellaneous settings

These **set** commands affect the current session only.

set background { **on** | **off** }
(undocumented) All statements placed between **set background on** and **set background off** are executed as a 'background task'. Be very careful with this undocumented and unsupported command, since the side-effects can be tricky! See my book *'Tips, Tricks & Recipes for Sybase ASE'* (**www.sypron.nl/ttr**) for more information.

set clientapplname *char_string*
set clienthostname *char_string*
set clientname *char_string*
In **master..sysprocesses**, sets the columns **clientapplname**, **clienthostname** or **clientname** to *char_string* (max. 30 chars).

(15.0) set delayed_commit { **on** | **off** }
When enabled (=**on**), a transaction commits immediately without waiting for the log records to be written to disk. When **off**, all log records are guaranteed to be written first. This option overrides the setting of **sp_dboption 'delayed commit'** for a database, which defines the default behaviour.

set fipsflagger { **on** | **off** }
When **on** (default = **off**), issues a warning for non-ANSI SQL compliant syntax.

set flushmessage { **on** | **off** }
When **off** (=default), accumulates output to the client into packets before sending it. When **on**, sends output immediately.

set nocount { **on** | **off** }
When **on** (default = **off**), suppressing the **'(*nnn* rows affected)'** messages in **isql**.

(12.5.1) set proc_output_params { **on** | **off** }
When **off** (default=**on**), result values for output parameters from stored procedures are not sent to the client. In **isql**, this suppresses the corresponding messages.

(12.5.1) set proc_return_status { **on** | **off** }
When **off** (default=**on**), the return status from a stored procedure is not sent to the client. In **isql**, this suppresses the **'(return status =**...**)'** messages.

set quoted_identifier { **on** | **off** }
When **on** (default=**off**), allows identifiers that would normally not be valid (➢p.9).

(12.5.4) set export_options { **on** | **off** }
(undocumented) When **on** (default=**off**), changes to some session-specific **set** options made inside a stored procedure, trigger, or execute-immediate, are carried over to the caller (otherwise, such changes are lost when execution returns). For login triggers, **export_options** is enabled by default in 12.5.4+; **set export_options off** disables exporting of **set** options, also from a login trigger.
Supported **set** commands are (NB: some commands are not described in this book):

ansi_permissions	**forceplan**	**quoted_identifier**	**proc_output_params**
ansinull	**nocount**	**remote_indexes**	**proc_return_status**
arithabort	**prefetch**	**sort_resources**	**raw_object_serialization**
arithignore	**replication**	**statement_cache**	**strict_dtm_enforcement**
cis_rpc_handling	**rowcount**	**self_recursion**	**string_rtruncation**
close on endtran	**sort_merge**	**textsize**	**textptr_parameters**
flushmessage	**showplan**	**triggers**	**transactional_rpc**
fmtonly	**stringsize**		

Notes:

- Various **set** options also require traceflag 4073 to be enabled in order to be exported from a login trigger.
- **datefirst**, **dateformat**, **identity_insert**, **language** are always global for a session (i.e. are automatically exported irrespective of **set export_options**).
- As this book went to press, not all of this functionality was yet supported in 15.0.
- Most new optimizer-related settings in 15.0, like **set plan optgoal**, **set nl_join** etc, (➢p.53) are global for a session and therefore always exported.

DBA Topics

41. Database devices & dump devices

disk init name = '*device_name*'**, physname =** '*pathname*'**,** [**(pre-12.5) vdevno=** *virtual_device_nr* **,**] **size =** *device_size* [**, vstart =** *virt_addr*] [**, cntrltype =** *controller*] [**, dsync =** { **true** | **false** }] [**, (15.0) directio =** { **true** | **false** }]
Creates a new database device named *device_name* at physical location *pathname*. On Unix, a symbolic link may be specified instead of the actual pathname. When using a raw device, it must already exist (NB: use the character device, not the block device!); when using a file system file, it must not yet exist (or an error results). For best performance, raw devices are recommended over file system devices, unless **directio** can be used.
The number of database devices is limited by the config option **'number of devices'** (static; 12.5:semi-dynamic); its maximum is 256 in pre-15 and 2 billion in 15.0.
In 12.5, the *device_size* can be specified as a quoted string consisting of a number and a size unit (**K**, **M**, **G** (=Kb, Mb, etc); in 15.0 also **T**). When the unit or quotes are omitted (as in pre-12.5), the unit defaults to 2Kb.
In 12.5, the **vdevno** clause may be omitted (the number will then be assigned automatically), but when specified *virtual_device_nr* must be a unique number for each database device (also see the note on **'16777216'** below).
dsync and **directio** apply to file system devices only. These options can be overridden on Unix level depending on how the filesystem is mounted/configured. These settings are ignored for raw devices, as well as on NT.
With **dsync=true** (=default), disk writes are guaranteed, but may be significantly slower; when **false**, writes may be buffered by the file system. With **directio=true**, disk writes are also guaranteed but bypass the file system completely; **directio** is fundamentally faster than **dsync**. **directio** and **dsync** cannot both be enabled at the same time. These settings can be changed with **sp_deviceattr**.
Note: after upgrading from pre-12.0, file system devices will have **dsync** set to **false** (except for the master device, where **dsync** is always **true**).
The clauses **vstart** (the starting offset, default=**0**) and **cntrltype** (controller type, default=**0**) are for special cases only.
Examples: **disk init name = 'dev1', physname = '/data/MY_SERVER.dev1', vdevno = 7, size = 51200** -- 51200*2Kb = 100 Mb

(15.0) disk init name = 'dev2', physname = '/data/MY_SERVER.dev2', size = '100M', directio = true

(pre-15) 16777216: the magic number in master..sysdevices
In pre-15.0, logical page numbers on a database device are based on the virtual device number **vdevno** (which is specified in **disk init**) and the magic number 16777216 (= 2^{24}): the first page on a device has page number **vdevno*16777216**. To find the **vdevno**'s currently in use, use this query:

select vdevno = low/16777216
from master..sysdevices where status & 2 = 2 order by 1

With >127 devices, this query may not work properly; use **sp_helpdevice** instead.

disk reinit name = '*device_name*'**, physname =** '*pathname*'**,** [**(pre-12.5) vdevno=** *virtual_device_nr* **,**] **size =** *device_size* [**, vstart =** *virt_addr*, **cntrltype =** *controller*] [**, dsync =** { **true** | **false** }]
Same as **disk init**, but only inserts a row into **sysdevices**; does not initialise the actual database device. This is a special troubleshooting command.

disk refit
Reconstructs the contents of the **sysusages** and **sysdatabases** tables from the actual database device contents. When completed, ASE will shut down automatically. This is a special troubleshooting command, typically run after **disk reinit**.

(12.5) disk resize name = '*device_name*'**, size =** *extra_device_size*
Increases the size of an existing database device by allocating additional space on OS level. The size can be specified with the same units as in **disk init**.
Example: **disk resize name = 'dev1', size = '50m'** -- adds 50Mb to device 'dev1'

sp_diskdefault *device_name*, { **defaulton** | **defaultoff** }
Enables (**defaulton**) or disables (**defaultoff**) the specified database device as a 'default disk' or 'default device', on which **create** / **alter database** can allocate space if no device has been specified explicitly. Always set the master device to **defaultoff**.

sp_deviceattr *device_name*, **'***option***'**, { **true** | **false** } (static)
Enables (**true**) or disables (**false**) the device option for the specified file system device, taking effect at the next ASE restart. *option* can be **dsync** or, in 15.0, **directio** (see **disk init** for details).

sp_addumpdevice *type*, *device_name*, *pathname* [, *tape_size*]
Creates a dump device named *device_name* (for use by **dump database** or **dump transaction** commands) mapping to the physical location *pathname*. *type* indicates the type of device and can be **'tape'** or **'disk'**. For tape devices, *tape_size* is the size in Mb. In 12.5.4, *type* can also be **'archive database'** (for use with archive databases only).

sp_dropdevice *device_name*
Drops the specified device. For a file system database device, the file is not deleted.

sp_helpdevice [*device_name*]
Displays information about all database devices and dump devices. With *device_name*, shows only that device.

42. Device mirroring

ASE allows database devices to be software-mirrored with the commands below. Note that this functionality is rarely used anymore these days as mirroring is typically done on storage level.

sp_configure 'disable disk mirroring', { **0** | **1** } (static)
Disables (**1**) or enables (**0**) the **disk [un][re]mirror** commands. Default is **1** in 12.5; **0** in pre-12.5.

disk mirror name = '*device_name***', mirror = '***pathname***' [,writes = {serial|noserial}]**
Starts software mirroring of the specified database device to the physical location *pathname*. Though slower, **serial** mirroring is safer than **noserial**. Note that hardware mirroring (outside ASE) is faster than software mirroring.
To mirror the master device, first run **disk mirror**, then add the '**-r** *master_mirror*' option to the **RUN_***servername* file.

disk remirror name = '*device_name***'**
Restarts disk mirroring after it is stopped by failure of a mirrored device or temporarily disabled by the **disk unmirror** command.

disk unmirror name = '*device_name***' [, side = { 'primary' | 'secondary' }] [, mode = { retain | remove }]**
For the specified database device, stops software mirroring (previously started with **disk mirror**). With **side='secondary'** (=default), *device_name* in the original **disk mirror** command continues as the database device; with **side='primary'**, the mirrored *pathname* will be the database device, and *device_name* is no longer used. **mode=retain** (=default) temporarily suspends mirroring, which can be restored with **disk remirror**; **mode=remove** removes the mirroring completely.

waitfor mirrorexit
Waits until a device mirror (set up with **disk mirror**) terminates abnormally.

43. Creating & maintaining databases

create [**(12.5.0.3) temporary** | **(12.5.4) archive**] **database** *db_name*
[**on** { **default** | *data_device_name* } [= *data_size*]] [,..*more data devices*...]
[**log on** *log_device_name* [= *log_size*] [,..*more log devices*...]
[**with** { **override** | **default_location** = '*location*' | **scratch_database** = *db_name* }]
[**for load** | **for proxy_update** }]
From the **master** database, creates a new database *db_name*. Space for data (default and system segments) is allocated on *data_device_name*, space for the transaction log is allocated on *log_device_name*. Optionally, multiple data and log devices can be specified. *data_size* and *log_size* are integers, specifying the amount of space (in Mb) to be allocated on each device. In 12.5, this size can also be specified as a quoted string consisting of a number and a unit indicator of **K**, **M**, **G** (=Kb, Mb...); in 15.0, also **T**. When not specifying a size, the value of the configuration option **'default database size'** is used (default=2Mb in pre-12.5; in 12.5, this default size increases with the server page size).
Without specifying a device name, allocates space on a default device (see **sp_diskdefault** on page 57). Without any options, creates a database of this default size on a default disk with mixed data and log segments.

with override must be specified when data and log segments are placed on the same database device. **for load** does not initialise the allocated space, which saves time when a dump will be loaded next. **for proxy_update** and **with default_location** are CIS-related options; for details, see the section on CIS on page 95.
In 12.5.0.3, with **temporary**, a **tempdb**-like temporary database is created (➢p.60).
In 12.5.4, with **archive**, an archive database is created (the **with scratch_database** clause is mandatory;➢p.60). In an archive database, the contents of a database dump file can be accessed (after loading it with **load database**) with regular SQL.
Examples: **create database my_db**
create database my_db on data_dev1 = 100 log on log_dev1 = 25
(12.5) create database my_db on data2 = '2.5G' log on log2 = '250M'
(12.5.0.3) create temporary database tempdb2 on my_device = '150M'
(12.5.4) create archive database arch_db on my_device = '10M'
with scratch_database = my_scratch_db

alter database *db_name* [**on** { **default** | *data_device_name* } [= *data_size*]] [,..*more data devices*...] [**log on** *log_device_name* [= *log_size*] [,..*more log devices*...] [**with override**] [**for load** | **for proxy_update**]
Expands the existing database *db_name* on the specified devices. **alter database** is otherwise identical to the **create database** statement. **for proxy_update** is a CIS-related option; for details, see the section on CIS on page 95.
Example: **(12.5) alter database my_db log on log3 = '100M'**

drop database *db_name1* [, *db_name2* ...]
Drops the specified database(s), which must not be in use and not contain any constraints referring to other databases. When a database is suspect, **drop database** will fail, and **dbcc dbrepair (***db_name*, **dropdb)** should be used instead.

sp_logdevice *db_name*, *log_device_name*
For a database which currently has its data and log segments mixed, moves the (yet-to-be-allocated) transaction log to the specified database device, and marks the data and log segments as separate.

sp_logiosize [{ **'all'**, **'default'**, **'2'**, **'4'**, **'8'**, **'16'** }]
(12.5) sp_logiosize [{ **'all'**, **'default'**, **'2'**, **'4'**, **'8'**, **'16'**, **'32'**, **'64'**, **'128'** }]
Defines the I/O size for transaction log I/O in the current database; without parameters, displays the current setting. **'all'** displays the current setting for all databases. **'default'** sets the I/O size to the server page size (=always 2Kb in pre-12.5); **'2'**, **'4'**, **'8'**, **'16'**, **'32'**, etc. set the log I/O size explicitly. By default, the log I/O size is 2*(server page size). Note that the specified log I/O size is used only when a buffer pool of the that size exists in the cache for the database; otherwise the smallest I/O size is used. The actual I/O size chosen at ASE boot time is shown in the errorlog.

sp_helplog
Displays the name of the database device that currently contains the first page of the transaction log of the current database.

sp_changedbowner *login_name* [, **true**]
Changes the owner of the current database to *login_name*. If **true** is specified, existing dbo aliases are kept; otherwise, they are dropped.

sp_dboption [*db_name*, *db_option*, **true** | **false**]
Enables (**true**) or disables (**false**) the specified database *db_option* for database *db_name*; in pre-12.5.1, the option will only become active after a **checkpoint** command is executed in the affected database. Without parameters, displays a list of database options that can be set (for a more user-friendly version, see **sp_rv_dboption** at **www.sypron.nl/new_ssp.html**).
The following database options can be set with **sp_dboption**. By default, all options are disabled (**false**). When enabled (**true**), the behaviour is as follows:

- **'abort tran on log full'** - when the transaction log is full, transactions will be aborted (by default, they get in LOG SUSPEND mode)
- **'allow nulls by default'** - a column is allowed to contain **NULL** values except when explicitly prohibited by **not NULL** in the **create table** statement
- **(12.5.0.3) 'async log service'** - handles transaction log I/O more efficiently (by reducing log semaphore contention) with two additional system processes. This option can be enabled only for ASE servers with at least 4 engines, and is useful only for high workloads.
- **'auto identity'** - ➢p.38, section 'Identity columns'.
- **'dbo use only'** - only the dbo user may access the database
- **'ddl in tran'** - allows DDL statements (such as **create table**) in a transaction.

- **(15.0) 'delayed commit'** - when enabled, a transaction in this database commits immediately without waiting for the log records to be written to disk. Can be overridden on session level by **set delayed_commit**.
- **'identity in nonunique index'** - ➢p.38, section 'Identity columns'
- **'no chkpt on recovery'** - after completing database recovery when the server starts, no checkpoint is written
- **'no free space acctg'** - disables free-space accounting on non-log segments for faster recovery; also disables thresholds on non-log segments
- **'read only'** - allows only read-only operations in the database
- **(12.5.4) 'scratch database'** - be a 'scratch' DB for an archive database (➢p.59)
- **'select into/bulkcopy/pllsort'** - allows 'minimally logged' operations such as **select...into** and fast **bcp** (➢p.121)
- **'single user'** - allows only a single user to access the database at a time
- **'trunc log on chkpt'** - truncates the transaction log at every automatic checkpoint (not for explicitly issued **checkpoint** commands)
- **'trunc. log on chkpt.'** - alternative spelling for **'trunc log on chkpt'**
- **'unique auto_identity index'** - ➢p.38, section 'Identity columns'

When specifying *db_option*, it is sufficient to specify a unique substring. Example:
sp_dboption my_db, 'pll', true -- enables **'select into/bulkcopy/pllsort'**

sp_helpdb [*db_name* [**(12.5.1), 'device_name'**]]
Displays information about the specified database, or, without *db_name*, about all databases. When *db_name* is the name of the current database, also displays information about segments. In 12.5.1, with **'device_name'**, displays device fragments in alphabetical order (default = order in which fragments were added to the database).

sp_renamedb *db_name*, *new_db_name*
Changes the name of database *db_name* (which must be in single-user mode) to *new_db_name*.

sp_spaceused
Without parameters, displays total space used by all tables in the current database.

sp_configure 'compression memory size', *size* (dynamic)
Defines the size (in 2Kb memory pages; default = **0**) of a shared memory pool for reading pages from an archive database based on a compressed dump file.

44. Temporary databases (12.5.0.3)

A temporary database, like **tempdb**, is the place where **#temp** tables and worktables are created for a session. A temporary database is assigned to a session when it logs into ASE; this does not change during the session. The global variable **@@tempdbid** contains the database ID of the session's temporary database; the built-in function **tempdb_id([*spid*])** returns the temporary database ID for any session. When a database is part of the **'default'** group (see below), all logins may use that database unless they have been bound to a different database with **sp_tempdb**.
A session may explicitly use any temporary database for creating regular (i.e. non-#temp) tables. Temporary databases are initialised with the contents of the **model** database during ASE startup, overwriting any existing database contents.
The **tempdb_space** resource limit (➢p.103) applies independently to all temporary databases.

create temporary database *db_name* **on** *device* ...[**log on** *device* ...]
Creates a temporary database. See **create database** (➢p.58) for command options. To drop a temporary database, use **drop database**. The database cannot be used by any sessions until it is either added to a group (with **sp_tempd 'add'**) or has a login or application bound to it (with **sp_tempdb 'bind'**).
The maximum number of user-defined temporary databases is 511.
Example: **create temporary database tempdb_for_sa on my_device = '100m'**
exec sp_tempdb 'bind', 'lg', sa, 'db', tempdb_for_sa

sp_tempdb [*subcommand*, *options*...]
Manages user-defined temporary databases. Possible subcommands and options:
- **'help'** (=same as no parameters at all) - displays brief usage information
- **'who'**, *tempdb_name* - displays sessions currently having *tempdb_name* as their temporary database.
- **'add'**, *tempdb_name*, *group_name* - adds a temporary database to a group (note: in 12.5.2, only the **'default'** group exists).
- **'remove'**, *tempdb_name*, *group_name* - removes a temporary database from a

group (required before dropping the database).

- **'bind', 'LG' | 'AP',** *name*, **'GR' | 'DB',** *bind_name* [**, NULL, 'hard' | 'soft'**] - binds a login (**'LG'**) or application (**'AP'**) with login name or **program_name** *name*, to a temporary database group (**'GR'**) or a specific database (**'DB'**), with name *bind_name*. With **'hard'**, a login fails when the specified database is not available; with **'soft'** (=default), the login succeeds and a different database is used.
- **'unbind', 'LG' | 'AP',** *name* - unbinds a login or application; see **bind**.
- **'unbindall_db',** *tempdb_name* - removes all bindings for this database.
- **show** *option* [,*name*] - when *option* is **'gr'**, **'db'**, **'login'** or **'app'**, displays details about groups, databases, login bindings or application bindings, optionally for the named object. When *option* is **'all'** or absent, displays all this information. To display temporary databases that are not in a group, use **sp_helpdb** or **dbcc pravailabletempdbs**.
- **'create',** *groupname* - creates an empty temporary database group. **tempdb** is always a member of **'default'** group. Note: in 12.5.2, no groups can be created; only the **'default'** group is supported.
- **'drop',** *groupname* - drops a temporary database group.

45. Dumping & loading databases

Making database dumps and transaction log dumps is the preferred method for backing up ASE databases. Direct OS-level backups of the underlying raw devices or OS files are usable as database backups only when ASE was first shut down, or when the database has been quiesced (➢p.63).
dump and **load** commands always use the Backup Server mapped to **SYB_BACKUP** in **master..sysservers** (use **sp_helpserver** to display this mapping), even when using a remote Backup Server. **SYB_BACKUP** usually runs on the same system as the ASE server, but it can also be located on another system (for example where multiple ASE servers share one Backup Server). When using a remote Backup Server, its name must exist in the **interfaces** file (NT: **SQL.INI** file). In order to make database dumps or transaction log dumps, the configuration option **'allow remote access'** must be set to 1 (dynamic).

dump database { *db_name* | *@variable* }
to { *stripe_device* | *@variable* } [**at** *remote_backup_server*] [*stripe_options*]
[**stripe on** { *stripe_device* | *@variable* } [**at** *remote_backup_server*] [*stripe_options*]
[...*more stripes*...] [**with** [*stripe_options*] [*dump_options*]]
Dumps database *db_name* to disk or tape, to one or more dump devices ('stripes') in parallel. *stripe_device* is either a dump device (created with **sp_addumpdevice**) or a tape or disk pathname (specified in quotes). By default, the dump is performed by the local Backup Server (on the same host as ASE), which is mapped to **SYB_BACKUP**. With **at** *remote_backup_server*, the dump is performed to the *stripe_device* located at the remote Backup Server specified. In pre-12.0, the maximum number of stripes is 32; in 12.0, this maximum is at least > 500 (or higher; this is platform-specific).
In 12.5 and 12.0.0.7, local dumps can be compressed by specifying *stripe_device* as **'compress::***level***::***stripe_device***'**. *level* ranges from **1** (minimum compression) to **9** (maximum compression); when *level* is not specified, but **compress::** is (and the second pair of colons is omitted), *level* defaults to **1**; *level* **0** means no compression. In 12.5.2, **with compression** (see below) can be used instead, also for remote dumps.

stripe_options can be one or more of the following (separate with commas):

- **capacity=***nr_kbytes* - the capacity of the device in Kb
- **dumpvolume=***volume_name* - the volume name when initialising a tape
- **file=***file_name* - the dump file name within the dump volume
- **blocksize=***nr_bytes* - the dump device block size (in bytes; multiple of 2048)
- **density=***value* - option is obsolete (OpenVMS only) from ASE 11.5 onwards

dump_options can be one or more of the following (separate with commas):

- **unload** - rewinds tape after dump, or **nounload** : doesn't rewind (=default)
- **retaindays =** *nr_days* - nr. of days before a disk dump can be overwritten
- **init** - overwrites tape contents, or **noinit** - appends to tape (=default)
- **notify =** { **client** | **operator_console** } - notification output for volume changes
- **dismount** - dismounts tape (=default), or **nodismount**
- **(12.5.2) compression = '***level***'** - compress the dump; *level* can be **1** (minimum compression) to **9** (maximum compression).
- **(12.5.2) passwd = '***password***'** - protects the dump with a password (6-30 characters); the same password must be specified when loading the dump.
- **(12.5.3) verify =** { **header** | **full** } - checks every dumped page; with **header** (=default) checks only the page header; with **full**, performs additional checks.

dump tran[saction] { *db_name* | *@variable* } [*...see* **dump database**...] [**with standby_access**]
Dumps the transaction log for database *db_name* to disk or tape, and then truncates the part of the log that was dumped. **with standby_access** will dump to the most recent point where no transactions were active; this option is required when, after loading this dump, the database is onlined with **for standby_access**. Otherwise **dump transaction** is similar to **dump database**.
In 15.0, **tran_dumpable_status()** indicates whether the log can be dumped (➢p.17).

dump tran[saction] { *db_name* | *@variable* } **with truncate_only**
Truncates the transaction log for database *db_name* without dumping it.

dump tran[saction] { *db_name* | *@variable* } **with no_log**
A last-resort method to truncate (but not dump) the transaction log for database *db_name* when **dump transaction**...**with truncate_only** doesn't work because the log is completely full. To ensure recoverability, a database dump should be made as soon as possible.

dump tran[saction] { *db_name* | *@variable* } [*...see* **dump database**...] [**with no_truncate**]
A special troubleshooting command: dumps the transaction log for database *db_name* to disk or tape even when the data devices are not accessible. Does not truncate the log after dumping it. Otherwise similar to **dump transaction**.

load database { *db_name* | *@variable* }
from { *stripe_device* | *@variable* } [**at** *remote_backup_server*] [*stripe_options*]
[**stripe on** { *stripe_device* | *@variable* } [**at** *remote_backup_server*] [*stripe_options*]
[*...more stripes...*]
[**with** [*stripe_options*] [*dump_options*] [, **listonly** [= **full**]] [, **headeronly**]
[**(12.5.3) , verify[only] = header** | **full**]] [**(12.5.4) , norecovery**]
Loads a database dump for database *db_name* from disk or tape, from one or more dump devices ('stripes') in parallel. *stripe_options* and *dump_options* are similar to **dump database**, except that the **capacity=** option cannot be used.
In 12.5.3, database dumps originating from a different platform can be loaded (also when those dumps are from earlier ASE versions, such as 12.0 and 11.9). All data conversions are performed automatically during **load database**; when the database is online, run **sp_post_xpload** to check and rebuild indexes.
In 12.5, to load dumps compressed with the **compress::** option, *stripe_device* must be specified as **'compress::***stripe_device***'**.

- **listonly** displays information about all files in the dump, but doesn't load any; with **=full**, displays more details.
- **headeronly** is identical to **listonly**, but only for the first file; in 12.5.4, **headeronly** also lists the disk fragments in the dump (i.e. the data in the **sysusages** rows). To display the contents of a dump (it's safe: it doesn't really load the dump!): **load tran tempdb from** *tape_device* **with listonly = full**. Note that **listonly** doesn't work for dumps compressed with **compress::**; it works fine for **with compression** (12.5.2).
- In 12.5.3, **verify[only]={header|full}** checks every loaded page; with **header** (= default) checks only the page header; with **full**, performs additional checks; with **verifyonly**, checks the pages but does not actually load them.
- In 12.5.4, and for archive databases only, **norecovery** skips database recovery after loading, and brings the database online automatically. Note that this may leave the database in an inconsistent state.

load tran[saction] { *db_name* | *@variable* }
from { *stripe_device* | *@variable* } [**at** *remote_backup_server*] [*stripe_options*]
[**stripe on** { *stripe_device* | *@variable* } [**at** *remote_backup_server*] [*stripe_options*]
[*...more stripes...*] [**with** [*stripe_options*] [*dump_options*]
[, **listonly** [= **full**]] [, **headeronly**] [{ **until_time = '***datetime***'** | **until_rid =** *log_rid* }]]
Loads a transaction log dump for database *db_name*. Similar to **load database**, except for the following options. The option **until_time** only loads transactions which were committed at the specified date/time. With **until_rid** (undocumented), only loads up to the specified log record.

online database { *db_name* | *@variable* } [**for standby_access**]
Brings database *db_name* online after loading a database dump or transaction log dump, or (in 12.5.1) creating a database with **mount database**. When the original database was from an older ASE version, also upgrades the database. With **for standby_access** (possible only after loading a log dump made with the **standby_access** option), the database will be in 'standby access' mode (i.e. the

database will be read-only accessible, and will not be checkpointed).

(12.5.3) sp_post_xpload
After loading a database dump from a platform with a different endian-ness (=byte-swapping), checks and rebuilds indexes in the current database. On databases larger than about 10Gb, it may be faster to manually drop and recreate all indexes instead.

sp_dumpoptimize [{ **'archive_space =** { **maximum** | **minimum** | **default** }**'** | **'reserved_threshold =**{ *%age* | **default** }**'** | **'allocation_threshold =**{ *%age* | **default** }**'** }]
Defines the amount of data dumped by Backup Server: **maximum** dumps all pages, whether allocated or not; **minimum** dumps only allocated pages; see the ASEdocumentation for details on the other options.

sp_volchanged *session_id*, *devname*, *action* [, *filename* [, *new_volume_name*]]
Instructs Backup Server to proceed with a dump or load operation after a tape has been changed. When Backup Server determined that a tape change was required, it printed the precise parameters to be used with **sp_volchanged** to the Backup Server errorlog file; make sure to use these parameter values. Only for the *action* parameter, choose between **'PROCEED'** or **'RETRY'** (to continue) or **'ABORT'** (to abort).

quiesce database *tag* **hold** *list-of-databases* [**(12.5) for external dump**]
[**(12.5.1) to** *manifest_file* [**with override**]]
quiesce database *tag* **release**
Allows copying a database by copying the database devices. **quiesce database**...**hold** freezes the database(s) by suspending all disk write activity until the corresponding **quiesce database...release** command, allowing a consistent copy of the database devices to be made. Existing devices in another server (which must be shut down) can be replaced with these copies, thus 'copying' the database. Uncommitted transactions in the original database are rolled back when the copy is recovered. *list-of-databases* is a comma-separated list; *tag* is an arbitrary string. **quiesce database** *tag* **release** resumes all databases specified in the **hold** command with the same *tag* (*tag* is also written to the errorlog, displayed by **dbcc resource** and, in 12.5.1, available in **monOpenDatabases.QuiesceTag**).
In 15.0, **is_quiesced()** indicates whether a database is currently quiesced (➤p.15). Returns 1 if the specified security service is active and 0 if not.

In pre-12.5.3, one command can handle ≤ 8 databases; in 12.5.3, there is no limit.
In 12.5, when using **for external dump**, and starting the server using the device copies with **-q**, the copied database(s) will remain offline to allow loading **standby_access** log dumps; without **for external dump**, no log dumps can be loaded. In 12.5.1, a manifest file (containing a binary copy of the quiesced database(s) as well as some metadata) can be created for use by **mount database**. Specify **with override** if a quiesced database contains references to non-quiesced databases.
Example: **(12.5) quiesce database blahblah hold prod_db for external dump**
...now copy the database devices for this database...
quiesce database blahblah release

(12.5.1) unmount database *list-of-database-names* **to** *manifest_file* [**with override**]
Unmounts a list of databases (≤ 8 in pre-12.5.3; no limit in 12.5.3) into a manifest file (containing a binary copy of the database(s) as well as some metadata), removing them from the current ASE server. They can be mounted again with **mount database**. Any open transactions in the unmounted databases are aborted. Specify **with override** if a database contains references to non-unmounted databases.
Example: **unmount database my_db to '/tmp/my_db.unmount'**

(12.5.1) mount database all from *manifest_file* [**with** { **verify, listonly** }] [**using** **'***pathname***'='***db_device_name***'** [, *...more devices...*]]
Mounts all databases in a manifest file, previously created with **quiesce database** or **unmount database**, in the current ASE server. The created databases remain offline, so **online database** should be run next. With the **using** clause, pathnames for database devices can be reassigned. **verify** performs additional checks while mounting the databases; **listonly** displays the device names, but does not mount databases. Note that the original and target ASE servers must have the same server page size.
Example: **mount database all from '/tmp/my_db.unmount'**

46. Segments

A segment is a 'label' for one or more database device fragments for the purpose of controlling object placement. As such, a segment does not have a size (though the underlying device fragment has), and cannot get 'full'. In the stored procedures below, *db_name* must match the current database.

sp_addsegment *segment_name*, *db_name*, *device_name*
In the current database, creates a new segment *segment_name* mapping to database device *device_name.*

sp_dropsegment *segment_name*, *db_name* [, *device_name*]
In the current database, drops the segment *segment_name*. *device_name* is optional except when the 'system', 'default' or 'logsegment' are dropped.

sp_extendsegment *segment_name*, *db_name*, *device_name*
In the current database, extends the mapping of the existing segment *segment_name* mapping to database device *device_name.*

sp_helpsegment [*segment_name*]
Displays information about all segments in the current database. With *segment_name*, displays only that segment.

sp_placeobject *segment_name*, *object_name*
Places an object on *segment_name*, which means that future space allocation for this object will only be performed on the database devices to which *segment_name* has been mapped. *object_name* can be a table name or an index name (specified as '*table_name.index_name*').

47. Thresholds

sp_addthreshold *db_name*, *segment_name*, *nr_free_pages*, *procedure_name*
Creates a new threshold in the current database, which must match *db_name*. When the free space on the devices for segment *segment_name* falls below *nr_free_pages* server pages, the stored procedure *procedure_name* is automatically executed in the background. Note: this procedure must be created by the DBA. the procedure name can be chosen freely, but the below parameter datatypes are mandatory :

```
create procedure sp_thresholdaction
    @dbname varchar(30), -- contains the database where the threshold fired
    @segment_name varchar(30), -- contains the segment for the threshold
    @free_pages int, -- contains the number of free server pages for the threshold
    @status int -- if 1, indicates a last-chance threshold; if 0, a user threshold
as begin ... T-SQL-statements... end
```

For logsegment thresholds, this procedure would typically perform a log dump.

sp_dropthreshold *db_name*, *segment_name*, *nr_free_pages*
Drops the specified user-defined threshold. Last-chance thresholds cannot be dropped. *db_name* must match the current database.

sp_helpthreshold [*segment_name*]
Displays all thresholds in the current database, or only on the specified segment.

sp_modifythreshold *db_name*, *segment_name*, *nr_free_pages* [, *new_proc_name* | **NULL** [, *new_nr_free_pages* | **NULL** [, *new_segment_name*]]]
Changes the stored procedure name, number of free server pages, or segment name for the specified user-defined threshold. For a last-chance threshold, only the stored procedure name can be changed. *db_name* must match the current database.

@@thresh_hysteresis
Contains the minimum amount of space (in server pages) that must be freed up above the threshold value before a threshold can be activated again. Thresholds on the same segment cannot be closer than twice this value.

(12.5.1) sp_dbextend [*subcommand* [, *...options...*]]
Configures automatic expansion of databases (based on thresholds). **sp_dbextend** is not installed by default; run the script *...***/$SYBASE_ASE/scripts/installdbextend** to install this procedure. For an overview of the many subcommands and their options, see the chapter *Automatic Database Expansion* in the ASE *System Administration Guide*. For brief online syntax help, run **sp_dbextend** without parameters.

48. Logins

A login is a name which is used to log into an ASE server; this always requires a password. Logins are stored in **master..syslogins**. To display all existing logins, use this query: **select name**, **suid from master..syslogins**

sp_addlogin *login_name*, *passwd* [, *def_db* [, *def_lang* [, *full_name* [, *passwd_expiration* [, *min_passwd_len* [, *max_failed_logins* [**(12.5.2)**, *authenticate_with*]]]]]]]
Creates a new login with the specified password and optional attributes; the latter can also be set with **sp_modifylogin**; see there (➤p.66) for details.

sp_droplogin *login_name*
Drops the specified login. Note that this will fail when the login is still mapped to a database user. In this case, download the stored procedure **sp_rv_helplogin** from **www.sypron.nl/new_ssp.html** to help resolve the problem.

sp_password *caller_password*, *new_password* [, *login_name*] [, **(12.5.1)** *immediate*]
Changes the password for a login. *caller_password* is the executing session's current login password; *new_password* is the new password being set. Without *login_name*, changes the password for the current session's login. To change the password for another login, specify *login_name* (but this requires **sso_role)**. For currently logged-in users, the change is not effective until they reconnect. When *immediate* = **1**, the change applies immediately to logged-in users; default=**0**(=pre-12.5.1 behaviour).

sp_displaylogin [*login_name* [, **'expand_up'** | **'expand_down'**]]
Displays attributes of the specified login. With **'expand_up'**, displays the parent roles of the roles assigned to *login_name*; **'expand_down'** displays all roles contained in the login's enabled roles. Note: to display all existing logins, use this query:
select name, **suid from master..syslogins**

sp_configure 'systemwide password expiration', *nr_days* (dynamic)
Defines the server-wide default number of days before a login or role password expires after being changed. Default = **0**, meaning a password never expires.

sp_configure 'minimum password length', *nr_characters* (dynamic)
Defines the server-wide minimum number of characters required for a login or role password (default = **6**); if **0**, blank passwords can be set.

sp_configure 'maximum failed logins', *nr_logins* (dynamic)
Defines the server-wide number of consecutive login failures (or **set role**...**on** failures) before a login (or the role) is locked. By default, *nr_logins* = **0**, meaning this feature is disabled (i.e. no such maximum applies).

sp_configure 'check password for digit', { **0** | **1** } (dynamic)
Enables (**1**) or disables (**0**, =default) whether passwords for logins (and roles) must include at least one digit (e.g. **0**..**9**).

(12.5.4) sp_passwordpolicy *subcommand*, *option*, '*value*'
Manages server-wide password policy options for login passwords (<u>not</u> for role passwords). These override the config option settings by **sp_configure** (described above). *subcommand* can be **'set'** or **'clear'** to set or delete *option* settings, or **'list'** to display current settings. When using **'clear'** without further parameters, all current dettings are deleted. Possible values for *option* (by default, these checks are all disabled):

- **'disallow simple passwords'** - when *value* = **1**, disallows password containing the login name; when **0** (=default), such 'simple' passwords are allowed
- **'systemwide password expiration'** - *value* is the number of days before a login password expires after being changed; if **0**, it never expires.
- **'password exp warn interval'** - *value* is the period (in days, **1**-**365**) before expiration of a login's password during which an expiration warning is displayed during login; if **0**, no warning is issued.
- **'minimum password length'** - *value* is the minimum number of characters required in a password; if **0**, blank passwords can be set.
- **'maximum failed logins'** - *value* is the number of consecutive login failures before a login is locked; if **0**, it never gets locked.
- **'expire login'** - when *value* = **1**, when a login is created or a login's password is changed by the DBA, it expires immediately, thus forcing the user to change the password at the next login.

The following *option*s specify the minimum number of certain characters required in login passwords; when set to **-1**, such a character is not allowed in a password at all. The default setting for all is **0** (i.e. the requirement doesn't apply).

- **'min digits in password'** - *value*= min. number of digits (**0**-**9**)
- **'min alpha in password'** - *value*= min. number of alphabetic chars (**a**-**z**, **A**-**Z**)
- **'min upper char in password'** - *value*= min. number of uppercase chars (**A**-**Z**)
- **'min lower char in password'** - *value*= min. number of lowercase chars (**a**-**z**)

- **'min special char in password'** - *value*= minimum number of special characters (i.e. **!@#$%^&*?=-+_.,:;\"{[(}])~`'** etc., but not a space)

Example: **sp_passwordpolicy 'set', 'min alpha in password' , 6**

(12.5.4) create procedure sp_extrapwdchecks
@caller_passwd varchar(30), -- the caller's current password
@new_passwd varchar(30), -- the new password specified for **@login_name**
@login_name varchar(30) -- login name whose password is set or changed
as begin ... T-SQL-statements... **end**

When this stored procedure exists in the **master** database, it is called when a login password is set or changed. When the procedure executes a **raiserror** statement for a user-defined message (error > 20000), **@new_passwd** will be rejected, otherwise it will be accepted. This allows implementing customised password checks, like checking a password history list or a dictionary.
By default, **sp_extrapwdchecks** does not exist; it must be created by the DBA (the *'New Features Guide'* for ASE 12.5.4 contains an example).

(12.5.4) create procedure sp_cleanpwdchecks
@login_name varchar(30) -- login name being dropped
as begin ... T-SQL-statements... **end**

When this stored procedure exists in the **master** database (by default, it does not exist), it is called when a login is dropped. This procedure can be used to clean up custom data used by **sp_extrapwdchecks**, such as password history lists.

sp_modifylogin *login_name*, *option*, '*value*'

Modifies properties of the specified login. Possible values for *option:*

- **'defdb'** - *value* is the default database for *login_name* after logging in
- **'deflanguage'** - *value* is the name default language of the login
- **'fullname'** - *value* is the full name of the login
- **'add default role'** - *value* is a user-defined role (which has been granted to this login), that is to be activated by default at login time
- **'drop default role'** - the reverse of **'add default role'**
- **'passwd expiration'** - *value* is the number of days (in quotes) before the password expires; if **'0'**, it never expires. Overrides server-wide settings.
- **'min passwd length'** - *value* is the minimum number of characters (in quotes) in a password; if **'0'**, a blank password can be set. Overrides server-wide settings.
- **'max failed_logins'** - *value* is the number of failed logins before the login gets locked (in quotes); if **'0'**, it never gets locked. Overrides server-wide settings.
- **(12.5) 'login script'** - *value* is the name of a login trigger for this login. This is a stored procedure in the login's default database, which is executed automatically in the background during login. Specify *value* = **NULL** to drop the setting, or a different name to change it. In 12.5.4, with *login_name* = **NULL**, defines or removes a global login trigger (see **sp_logintrigger** for full details).
- **(12.5.2) 'authenticate with'** - *value* is the name of the authentication mechanism to be used for the login; this can be **'ASE'** (=classic **syslogins** authentication), **'LDAP'**, **'PAM'** or **'ANY'**; in 12.5.4, also **'KERBEROS'**.

When specifying **'passwd expiration'**, **'min passwd length'** or **'max failed_logins'** for *option*, and **'all overrides'** for *login_name*, the setting is applied to all logins with a non-default setting; with also **'-1'** for *value*, all non-default settings are dropped.

(12.5.4) sp_logintrigger ['[*db_name*..]*proc_name*' | **'drop'**]

Defines of modifies (with *proc_name*) or removes (with **'drop'**) a global login trigger. This is a login trigger which is executed for all logins, before a login's own login trigger (if any is defined; see **sp_modifylogin**). If no database name is specified for the login trigger, it is assumed to exist in the login's default database.
Without parameter, shows the current setting, which is also in **@@logintrigger**. Modified settings are not shown by **sp_logintrigger** / **@@logintrigger** until a user logs in. Running **sp_logintrigger...** is equivalent to **sp_modifylogin NULL, 'login script',...** The global login trigger is disabled with traceflag 4072 (undocumented).
Example: **sp_logintrigger 'my_db.dbo.p_globaltrg'**

suser_id ([*login_name*] **)**

A built-in function which returns the login ID (suid) for the specified *login_name*. Without *login_name*, returns the current session's login ID.

suser_name ([*suid*] **)**

A built-in function which returns the login name for the specified login ID (*suid)*, which uniquely identifies a login. Without *suid*, returns the current session's login name.

set proxy *login_name*
set session authorization *login_name*
Changes the current session's login name (suid) to *login_name*, inheriting all roles and permissions granted to *login_name*. To return to the session's original login name, specify the original *login_name*. In 12.5.2, the inherited roles can be restricted with grant **set proxy**...**restrict role** (➢p.70).
Before **set proxy** can be used, a user having **sso_role** must execute **grant set proxy to...** in the **master** database. Note: granting **set proxy** may have security implications. Note 2: **set session authorization** and **set proxy** are identical (but **set session authorization** is ANSI-compliant).

sp_locklogin [*login_name*, { **'lock'** | **'unlock'** } [**(15.0),** *exempt_name*]]
Locks or unlocks the specified login. In 15.0, a wildcard pattern can be specified, affecting all matching logins. except **sa** which is locked only when specified explicitly. Without parameters, displays all locked logins. A login specified in *exempt_name* is not affected; when a role name is specified, the logins with that role are not affected.

(12.5.2) sp_maplogin [*auth_mech* [, *client_login_name* [, *action* | *ASE_login_name*]]]
Maps login requests to ASE logins and authentication methods. *auth_mech* can be **'ASE'** (=classic **syslogins** authentication), **'LDAP'**, **'PAM'**, **'ANY'**, **NULL**(=**'ANY'**) or (in 12.5.4) **'KERBEROS'**, and specifies the method to authenticate *client_login_name*, which is the identification used by a client. This is either mapped to an existing *ASE_login_name*, or, when *action* = **'create login'**, a new ASE login is created for this client if it doesn't exist; when *action* = **'drop'**, the ASE login is dropped. When *client_login_name* = **NULL**, any name is valid. Note that LDAP and PAM are not covered in this book.

(12.5.2) sp_helpmaplogin [*auth_mech* [, *client_login_name*]]
Displays login mappings made by **sp_maplogin**; the parameters act as a filter.

49. Database users

Formally, an ASE 'database user' (often abbreviated to 'user') is not the same as a login or an active session : a 'user' is a database-specific name for a login, used while accessing that database. 'dbo' and 'guest' are examples of user names. Users and user groups are stored in the **sysusers** table; alias users in the **sysalternates** table.

user
A built-in function which returns the current session's database user name, equivalent to **user_name()**. Note: **user** is the only built-in function that requires no parentheses.

user_id ([*db_user_name*] **)**
A built-in function which returns the database user ID number for the specified user name, as stored in the **sysusers** table in the current database. If no *user_name* is supplied, it returns the ID of the current session's database user. Note: this should not be confused with server-wide login IDs as returned by the **suser_id()** function.

user_name ([*db_user_id*] **)**
A built-in function which returns the database user's name for the specified user ID number. If no *user_id* is supplied, it returns the name of the current session's database user. Note: this should not be confused with server-wide login names as returned by the **suser_name()** function.

setuser [**'***db_user_name***'**]
Changes the current session's user ID (uid) to that of *db_user_name* in the current database. Without parameter, restores the session's original user ID. Note that the quotes are mandatory.

sp_addalias *login_name*, *db_user_name*
Adds a database user for login *login_name* as an alias user of database user *db_user_name* in the current database. *login_name* must not already be a normal database user in this database.

sp_addgroup *group_name*
Adds a group (a named collection of database users) to the current database. Groups are stored in the **sysusers** table; a group's uid is ≥ 16384, except for the group **public**, which has uid = 0.

sp_adduser *login_name* [, *db_user_name* [, *group_name*]]
Adds server login *login_name* as database user *db_user_name* in the current database. Without *db_user_name*, the user name will be equal to *login_name*. With

group_name, also adds the new database user to this group. Database owner user **dbo** has uid=1; the **guest** user (if present) has uid=2.

sp_changegroup *group_name*, *db_user_name*
Moves a database user into the group *group_name*, removing it from the group it was previously part of (if any). Note that a user will always be in the group **public**. To remove a user from a group, run: **sp_changegroup 'public'**, *db_user_name*

sp_dropalias *login_name* [**(12.5, 12.0.0.4) , 'force'**]
Removes an alias database user for the specified login. **'force'** will drop the alias even when the login still owns database objects (these objects are not dropped).

sp_dropgroup *group_name*
Removes a group, which must be empty.

sp_dropuser *db_user_name*
Removes a database user, which must not own any objects.

sp_helpgroup [*group_name*]
Displays information about one or all groups in the current database.

sp_helpuser [*db_user_name*]
Displays details on database users, groups, or aliases in the current database.
Example: **sp_helpuser dbo** - displays all aliases of the database owner

50. Roles

Roles (both user-defined roles and system roles) are stored in **master..syssrvroles**. Role assignments to logins are stored in **master..sysloginroles**.
System roles are the following predefined roles:

- **sa_role** - skips most permission checks and implies **dbo** rights in all databases
- **sso_role** - required for most security-related actions
- **oper_role** - allows dumping and loading of database and transaction logs
- **sybase_ts_role** - required for most **dbcc** commands
- **replication_role** - required for replication-related tasks (such as **set triggers**, **set replication** and **truncate table**, **dbcc gettrunc/settrunc**)
- **mon_role** - required for monitoring tasks (MDA tables, Monitor Server)
- **dtm_tm_role** - required for tasks related to DTM
- **ha_role** - required for configuring High Availability
- **(12.5.1) js_admin_role, js_client_role, js_user_role** - Job Scheduler (➢p.108)
- **(12.5.2) messaging_role** - required for real-time data services tasks
- **(15.0) webservices_role** - required for webservices tasks (➢p.49)
- **(pre-11.0) navigator_role** - obsolete (was required for Sybase MPP)

By default, the 'sa' login has been granted **sa_role**, **sso_role** and **oper_role**. User-defined roles are created with **create role**.

create role *role_name* [**with passwd** *new_password*]
create role *role_name* [**with** [**passwd** *new_password*] [**, passwd expiration** *nr_days*] [**, min passwd length** *min_length*] [**max failed_logins** *max_number*]]
Creates a user-defined role. *role_name* must be unique in the server, and cannot be the name of an existing database user or group. When specifying a password, ASE users must specify this password to activate the role.
passwd expiration is the number of days before the password expires, overriding the server-wide setting - if **'0'**, the password never expires (=default); **min passwd length** is the minimum length required for a password; **max failed_logins** is the number of times a wrong password can be specified before the role is locked.

alter role *role_1* { **add** | **drop** } **exclusive** { **membership** | **activation** } *role_2*
alter role *role_name* { **add passwd** *new_passwd* | **drop passwd** } { **lock** | **unlock** }
alter role { *role_name* | **'all overrides'** } **set** { **passwd expiration** *nr_days* |
min passwd length *min_length* | **max failed_logins** *max_number* }
Defines mutually exclusive relationships between roles and adds, drops, and changes the password for a role. Also locks or unlocks a role and sets additional properties (see **create role** above); with **'all overrides'** (including quotes) instead of *role_name*, the setting is applied to all roles with a non-default setting; when also specifying **'-1'** as the setting value, all non-default settings will be dropped.

drop role *role_name* [**with override**]
Drops the user-defined role *role_name*. **with override** also drops all associated permissions in all databases; otherwise, these permissions must be dropped first.

grant role *role_1* [, *role_2* ...] **to** *login_or_role_name* [, *login_or_role_name*...]
Grants roles to logins or other roles. Roles cannot be granted to database user or groups. When granting a user-defined role to a login, by default it is not enabled at login time. This can be modified with **sp_modifylogin**.

revoke role *role_1* [, *role_2* ...] **from** *login_or_role_name* [, *login_or_role_name*...]
Revokes previously granted roles.

sp_role { **'grant'** | **'revoke'** }, *role_name*, *login_name*
Grants or revokes *role_name* to/from *login_name*. Equivalent to { **grant** | **revoke** } **role** *role_name* { **to** | **from** } *login_name* .

sp_helprotect @*role_name* = *some_role*
Displays permissions granted to/revoked from role *some_role* in the current database.

set role *role_name* { [**with passwd** *password*] **on** | **off** }
Enables or disables *role_name* for the current session. Only roles that have been granted directly can be enabled; contained roles cannot be enabled independently.

sp_activeroles [**'expand_down'**]
Displays enabled roles for the current session. With **'expand_down'**, displays all roles contained in the enabled roles.

sp_displayroles [*role_name* | *login_name* [, *option*]]
Displays all roles granted to a role or login (default = current session's login). Values for *option*: **'expand_up'** displays the parent roles; **'expand_down'** displays all roles contained in the enabled roles.
When option = **'display_info'**, only shows info on *role_name*, but does not show if it is locked. To display all locked roles (all ASE versions), use this query: **select name from master..syssrvroles where status&2=2**

sp_modifylogin *login_name*, **'{ add** | **drop** } **default role'**, *role_name*
Enables/disables a user-defined role at login time for the specified login; by default, a user-defined role is not automatically enabled. **'add default role'** enables the role; **'drop default role'** restores the default state. **sp_modifylogin** can only be used for roles that have been granted to the login directly (i.e. not for contained roles).

(pre-12.5) sp_configure 'max roles enabled per user', *nr_of_roles* (static)
Defines the maximum # directly enabled roles per login. The maximum is 127, also in 12.5. This does not apply to indirectly enabled roles (i.e. roles granted to other roles).

The configuration options **'systemwide password expiration'**, **'minimum password length'**, **'maximum failed logins'**, **'check password for digit'** also apply to role passwords (⮚p.65).
The built-in functions **mut_excl_roles()**, **proc_role()**, **has_role()**, **role_contain()**, **role_name()**, **role_id()**, and **show_role()** provide role-related information (⮚p.19).

51. Permissions

grant *permissions* **on** { *table_name* [**(** *list_of_columns* **)**] |
view_name [**(** *list_of_columns* **)**] |
procedure_name |
encryption_key_name }
to { **public** | *user_names* | *group_names* | *role_names* } [**with grant option**]
Grants the specified permissions on a specific object (a table, view or stored procedure) to users, groups (including **public**) or roles. Multiple users, groups or roles can be specified, separated by commas.
The permissions which can be granted depend on the object:

- for a table, *permissions* can be **select**, **insert**, **update**, **delete** & **references**; in **12.5.2**, also **truncate table**, **update statistics** & **delete statistics**; in **12.5.3a**, also **decrypt** (⮚p.29)
- for a column of a table, *permissions* can be **select**, **update** & **references**; in **12.5.3a**, also **decrypt**
- for a view, *permissions* can be **select**, **insert**, **update** & **delete**
- for a column of a view, *permissions* can be **select** & **update**
- for a stored procedure, *permissions* can only be **exec**[**ute**]
- **(12.5)** for application context functions (⮚p.71), *permissions* can only be **select**
- **(12.5.3a)** for encryption keys (⮚p.28), *permissions* can only be **alter encryption key**, **select** or **all** (=both)

When specifying **all** or **all privileges** as object permission, this includes all possible

permissions for the specified object, except **decrypt**.
with grant option is possible only for users (not roles or groups), and allows the user to grant the granted permissions to other users.
Examples: **grant select on my_table to employee_group, jsmith, secretary_role**
grant all on my_table2 to jbrown

grant *cmd_permissions* **to** { **public** | *user_names* | *group_names* | *role_names* }
[**(12.5.2) restrict role** { *list_of_roles* | **all** | **system** }]
Grant the specified T-SQL command permissions to users, groups (including **public**) or roles. Multiple users, groups or roles can be specified, separated by commas. Possible command permissions are:

- **create default / create procedure / create rule**
- **create table / create view**
- **connect** (must be granted in **master** database)
- **create database** (must be granted in **master** database)
- **set proxy / set session authorization** (must be granted in **master** database)
- **(12.5.3a) create encryption key**

When specifying **all** or **all privileges** as command permission, this covers all the above commands except **set proxy/set session authorization**.
In 12.5.2, **restrict role** applies only to **set proxy** and **set session authorization**, and does not allow executing **set proxy** *login_name* to a login having roles that are not already granted to the user running **set proxy**. In addition, *list_of_roles* specifies an explicit list of roles that *login_name* must not have; **system** means that *login_name* must not have any system roles; **all** is similar to **system** but applies to all roles.
Examples: **grant create table, create procedure to guest**
(12.5.2) grant set proxy to dba_role restrict role system

revoke [**grant option for**] *object_permissions* **on**
{ *table_name* [**(** *list_of_columns* **)**] |
view_name [**(** *list_of_columns* **)**] |
procedure_name }
from { **public** | *user_names* | *group_names* | *role_names* } [**cascade**]
Revokes permissions previously granted. **grant option for** revokes a **with grant option** that was granted previously. **cascade** revoke the permissions that were granted to others as a result of having been granted **with grant option** previously. Otherwise, the syntax is similar to the **grant** *object_permissions* command.
Example: **revoke all on my_table from jwilson**

revoke *cmd_permissions* **from** { **public** | *user_names* | *group_names* | *role_names* }
Revokes the specified T-SQL command permissions granted previously; the syntax is similar to the **grant** *cmd_permissions* command.

(12.5) grant dbcc *command* [**on** { **all** | *db_name* } [**,** *...more grants...*]] **to** { *user_names* | *role_names* }
Grants execute permission on **dbcc** commands to users or roles (not to groups). The **dbcc** commands can be granted on a specific database or on **all** databases (except for **dbcc tune**, for which the **on** clause must be omitted). To execute a granted **dbcc** command, the executing login must have access to the database to which the **dbcc** command applies. *command* can be (➢p.86 for **dbcc** command details):

checkalloc	**checkstorage**	**reindex**
checkcatalog	**checkverify**	**tablealloc**
checkdb	**fix_text**	**textalloc**
checktable	**indexalloc**	**tune**

Example: **grant dbcc checkalloc on all to special_role**
grant dbcc checkstorage on my_db, dbcc checkverify on my_db to jsmith, jbloggs, special_role
grant dbcc tune to special_role

(12.5) revoke dbcc *command* [**on** { **all** | *db_name* } [**,** *...more revokes...*]] **from** { *user_names* | *role_names* }
Revokes execute permission on **dbcc** commands (previously granted by **grant dbcc**).

(12.5.2) grant default permissions on system tables
(12.5.2) revoke default permissions on system tables
Grants/revokes a set of basic **select** permissions on system tables in the current database to/from **public** (default=granted). If revoked, **sp_help** etc. can still be used.

grant role *role_1* [, *role_2* ...] **to** *login_or_role_name* [, *login_or_role_name...*]
revoke role *role_1* [, *role_2* ...] **from** *login_or_role_name* [, *login_or_role_name...*]
sp_role { **'grant'** | **'revoke'** }, *role_name*, *login_name*
Grants/revokes roles to logins or other roles (➢p.69).

sp_helprotect [*name* [, *user_name* [, **'grant'** [, **'none'** | **'granted'** | **'enabled'** | *role_name*]]]
Displays information about granted and/or revoked permissions in the current database. Without parameters, provides information about everything; specify parameters to display only specific information. Possible parameters are the following (specify **NULL** to omit a parameter):

- *name* - the name of the table, view, stored procedure, a user, group or role.
- *user_name* - specifies the user name of the owner of the table, view or procedure specified by *name*
- **'grant'** - only displays the privileges granted to *name* with **with grant option**
- **'none'** - does not display role-related information
- **'granted'** - includes information about roles granted to the user
- **'enabled'** - includes information about roles granted and activated by the user
- *role_name* - displays information for the specified *role_name*, whether granted to the user or not.

create schema authorization *current_db_user_name* [**create table** *statements*] [**create view** *statements*] [**grant** *statements*] [**revoke** *statements*]
Creates tables and/or views, and sets permissions, in a transaction (➢p.28).

52. Row-level access control (12.5)

Row-level access control (also known as 'fine-grain access control') allows access protection on individual rows in a table by means of access rules; an access rule will effectively (but invisibly) be part of the **where** clause of any query referring to a table to which this access rule is bound. Access rules are designed to be used with application context functions (see below) or Java functions (➢p.46); the application context is designed to be defined by a login trigger (➢p.66).

sp_configure 'enable row level access', { **0** |**1** } (dynamic)
Enables (**1**) or disables (**0**,=default) row-level access control. To enable, the **ASE_ASM** option must be licensed; in 15.0esd2, **ASE_RLAC** must be licensed instead.

create [**and** | **or**] **access rule** *rule_name* **as** *rule_expression*
Creates an access rule with the specified name (➢p.34 for details). To run this command, the config option **'enable row level access'** (see above) must be enabled.
Example: **create access rule ar1 as @owner = suser_id()**

create access rule ar2 as
@owner = get_appcontext ('my_context', 'auth_code')

Application contexts are managed with the following built-in functions. To allow non-privileged logins to use these functions, permissions must be granted first (note the absence of parentheses with the built-in function name):
Example: **grant select on list_appcontext to special_privs_role**

get_appcontext ('*app_context_name*', '*attribute_name*' **)**
Returns the value of the specified attribute in the specified application context.
Example: **select get_appcontext ('my_context', 'attrib_1')**

list_appcontext ('*app_context_name*' | **'*'** , '*attribute_name*' | **'*'** **)**
Displays the specified attribute(s) in the specified application context(s). To display all attributes and/or contexts, specify **'*'** values for the parameters.
Example: **select list_appcontext ('*', '*')**

rm_appcontext *(* '*app_context_name*', '*attribute_name*' *)*
Deletes the specified attribute from the specified application context.
Example: **select rm_appcontext (** '*my_context*', '*attrib_1*' **)**

set_appcontext ('*app_context_name*', '*attribute_name*', '*attribute_value*' **)**
Creates an attribute in the specified application context; if the context does not yet exist, it will be created as well.
Example: **select set_appcontext ('my_context', 'attrib_1', 'value_1')**

Some session-specific attributes can be accessed through the read-only application context **SYS_SESSION** (note: these are not listed by **list_appcontext**):

Attribute	Description	Equivalent to
applname	application name	**sysprocesses.program_name**
character_set	client character set	**@@client_csname**
client_applname	client-defined appl. name	**sysprocesses.clientapplname**
client_hostname	client-defined host name	**sysprocesses.clienthostname**
client_name	client-defined name	**sysprocesses.clientname**
dateformat	setting of **set dateformat**	no direct equivalent
db_userid	user ID in database	**user_id()**
dbid	current database ID	**db_id()**
dbname	current database name	**db_name()**
groupid	group ID in database	no direct equivalent
hostname	client host name	**sysprocesses.hostname**
flanguage	session language	**@@language**
proxy_suserid	indicates **set proxy** is active	**sysprocesses.origsuid**
spid	process ID	**@@spid**
suserid	login ID	**suser_id()**
username	login name	**suser_name()**

Example: **select get_appcontext ('SYS_SESSION', 'dateformat')**

53. Managing server configuration options

sp_configure ['*configuration_option*' [, *config_value* [, **'default'**]]
(12.5) sp_configure '*configuration_option*', *0*, '*config_value***P|K|M|G'**
Without parameters, displays the current settings for all configuration options (subject to the settings by **sp_displaylevel**). When specifying (a substring of) a configuration option, or when wildcard characters ('**%**' and '_'; ➤p.9) are specified, displays only those options matching the specified substring and/or wildcards. The column 'Memory Used' is usually expressed in Kb.
With *config_value* (an integer value), sets the specified configuration option to this value; in this case, the specified string must uniquely identify the configuration option. When specifying **'default'**, and *config_value* is set to **0**, the configuration option is reset to its default value.
In 12.5, **sp_configure** also displays the unit of measurement for the config option, and whether it is static, dynamic or read-only (➤p.6 for the difference between semi-dynamic and dynamic config options as used in this book).
In 12.5, the value to be configured can also be specified in a quoted string with a unit indicator, which can be **P**(=2Kb memory pages, or 2048), **K**(=Kb, or 1024), **M**(=Mb, or 1048576) or **G** (=Gb, or 1073741824); *config_value* must be **0**. When the unit is omitted from the string, it defaults to **K**. In this book, this **sp_configure** parameter is shown only where relevant (for example, in the section about memory allocation).
Examples: **sp_configure 'upd', 1** -- enables **'allow updates to system tables'**
(12.5) sp_configure 'procedure cache size', 0, '150M' -- 150 Mb
(12.5) sp_configure 'number of locks', 0, '250K' -- 256000 locks

Note: for static configuration options, an ASE server restart is required to make the change effective. Changes to dynamic options are effective directly. To determine whether an option is static or dynamic, use **sp_configure** or **sp_helpconfig** in 12.5; in pre-12.5, run the following query:
select name, case when status&8 = 0 then 'static' else 'dynamic' end
from master..sysconfigures where name like '%some_substring%'

sp_configure 'configuration file', 0, *option*, '*file_name*'
Performs specific operations on the configuration options and the specified file name. *option* can be:

- **'write'** - writes the current run (= active) values to the specified file.
- **'restore'** - writes the currently configured values (not the run values) to the specified file.
- **'read'** - sets the configuration options to the values in the specified file after validating them.
- **'verify'** - only validates the configuration options in the specified file.

With only **'configuration file'**, shows the actual pathname of the server's configuration file, but unfortunately, this tends to be truncated. To display the full pathname, use this query: **select value2 from master..syscurconfigs where config = 114**

sp_displaylevel [*login_name* [, *display_level*]]
Sets or displays the 'display level' for **sp_configure**, which determines the level of detail for displaying configuration options. Without parameters, displays the setting for the current session's login; with only *login_name*, displays the setting for that login.
To set the display level to *display_level* for the current session, specify **NULL** for

login_name; to set the level for a specific login, specify the *login_name*. *display_level* can be **'basic'** (displays only some config options), **'intermediate'** (displays more, but not all, config options), and **'comprehensive'** (=default, displays all config options).

sp_helpconfig '*configuration_option*', ['*config_value*' | '*size***P|M|K|G'**]
Displays a short description, and the minimum & maximum values allowed for the specified configuration option, which can be specified as a unique substring. When *config_value* is specified, it also displays the amount of memory required when the configuration option would be set to this new *config_value*. When a memory size is specified instead (like **'1M'** or **'200K'**; **P**=Pages, **K**=Kb, **M**=Mb, **G**=Gb), displays the highest possible configuration value for this configuration option which can fit in this size. *configuration_option* may contain wildcard characters ('**%**' and '_'; ➢p.9).
In 12.5, also displays the config option's unit of measurement and whether it is 'static', 'dynamic' or 'read-only'. Specifying **'static options'**, **'dynamic options'** or **'read-only options'** for *configuration_option* displays all config options of that type.
Example: **sp_helpconfig 'f loc', 10000** -- displays memory required for setting the configuration option **'number of locks'** to 10000.

sp_countmetadata *option* [, *db_name*]
Counts the total number of objects, indexes or databases existing in the server; with *db_name*, determines the total for the specified database only. The total is displayed along with the corresponding configuration option. These totals can often be used as an upper limit for these configuration options. *option* can be:

- **'open databases'** - counts the total number of databases; displays the current setting for the config option **number of open databases** (static; 12.5:semi-dyn.)
- **'open indexes'** - counts the total number of indexes; displays the current setting for the config option **number of open indexes** (static; 12.5:semi-dynamic)
- **'open objects'** - counts the total number of objects; displays the current setting for the config option **number of open objects** (static; 12.5:semi-dynamic)
- **(15.0) 'open partitions'** - counts the total number of partitions; displays the current setting for the config option **number of open partitions** (semi-dynamic)

sp_monitorconfig '*config_option*' | **'all'** [**(12.5.0.3),** *result_table_name* [**(12.5.2), 'full'**]
For one or more configuration options, displays how much of the configured value is currently free, how much is in use (free + in use = configured value), and the highest amount used since the server was started; this can be used for adjusting configuration values (with **sp_configure**). In pre-12.5.2, indicates whether or not configuration data was re-used; in 12.5.2, indicates the number of times re-use occurred. With **'full'** in 12.5.2, three additional columns are displayed.
The supported config options are listed below. *config_option* may contain wildcard characters ('**%**' and '_'; ➢p.9), but full output is displayed only when matching exactly one config option. For a full display of all supported options, specify **'all'**. In 12.5.0.3, the results are optionally inserted into *result_table_name*. This table must already exist with the following datatypes (different table/column names can be used):

create table moncfg_data (Name varchar(35), Num_free int, Num_active int, Pct_act char(6), Max_Used int, Reuse_cnt int, Date varchar(30))

In 12.5.1, three additional columns must be specified:

create table moncfg_data (Name varchar(35), Config_val int, System_val int, Total_val int, Num_free int, Num_active int, Pct_act char(6), Max_Used int, Reuse_cnt int, Date varchar(30))

Starting with 12.5, most of the sampling by **sp_monitorconfig** is disabled by starting ASE with traceflag 3631. Unless specified otherwise, all config options below are 'static' in pre-12.5 and 'semi-dynamic' (➢p.6) in 12.5.
Configuration options supported by **sp_monitorconfig** in ASE 12.0:

number of aux scan descriptors	**number of open indexes**
number of open databases	**number of open objects**
number of dtx participants	**txn to pss ratio**

Additional configuration options supported by **sp_monitorconfig** in ASE 12.5:

additional network memory	**number of messages**
audit queue size	**number of remote connections** (static)
heap memory per user	**number of remote logins** (static)
size of unilib cache	**number of remote sites** (static)
max cis remote connections	**number of sort buffers** (dynamic)
max memory	**number of user connections**
max online engines (static)	**max number network listeners** (static)
memory per worker process	**number of worker processes**
number of alarms	**partition groups**
number of devices	**permission cache entries**

number of java sockets	procedure cache size
number of large i/o buffers	size of global fixed heap
number of locks	size of process object heap
number of mailboxes	size of shared class heap

Additional configuration options supported by **sp_monitorconfig** in ASE 12.5.2:

disk i/o structures

Additional configuration options supported by **sp_monitorconfig** in ASE 15.0:

number of open partitions

reconfigure [**with override**]
As of ASE 11.0, this command is obsolete and performs no function anymore.

54. Memory allocation in ASE 12.0

Up to ASE 12.0, all changes to configuration options related to memory allocation are static, meaning that an ASE server restart is required to make the change effective.

sp_configure *option*, *numeric_value*
Sets configuration options related to memory allocation. *option* can be:

- **'total memory'** (static) - sets the total amount of memory to be allocated by the server, expressed in 2Kb memory pages.
- **'procedure cache percent'** (static) - sets the percentage of the total cache size to be allocated for the procedure cache (default = 20).
- **'total data cache size'** (read-only) - displays the total size of all data caches.

55. Memory allocation in ASE 12.5+

Starting with ASE 12.5, memory allocation has become more dynamic than before, and often does not require an ASE server restart anymore. See page 6 for the difference between semi-dynamic and dynamic config options as indicated in this book. Also, note that the size of the default data cache must explicitly be set in 12.5+:
  sp_cacheconfig 'default data cache', '1.5G' -- 1.5 Gb (static)

sp_configure *option*, { *config_value* | **0** } [, **'***config_value***P|K|M|G'**]
Sets configuration options related to memory allocation. *option* can be:

- **'memory'** (read-only) - displays memory-related configuration options as well as the amount of memory available for reconfiguration.
- **'max memory'** (semi-dynamic) - sets the maximum amount of memory that can be allocated by the server.
- **'allocate max shared memory'** (dynamic) - when set to **0** (=default), allocates only as much memory as required for the current configuration (=**'total logical memory'**); when set to **1**, allocates up to **'max memory'**.
- **'dynamic allocation on demand'** (dynamic) - defines memory allocation behaviour: when set to **1** (=default), allocates additional memory for a changed config option only when actually needed by ASE; when set to **0**, immediately allocates all additional memory for a changed config option.
- **'total logical memory'** (read-only) - indicates the total amount of memory required (but not necessarily allocated) for the current configuration, both at boot time ('Config Value') and currently ('Run Value'); the latter can both increase and decrease when configuration options are changed.
- **'total physical memory'** (read-only) - indicates the total amount of memory currently allocated ('Run Value'); this can decrease only after a restart.
- **'procedure cache size'** (semi-dynamic) - sets the size of the procedure cache as an absolute value.
- **'total data cache size'** (read-only) - displays the total size of all data caches.

56. Named caches & buffer pools

In this section, sizes of caches and pools are specified as **'***size***P|K|M|G'**. *size* is a number indicating the cache size, expressed in one of the subsequent units: **P** (= server pages; =2Kb in pre-12.5), **K** (=Kb=default), **M** (=Mb) or **G** (=Gb). For **M** and **G**, *size* can be a floating-point number. Note that the minimum size for a cache or pool is 256 times the server pagesize. Examples: **'5120P'**, **'2000K'**, **'100M'**, **'1.5G'**.

sp_cacheconfig [cache_name [,'size**P|K|M|G'**] [, cache_type] [, lru_policy]
Creates, drops or modifies named caches. In pre-12.5.1, most changes by **sp_cacheconfig** are static and take effect after a server restart. In 12.5.1, creating, dropping and enlarging a cache, and changing the cache type, is dynamic; to dynamically reduce cache size, drop/recreate the cache. To drop a cache (in any ASE

version), specify the size as **'0'**.
By default, *cache_type* is **'mixed'** (for both data and log I/O); a **'logonly'** cache is for log I/O only. By default, *lru_policy* (LRU replacement policy) is **'strict'**; **'relaxed'** LRU caches are for special cases.
With only *cache_name*, displays its status (without *cache_name*, for all caches). To display cache bindings, use **sp_helpcache** instead. Examples:

- create or resize cache MY_CACHE: **sp_cacheconfig MY_CACHE, '100M'**
- change MY_CACHE to **'logonly'** : **sp_cacheconfig MY_CACHE, 'logonly'**
- drop MY_CACHE: **sp_cacheconfig MY_CACHE, '0'**

In pre-12.5, the size of the default data cache cannot be set directly, but will always automatically be as large as possible, minus the memory requirements for config options and other named caches. In 12.5 however, the size of the default data cache must explicitly be defined as follows:

(12.5) sp_cacheconfig 'default data cache', '800M' -- 800 Mb

sp_cacheconfig *cache_name* **, 'cache_partition=1 | 2 | 4 | 8 | 16 | 32 | 64'** (static)
sp_configure 'global cache partition number', { 1 | 2 | 4 | 8 | 16 | 32 | 64 } (static)
Defines the number of cache partitions for data caches (in multi-engine servers, cache partitions can reduce spinlock contention on data caches). **sp_configure** defines a default setting for all caches; **sp_cacheconfig** defines a setting for the specified cache, overriding the default. In 12.5.2, the number of cache partitions for the default data cache is automatically configured for multi-engine servers (provided no settings have already been established with **sp_cacheconfig** or **sp_configure**).

sp_poolconfig *cache_name* [**,'***size***P|K|M|G', '***pool_id***'** [**, '***affected_pool_id***'**]]
sp_poolconfig *cache_name***, '***pool_id***', 'wash=***size***P|K|M|G'**
sp_poolconfig *cache_name***, '***pool_id***', 'local async prefetch limit=***percentage***'**
Creates, drops or modifies buffer pools. Changes by **sp_poolconfig** take effect immediately. In the first form, creates, drops or resizes a pool of the specified size in *cache_name*. To drop a pool, specify **'0'** for the size. With only *cache_name*, displays the pools in the cache.
pool_id identifies the pool's buffer size and must either be the server page size, or a 2, 4 or 8 multiple of this (for a 2Kb server page size, possible pool sizes are **'2K'**, **'4K'**, **'8K'** or **'16K'**; likewise, in 12.5, for a 16Kb server page size, these are **'16K'**, **'32K'**, **'64K'** or **'128K'**). *affected_pool_id* identifies the pool where the space is taken from or added to; default is the pool with the smallest buffer size.
The second and third from change the pool's wash size and APF limit, respectively.
Example: **sp_poolconfig 'default data cache', '50M', '16K'** -- a 16K pool of 50Mb

sp_helpcache [*cache_name* | **'***size***P|K|M|G'**]
Displays cache bindings for the specified cache (without *cache_name*, for all caches). When specifying a size, computes the overhead for a cache of that size.

sp_bindcache *cache_name*, *db_name* [, *table_name* [**,** *index_name* | **'text only'**]]
Binds objects to *cache_name* (if already bound to a different cache, it is re-bound to *cache_name*). Changes by **sp_bindcache** take effect immediately. An object can be a database (specify only *db_name*), a table (also specify *table_name)*, an index (also specify *index_name*) or a table's **text** or **image** columns (specify **'text only'** instead).

sp_unbindcache *db_name* [, *table_name* [**,** *index_name* | **'text only'**]]
Like **sp_bindcache**, but unbinds an object from the cache it is currently bound to.

sp_unbindcache_all *cache_name*
Unbinds all objects bound to *cache_name* (takes effect immediately).

sp_cachestrategy *db_name***,** *table_name* [**,** *index_name* | **'text only'** | **'table only'** [**, 'prefetch'** | **'mru', 'on'** | **'off'**]]
For an object, enables (**'on'**) or disables (**'off'**) large I/O (**'prefetch'**) or **'mru'** buffer replacement; both are enabled by default. An object can be a table (specify **'table only'**), an index (specify *index_name*) or the table's **text** or **image** columns (specify **'text only'**). With only *db_name* and *table_name*, displays current settings.

(12.5.2) sp_configure 'extended cache size', *size_in_2Kb_pages* (semi-dynamic)
(32-bit Linux only) Creates a secondary data cache, as an extension to the regular data caches; this space is allocated from the host RAM, not from **'max memory'** (only a small amount of memory is used as overhead). By setting the size to 0, the extended cache is dropped immediately. Before enabling the extended cache, **/dev/shm** must be mounted (on OS level) as a shared memory file system ('shmfs').

57. Update statistics

update statistics should be run regularly for all user tables to help avoid performance problems. The **update statistics** commands automatically run at transaction isolation level 0 for DOL tables, and at level 1 for APL tables. In the statements below, *table_name* can optionally be qualified with the database name and/or owner name.
Table and index statistics, as stored in **systabstats** and **sysstatistics**, can be viewed, and **sysstatistics** edited, with the **optdiag** utility (➢p.114). To find the date/time an **update statistics** command was last run for a table, use **optdiag**, or use this query: **select moddate from sysstatistics where id = object_id('*table_name*')**
The statistics in **syssstatistics** consist of histogram statistics (used for costing search arguments), and density statistics (for costing joins).

update statistics *table_name* [**(15.0) partition** *ptn_name*] [*index_name*] [*options*]
update statistics *table_name* [*index_name* [**(15.0) partition** *ix_ptn_name*]] [*options*]
Creates/updates a histogram (**sysstatistics**) for the leading index column in all indexes on *table_name* (when specified, only for the specified index or partition), and density statistics for all prefix subsets of the index columns.

update statistics *table_name* **(** *column_list* **)** [*options*]
For *table_name*, creates/updates a histogram for the first column in the list and density statistics for all prefix subsets of the specified columns.

update index statistics *table_name* [**(15.0) partition** *ptn_name*][*index_name*][*options*]
update index statistics *table_name* [*index_name* [**(15.0) partition** *ix_ptn_name*]] [*options*]
Creates/updates a histogram for all indexed columns in all indexes on *table_name* (when specified, only for the specified index or partition), and density statistics for all prefix subsets of the index columns. **update index statistics** provides more information to the optimizer than **update statistics**, but requires space in the procedure cache and **tempdb**.

update all statistics *table_name* [**(15.0) partition** *ptn_name*] [*options*]
Runs **update index statistics** for all indexes on *table_name* (when specified, only for the specified partition), and creates/updates a histogram for all non-indexed columns; for partitioned tables, also performs **update partition statistics**. Note: **update all statistics** should be used reluctantly, especially for tables with many columns, since it may consume a significant amount of space in the procedure cache and in **tempdb**.

In the above **update** [...] **statistics** commands, *options* can be one or more of:

- **using** *nr_steps* **values** - uses *nr_steps* histogram steps; in pre-12.5, the default is 20; in 12.5 and 12.0.0.4, the default is the value of **'number of histogram steps'** (see below). Once statistics are created, the number of steps is retained unless overridden with **using** *nr_steps* **values** or until the statistics are deleted.
- **with consumers =** *nr_consumers* - forces I/O parallelism (for partitioned tables)
- **(12.5.0.3) with sampling =** *percentage* **percent** - for non-leading index columns and non-indexed columns only, reads the specified percentage of the rows from the table, instead of all rows.

(12.5, 12.0.0.4) sp_configure 'number of histogram steps', *nr_steps* (dynamic)
Sets the server-wide default number of histogram steps for **update statistics**.

(12.5.0.3) sp_configure 'sampling percent', *percentage* (dynamic)
Sets the server-wide default sampling percentage (**1..100**; default=**0**=sampling is disabled) for **update statistics** (applies to non-leading index columns and non-indexed columns only).

(12.5.2) sp_configure 'histogram tuning factor', *value* (dynamic)
Increases the maximum number of histogram steps, aiming to identify duplicate data values (frequency cells). During histogram generation, *value* (default=**1**) multiplies the number of steps specified by ...**using** *nr_steps* **values** or **'number of histogram steps'**; the steps in the final histogram are again reduced to these settings if possible.

(15.0) update table statistics *table_name* [**(15.0) partition** *ptn_name*]
[**(15.0.1)** *index_name* [**partition** *ix_ptn_name*]]
(pre-15) update partition statistics *table_name* [*partition_nr*]
Updates table/partition statistics (in **systabstats**) for all table partitions, or only for the specified partition. With *index_name*, updates only the index partitions for this index; optionally, updates the specified index partition only.

delete statistics *table_name* [**(** *column_list* **)**]
Deletes all statistics (both actual and simulated) for *table_name* from **sysstatistics**. With *column_list*, deletes only the statistics for those columns.

delete shared statistics
Deletes simulated statistics for configuration settings from **master..sysstatistics**.

(15.0) datachange (*table_name*, *partition_name*, *column_name* **)**
Returns the amount of modified rows (as a percentage of the table's total #rows) for the table, partition, or column since the last **update statistics**; see p.14 for details.

sp_flushstats [*table_name*]
For the specified table, updates **systabstats** with statistics information currently stored in memory. Without *table_name*, for all tables in the current database.

(15.0) sp_configure 'sysstatistics flush interval', *nr_of_minutes* (dynamic)
Defines the number of minutes (**1**..**32767**; **0** =disabled =default) until the housekeeper writes **sysstatistics** data to disk.

sp_modifystats *table_name*, *column_name*, **'REMOVE_SKEW_FROM_DENSITY'**
(12.5) sp_modifystats *table_name*, **'***column_list***'**, **'MODIFY_DENSITY'**, { **range** | **total** }, { **absolute** | **factor** }, **'***value***'**
Manipulates column statistics in **sysstatistics**. Use only when you understand what you're doing! The first form sets the total density of the specified column to the range cell density (this may be useful for heavily skewed column data). The second form (12.5), sets or modifies the density for the (comma-separated) list of column names in *column_list* (**'all'** matches all columns, **%** can be used as a wildcard for single columns). **range** and **total** modify the range cell and total cell density, respectively. **absolute** sets the density to *value*; **factor** multiplies the density by *value.*
Example: **sp_modifystats t1, 'col1,col2', MODIFY_DENSITY, total, factor, '0.1'**

sp_recompile *table_name*
Ensures that any stored procedure or trigger accessing *table_name* will have its query plan recompiled (= re-optimized) the next time it is executed. **sp_recompile** should be run after updating the statistics for a table or index, or after adding indexes, to ensure these can also be used by already compiled queries.

58. sp_sysmon

sp_sysmon displays statistics about the internal resource usage of the server, as well as other information that may be useful for performance tuning.

sp_sysmon 'begin_sample'
sp_sysmon { **'end_sample'** | **'***hh:mm:ss***'** } [**,** *section* [**,** *application* [**(12.5.1),** *filter* [**(12.5.2),** *dump_counters* [**(12.5.3), 'noclear'**]]]]]
The simplest way to invoke **sp_sysmon** is to specify a sample interval using **'***hh:mm:ss***'**. Using both the **'begin_sample'** and **'end_sample'** calls, sampling can also cover specific actions or statements.
Warning: in pre-12.5.3, only a single **sp_sysmon** session should run at a time, as multiple concurrent invocations may interfere and produce invalid results. In 12.5.3, specify the **'noclear'** parameter to avoid such interference (also see **@@monitors_active**;➢p.119).
When *dump_counters* = **'y'** (default = **'n'**), also displays the raw monitor counters (this option is undocumented).
Because the default **sp_sysmon** output can be large, it can be limited to a specific section by specifying the *section* parameter as below (in **sp_sysmon** output order). The **'cache wizard'** section is not included by default; it must be specified explicitly.

section **parameter**	**Resulting sp_sysmon output**
kernel	Kernel Utilization
wpm	Worker Process Management
parallel	Parallel Query Management
taskmgmt	Task Management
appmgmt	Application Management
esp	ESP Management
housekeeper	Housekeeper Task Activity
monaccess	Monitor Access to Executing SQL
xactsum	Transaction Profile
xactmgmt	Transaction Management
indexmgmt	Index Management
mdcache	Metadata Cache Management

locks	Lock Management
dcache	Data Cache Management
pcache	Procedure Cache Management
memory	Memory Management *(note: this is hardly useful…)*
recovery	Recovery Management
diskio	Disk I/O Management
netio	Network I/O Management
(12.5.0.3) repagent	ASE RepAgent threads
(12.5.1) 'cache wizard'	Recommendations and statistics for data caches

The *application* parameter is valid only when specifying either **'appmgmt'**, **NULL** or **'cache wizard'** as the *section* parameter; it is ignored otherwise.
For **'cache wizard'** (12.5.1), *application* is an integer number (specify as a quoted string) specifing the top-N objects to be reported (by default, N=10).
For **'appmgmt'** or **NULL,** *application* is as follows:

appl_only	CPU, I/O, priority changes, and resource limit violations by application name.
appl_and_login	ibid., by application name and login name.
no_appl	Skips the application and login section (=default)

When specifying **'cache wizard'** as the *section* parameter, *filter* can specify a data cache name to limit the report to (default = all caches); *filter* is ignored otherwise.

59. Reorg

The **reorg** command can be used for garbage collection and defragmentation of DOL tables; in 15.0, **reorg rebuild** *table_name* can also be used with APL tables.
The option **with resume** lets **reorg** continue at the point where it stopped when it ran previously for this table. The option **with time =** *nr_minutes* lets the **reorg** command run for the specified number of minutes, after which it stops.

reorg forwarded_rows *table_name* [**(15.0) partition** *ptn_name*]
[**with** { **resume, time =** *nr_minutes* }]
Moves forwarded rows back to their originating page.

reorg reclaim_space *table_name* [*index_name*] [**(15.0) partition** *ptn_name*]
[**with** { **resume, time =** *nr_minutes* }]
Reclaims unused space from deleted or updated rows on individual pages of the specified table/index/partition (but doesn't move rows across pages so as to deallocate resulting empty pages).

reorg compact *table_name* [**(15.0) partition** *ptn_name*]
[**with** { **resume, time =** *nr_minutes* }]
Performs both the **reclaim_space** and **forwarded_rows** actions; **reclaim_space** is performed only for the data pages of the table or partition, not for the indexes.

reorg rebuild *table_name*
Defragments the table and its indexes; this requires sufficient free space (> 100% of the table size) and blocks all access to the table (using an Exclusive-Table lock). The database option **select into/bulkcopy/pllsort** must be enabled; it is recommended to make a database dump afterwards.

reorg rebuild *table_name index_name* [**(15.0) partition** *ix_ptn_name*]
Rebuilds the specified index, or index partition, while the table and index remain accessible (using an Exclusive-Intent lock). When rebuilding a clustered index, data pages are not affected.

sp_configure 'enable housekeeper GC', *value* (dynamic)
Defines behaviour of the housekeeper for 'Garbage Collection' ('GC'; cleaning up empty pages in DOL tables). In pre-12.5.0.3, enables (*value*=**1**, =default) or disables (*value* =**0**) GC; this is done by the 'HOUSEKEEPER' thread. In 12.5.0.3, defines GC by the 'HK GC' thread, and also GC for **delete** operations. *value* can be:

- **0** - disables GC by 'HK GC'; lazy GC for **delete** operations
- **1** (=default) - use lazy GC for both 'HK GC' and for **delete** operations
- **4** - use aggressive GC for both 'HK GC' and for **delete** operations
- **5** - use aggressive GC for 'HK GC', and lazy GC for **delete** operations

Aggressive GC is more effective, but requires more CPU, than lazy GC.

60. Languages & messages

The language for error messages is 'us_english' by default; this can be changed by installing additional languages. To install a Sybase-provided language, use **langinstall** (➢p.113). To install a custom language, use the commands described below.

sp_addlanguage *language_name*, *language_alias*, *month_list*, *shortmonth_list*, *day_list*, *dateformat*, *datefirst*
Installs a custom language (i.e. one not provided by Sybase) in the current server (to install Sybase-supported languages, use **langinstall** instead). This language can be referred to as *language_name* or its alias *language_alias*. *month_list*, *shortmonth_list* and *day_list* are quoted strings containing comma-separated lists of names of the months, abbreviated months and days in this language, respectively. *dateformat* is one of **'mdy'**, **'myd'**, **'dmy'**, **'dym'**, **'ydm'** or **'ymd'**, defining the day-month-year order to be used for dates. *datefirst* defines the first day of the week. Example:

```
sp_addlanguage dutch, nederlands,
'januari,februari,maart,april,mei,juni,juli,augustus,september,oktober, november,december', 'jan,feb,mar,apr,mei,jun,jul,aug,sep,okt,nov,dec',
'maandag,dinsdag,woensdag,donderdag,vrijdag,zaterdag,zondag', dmy, 1
```

sp_droplanguage *language_name* [, **'dropmessages'**]
Drops the language *language_name*, for languages installed either with **langinstall** and **sp_addlanguage**. When messages exist for this language, **'dropmessages'** must be specified to drop these messages.

sp_helplanguage [*language_name*]
Displays information about the specified language. Without parameter, displays all installed languages.

sp_modifylogin *login_name*, **'deflanguage'**, *language_name*
Sets the default language for the specified login to *language_name*. This overrides the server-wide default language. When creating a new login, a default language can also be specified with **sp_addlogin**.

sp_setlangalias *language_name*, *language_alias*
Defines *language_alias* as the alias for *language_name*, replacing any existing alias. Example: **sp_setlangalias spanish, castellano**

sp_configure 'default language id' , *language_id* (dynamic)
Sets the server-wide default language.

set language *language_name*
Sets the current session's language, overriding the server-wide default language and the login's default language. Either the language name or the language alias can be specified for *language_name*. The global variables **@@language** and **@@langid** contain the name and ID of the current session's language, respectively.

sp_addmessage *error_nr*, *msg_text* [, *language_name* [, *with_log* [, **'replace'**]]]
Creates a user-defined message (stored in **sysusermessages)**, identified by *error_nr* (must be ≥ 20000). *msg_text* is the message text, including formatting placeholders (like **%1!**). *language_name* specifies the language this message belongs to; if omitted, the session's default language is used.
If *with_log* = **true**, whenever the error occurs (or is raised with **raiserror)**, the message text is also written to the server errorlog. If *with_log* = **false** (=default), the message may or may not be logged, depending on the severity. If a message with the same *error_nr* already exists, the existing message is overwritten if **'replace'** is specified; otherwise, **sp_addmessage** fails. Examples:

```
sp_addmessage 23456, "Please don't update the key of table '%1!' "
sp_addmessage 23457, "Blijf met je tengels van tabel '%1!' af !", dutch
```

To display the user-defined message for error nr. 23456 in the current database:

```
select * from sysusermessages where error = 23456
```

To display the system-defined message for error nr. 208:

```
select * from master..sysmessages where error = 208
```

sp_altermessage *error_nr*, **'with_log'**, { **true** | **false** }
Enables (**true**) or disables (**false**) that the (user-defined or system-defined) message for the specified *error_nr* is written to the server errorlog whenever the error occurs.

sp_dropmessage *error_nr* [, *language_name*]
Drops the message for *error_nr* in the session's current language, or, with *language_name*, in the specified language.

sp_getmessage *error_nr*, *@result* **output** [, *language_name*]
Retrieves the message for *error_nr* in the session's current language, or, with *language_name*, in that language. The result is placed in the variable *@result* which must be of datatype (**var**)**char**, and can be used in a subsequent **print** statement.

sp_bindmsg *constraint_name*, *error_nr*
Binds the message corresponding to *error_nr* to the specified constraint (➢p.32).

sp_unbindmsg *constraint_name*
Unbinds the message bound to the specified constraint.

raiserror *error_nr* [, *value_list*]
Retrieves, formats and prints the message for *error_nr*; ➢p.40 for more details.

61. Character set & sort order

The character set and sort order used by the server must be chosen when the server is created. This can be changed later, but this is normally not recommended as this may invalidate existing indexes (when changing to a multibyte character set, **text** columns may also be affected). See the *ASE System Administration Guide* for more information. To install additional character sets, or additional sort orders for already installed characters sets, use the **charset** utility (➢p.112).

sp_configure 'default sortorder id', *sortorder_id* (static)
Changes the sort order for the current default character set. After restarting the ASE server, run **sp_indsuspect** to check for invalid indexes.
To display the available sort orders (and their IDs) in the server:
select id, csid, name, description from master..syscharsets where type >= 2000

sp_configure 'default character set id', *charset_id* (static)
Changes the default character set used by the server. When ASE is restarted, the default character set will be changed and ASE will shutdown automatically.
To display the available character sets (and their IDs) in the current server:
select id, csid, name, description from master..syscharsets where type < 2000

sp_configure 'disable character set conversion', { **0** | **1** } (static)
Enables (**0**, =default) or disables (**1**) automatic conversion between the character sets of the server and the client.

sp_checknames
Displays all identifiers in the current database that contain non-7-bit-ASCII characters.

sp_helpsort
Displays the default character set and sort order used by the server.

sp_indsuspect [*table_name*]
Checks the specified *table_name* (if omitted, checks all tables in the current database) for indexes marked as suspect during recovery as the result of changing the server sort order. Suspect indexes can be fixed by running **dbcc reindex**.

set char_convert on [**with** { **error** | **no_error** }]
set char_convert off
set char_convert *character_set* [**with** { **error** | **no_error** }]
Defines conversion between the character sets of server and client. **on** (=default) enables character set conversion; **off** disables it; *character_set* explicitly specifies the client character set to convert to. **with no_error** specifies that no error message is raised for conversion errors (ASE-to-client only); default=**with error**. **@@char_convert** indicates if character set conversion is currently in effect (**1**) or not (**0**).

The global variables **@@maxcharlen**, **@@ncharsize** and **@@unicharsize** (12.5) also contain information related to character sets (➢p.117,118).

62. Setting up sybsyntax, pubs3 & sybsystemprocs

The **sybsyntax** database provides on-line syntax information about T-SQL commands and system stored procedures (note: **sybsyntax** was removed in 12.0, but an unofficial version can be downloaded from **www.sypron.nl/syntax120.html**). To install **sybsyntax**, create a database named **sybsyntax** of 2Mb (3Mb in 12.5), and run the script **scripts/ins_syn_sql** (NT: **scripts\ins_syn_sql**), located in **$SYBASE/$SYBASE_ASE**, using **isql**. **sp_syntax** can then be used as follows:
sp_syntax 'select' -- note the quotes; these are mandatory around keywords!

sp_syntax sp_recompile

The **pubs3** database is a small database on which all example queries in the Sybase documentation are based. To install **pubs3**, run the script file **scripts/installpubs3** (NT: **scripts\instpbs3**) using **isql**. This will create a 3Mb **pubs3** database on the default device. To create the database elsewhere, edit the script. The optional script **installpix2** (NT: **instpix2**) contains **image** data. **pubs2** is an older version of **pubs3**.

To (re)install the **sybsystemprocs** database manually, first create a database named **sybsystemprocs** of at least 60Mb (100Mb in 12.5) (mixed data and log is OK). Then run the script file **scripts/installmaster** (NT: **scripts\instmstr**) using **isql**.

(12.5.3) sp_version [*script_name* [**, 'all'**]]
Without parameters, displays the version of each system script (e.g. **installmaster**, etc.) most recently executed. With *script_name* (wildcards allowed), displays only for matching scripts. With **'all'**, also displays script execution start & end times.
Example: **sp_version 'installm%', 'all'**

63. Configuring parallel processing

Parallel processing is an optimization to deliver faster response time by using more server resources. Parallel query processing is possible only for **select** statements and index creation (as well as for **dbcc checkstorage**; ➢p.84).
To enable parallel query processing, some server config options must be set. Whether the optimizer will indeed use a parallel query plan depends on many different factors; see the *ASE Performance and Tuning Guide* for details.
To enable parallel processing, follow these steps:

1. **sp_configure 'number of worker processes'**, *nr_workers* (static; 12.5:semi-dynamic) - defines the maximum number of worker processes available for parallel processing. To enable parallel processing, *nr_workers* must be ≥ 2. As a rule of thumb, do not set *nr_workers* higher than (**'max online engines'** * 3).
2. In pre-12.5, stop and restart the ASE server.
3. **sp_configure 'max parallel degree',** *degree* (dynamic) - defines the server-wide upper limit on the number of worker processes that can be used by any query at a time; this is also the maximum parallelism for so-called 'partition scans'. To enable parallel processing, *degree* must at least be 2. *degree* cannot be higher than the current setting of **'number of worker processes'**.
4. **sp_configure 'max scan parallel degree'**, *degree* (dynamic) - defines the server-wide upper limit on the number of worker processes that can be used by any query at a time for 'hash scans' on non-partitioned tables. *degree* cannot be higher than the current setting of **'max parallel degree'**. As a rule of thumb, do not set **'max scan parallel degree'** higher than 3 to 5.

Note: when partitioning tables with the intention to use parallel partition scans, choosing the number of partitions is important: when a table has more partitions than **'max parallel degree'**, a parallel partition scan will never be used.

set parallel_degree *degree*
For the current session, sets the upper limit on the number of worker processes that any query may use at a time; *degree* must be ≤ **'max parallel degree'**. If *degree* is 0, the session-specific limit is removed and **'max parallel degree'** takes effect again.

set scan_parallel_degree *degree*
For the current session, sets the upper limit on the number of worker processes that any query may use at a time for 'hash scans' on non-partitioned tables; *degree* must be ≤ **'max scan parallel degree'**. If *degree* is 0, the session-specific limit is removed and **'max scan parallel degree'** takes effect again.

@@parallel_degree / @@scan_parallel_degree
Contain the current session's maximum parallel degree settings for partition scans and hash scans, repectively.

set process_limit_action *action*
Defines behaviour when parallel query plans are adjusted at run-time due to a lack of resources. *action* can be: **abort** - the query is aborted with error 11015; **warning** - the query continues, and error 11014 is issued; **quiet** - the query continues (=default)

Parallel index creation is a complex topic which can't be covered here; see the *ASE Performance and Tuning Guide* for details. Still, here are some tips:

- When creating indexes in parallel, it may be required to enable to the database option **select into/bulkcopy/pllsort**; this can have implications for recoverability, as transaction log dumps cannot be made anymore.

- When creating indexes, the command **set sort_resources on** shows the 'query plan' that would be used for creating the index (but does not create it):
  set sort_resources on
  create index new_ix on my_table(col_a, col_b)
  set sort_resources off

The config option **'number of sort buffers'** (dynamic) defines the max. number of buffers in the smallest buffer pool that a worker process can use for sorting tasks, like index creation. Increasing this setting may improve index creation performance.

64. Miscellaneous DBA commands

kill *spid* [**with trace**]
(12.5.2) kill *spid* **with statusonly**
Kills the specified session. The undocumented option **with trace** prints a stacktrace for the killed session to the errorlog (this may not always work). **kill**...**with statusonly** does not kill, but only reports progress when the session is performing a rollback.

shutdown [**with nowait** | **with wait** [**(12.5.4) =** '*hh:mm:ss*']]
Shuts down the ASE server. With **with wait** (=default), when users are still active, the server will shut down once all activity has stopped (even if this takes a long time). In 12.5.4, an additional wait interval can be specified: if users are still active after this interval, a **shutdown with nowait** is performed. **shutdown with nowait** shuts down immediately, regardless of user activity and without performing housekeeping tasks.
Warning: **'shutdown with nowait'** ***is a last-resort measure which may result in long recovery times and may cause large gaps in identity columns. Do not use*** **'shutdown with nowait'** ***unless a regular*** **'shutdown'** ***does not work.***

shutdown { **SYB_BACKUP** | *remote_backup_server_name* }
From within the ASE server, shuts down the local Backup Server (mapped to **SYB_BACKUP** in **master..sysservers**), or shuts down a remote Backup Server.

sp_configure *option*, *value*
Some common configuration settings; *option* can be:

- **'allow updates to system tables'** (dynamic) - when set to **1**, allows manual updating of the system tables by the **dbo**. ***Warning:*** updating system tables is not supported by Sybase; this may damage your database, so be very careful!
- **'number of user connections'** (static; 12.5:semi-dynamic) - defines the maximum number of users that can connect to the server concurrently. In 12.5.1, the last available connection is reserved for the DBA and will be disconnected after 15 minutes (to avoid locking out the DBA when all connections are in use).
- **'housekeeper free write percent'** (dynamic) - a percentage (**1**..**100**; default=**1**) defining the max. allowed activity for writing dirty pages to disk by the 'HOUSEKEEPER' thread in pre-12.5.0.3 or the 'HK WASH' thread in 12.5.0.3. When set to **0**, no dirty pages will be written to disk. In pre-12.5.0.3, the HOUSEKEEPER thread also performs garbage collection for DOL tables and updates **systabstats** and **syblicenseslog**. In 12.5.0.3, the latter are performed by 'HK GC' (➢p.78) and 'HK CHORES', respectively.
- **'default network packet size'** (static) - default network packet size (in bytes) used for client connections. (default=**2048** in 15.0; **512** in pre-15) Don't change!
- **'max network packet size'** (static) - largest possible non-default network packet size (in bytes) that can be used for client connections.
- **'additional network memory'** (static; 12.5:semi-dynamic) - memory available (in bytes) for client connections using a larger-than-default network packet size.
- **'tcp no delay'** (static) - enables (**0**) or disables (**1**, recommended) TCP/IP packet batching. Default: **1** in 12.5+; **0** in pre-12.5.
- **(pre-12.5) 'min online engines'** (static) - don't change; leave it at **1** (=default).
- **(12.5) 'number of engines at startup'** (static) - the number of server engines started for this server at ASE boot time (default=**1**).
- **'max online engines'** (static) - pre-12.5: the number of server engines started for this server at ASE boot time; 12.5: the max. number of engines that can be started at any time using **sp_engine** (default=**1**).
- **(15.0) 'enable logins during recovery'** (dynamic) - when **0** (default=**1**), logins without **sa_role** cannot log in until all user database are recovered.

(12.5) sp_engine { **'online'** | **'offline'** [, *engine_nr*] | **'shutdown'** [, *engine_nr*] | **'can_offline'** [, *engine_nr*] }
Dynamically starts (**'online'**), stops (**'offline'** and **'shutdown'** (stronger than **'offline'**)) the specified server engine; **'can_offline'** tells whether the engine may be stopped. Without *engine_nr*, these commands apply to the highest-numbered engine. If an

engine cannot be taken offline within 5 minutes, all tasks running on that engine will be killed. The number of running engines must remain less than the config option **'max online engines'** (static). Engine 0 cannot be taken offline.
To display engine status, use this query: **select * from master..sysengines**

(15.0) sp_fragmentation [*'table_name'* , …more parameters…]
(undocumented) Displays details about space usage/fragmentation for the specified table(s); table-name may contain wildcard. Without parameters, shows usage info.

(12.5.1) sp_listener 'status'
(12.5.1) sp_listener *'command'*, *'port_spec'*, { *'engine_no'* | **'remaining'** }
Manages dynamic ASE listeners (NETWORK HANDLER threads). With **'status'**, displays the current listeners. *command* can be **start**, **stop**, **suspend** or **resume**, operating on the listeners specified by *port_spec*: this can be the ASE servername (corresponds to all listeners in the **interfaces** file), or [*protocol*:]*host*:*port* to specify a different listener. *protocol* can be **tcp**, **tli**, etc. (like in the **interfaces** file). *engine_no* is a list of ASE engines to which *command* applies; **'remaining'** means all engines. Changes take effect immediately; no ASE restart is required. The config option **'max number network listeners'** (static; 12.5: dynamic) defines the max. number of listeners. Note that changes made by **sp_listener** are not maintained over an ASE restart.
Example: **sp_listener 'start', 'tcp:pluto:7010', 'remaining'**

sp_clearstats [*login_name*]
Clears accounting statistics in **master..syslogins** for all logins, or only for *login_name*.

sp_reportstats [*login_name*]
Displays accounting statistics for all logins, or only for *login_name*, when specified.

(12.5) sp_ssladmin addcert, *certificate_file_pathname* **[,** *password* | **NULL**]
(12.5) sp_ssladmin dropcert, *certificate_file_pathname*
(12.5) sp_ssladmin { **lscert** | **help** }
(12.5.3) sp_ssladmin setcipher { **'FIPS'** | **'Strong'** | **'Weak'** | **'All'** | *'list-of-ciphers'* }
(12.5.3) sp_ssladmin lscipher
Manages SSL certificates. **lscert** lists the currently installed certificates; **help** prints usage help information. **addcert/dropcert** adds/drops the certificate in the specified file, respectively. *password* is used to encrypt the public key; when **NULL** is specified instead, the password must be entered during ASE startup; this requires starting the **dataserver** executable with the **-y** parameter.
In 12.5.3, **setcipher** sets cipher suite preferences (**'FIPS'** includes AES, 3DES, DES and SHA1; **'Strong'**: >64 bit keys); **lscipher** displays current settings.

Advanced DBA Topics

65. Setting up the 'dbccdb' database

To run **dbcc checkstorage** and **dbcc checkverify** (➢p.86), the **dbccdb** database must be set up first. Also, some configuration is required for each database that will be checked. Here's a summary of the steps to prepare for a database named **my_db**:

1. From within the **master** database, run **sp_plan_dbccdb 'my_db'** to obtain sizing and configuration recommendations (when omitting the parameter **'my_db'**, **sp_plan_dbccdb** will print recommendations for all databases).
2. If the **dbccdb** database doesn't exist yet:
   - create the **dbccdb** database on separate data and log devices according to the size recommendations. Note: the log device should be large, or it may be difficult to cleanup **dbccdb** using **sp_dbcc_deletehistory**.
   - using **isql**, run the script **scripts/installdbccdb** (in the **$SYBASE/$SYBASE_ASE** directory tree)
3. Run **sp_configure 'number of worker processes'**, *nr_workers* to set this value at least as high as recommended by **sp_plan_dbccdb**; in pre-12.5, re-start ASE before proceeding.
4. (Optional) Create a dedicated named cache for **dbcc checkstorage** (otherwise, the 'default data cache' is used) : **sp_cacheconfig** **'***cache_name***'**, **'***size***M'**; in pre-12.5.1, restart ASE before proceeding.
5. In the cache used by **dbcc checkstorage**, configure an extent-size pool (16 Kb for 2Kb server pages): **sp_poolconfig '***cache_name***'**, **'***size***P|K|M|G'**, **'16K'**. *size* must be at least 40 extents**(recommended nr. of worker processes)* (for a 2Kb server page size, 40 extents = 640Kb). Since **dbcc checkstorage** does not use the smallest pool, this may be kept at minimum size in a dedicated cache.
6. (Optional in 12.5.0.3) From within the **dbccdb** database, create scan and text workspaces (this step may be omitted already existing workspaces are reused):
   sp_dbcc_createws dbccdb, 'default', scan_my_db, scan, '*size***P|K|M|G'**
   sp_dbcc_createws dbccdb, 'default', text_my_db, text, '*size***P|K|M|G'**
7. (Optional in 12.5.0.3) From within the **dbccdb** database, complete configuration issues (the **values** specified below should match the steps 3-6 above):
   sp_dbcc_updateconfig my_db, 'max worker processes', '*number***'**
   sp_dbcc_updateconfig my_db, 'dbcc named cache', '*cache_name***', '***cache_size***P|K|M|G'**
   sp_dbcc_updateconfig my_db, 'scan workspace', 'scan_my_db'
   sp_dbcc_updateconfig my_db, 'text workspace', 'text_my_db'
8. Now you're ready to run **dbcc checkstorage (my_db)**

After completing **dbcc checkstorage**, run **dbcc checkverify**. The results can then be displayed using **sp_dbcc_summaryreport** and **sp_dbcc_faultreport**. Periodically, review the **dbccdb** configuration with **sp_dbcc_evaluatedb**. When running **dbcc checkstorage** on **dbccdb** itself, the results are stored in the **dbccalt** database if it exists; otherwise, in **dbccdb**. Note that **dbcc checkstorage** can find corruptions, but <u>cannot</u> fix these; use **dbcc checkalloc / tablealloc / indexalloc** with the **'fix'** option for this. Repair fault code 100035 with **dbcc checktable(... , 'fix_spacebits')**.

66. 'dbccdb' stored procedures

sp_plan_dbccdb [*db_name*]
Recommends values for setting up and configuring **dbccdb** for all existing databases, or only for database *db_name*, when specified. When specifying **dbccdb** for *db_name*, recommends values for **dbccalt**, and vice versa.

Note: in pre-12.5.0.3, all stored procedures **sp_dbcc_*** below, can be executed only in the **dbccdb** database. In 12.5.0.3, they can be executed in any database.

sp_dbcc_alterws *db_name*, *ws_name*, **'***size***P|K|M|G'**
Changes the size of a workspace in database *db_name* to the specified size (**P**=pages (=default); **K**=Kb; **M**=Mb; **G**=Gb). *db_name* must be **dbccdb** or **dbccalt**.

sp_dbcc_configreport [*db_name* [**, (12.5.0.3) 'true'**]
Displays the **dbccdb** configuration settings used for all databases, or only for database *db_name*. When **'true'** is specified and *db_name* = **NULL**, displays only default settings created with **sp_dbcc_updateconfig**.

sp_dbcc_createws *db_name*, *segment_name*, [*ws_name*], *ws_type*, **'***size***P|K|M|G'**
Creates a workspace of the specified size (**P**=pages (=default); **K**=Kb; **M**=Mb; **G**=Gb)

on *segment_name* in database *db_name*. If *ws_name* = **NULL**, a name is generated. *ws_type* must be **'scan'** or **'text'**. *db_name* must be **dbccdb** or **dbccalt**. To drop a workspace, use **drop table** *ws_name*.

sp_dbcc_deletedb [*db_id* | *db_name*]
Deletes **dbccdb** config settings for all databases, or only for the specified database.

sp_dbcc_deletehistory [**'***delete_until_datetime***'** [, *db_name*]]
Deletes results from **dbcc checkstorage** runs which completed before or on *delete_until_datetime* from **dbccdb**, for all databases or only for *db_name*. Without a date/time, all but the most recent results are deleted. When deleting many results, this may fill the **dbccdb** transaction log. To keep only the results of the last 30 days, run:

declare @dt datetime select @dt = dateadd(dd, -30, getdate())
exec sp_dbcc_deletehistory @dt, my_db

sp_dbcc_differentialreport [*db_name* [, *object_name*]] [, **'checkstorage'**] [, **'***date1***'** [, **'***date2***'**]]
Displays differences between two **dbcc checkstorage** results for all databases, or only for *db_name*, and for all objects or only for *object_name*. With both dates, compares results from those dates. With one date, compares that date's result with the preceding result. Without dates, compares the two latest results.

sp_dbcc_evaluatedb [*db_name*]
Re-computes recommended values for **dbccdb** config settings and compares these to the current settings, for all databases, or only for *db_name*. **sp_dbcc_evaluatedb** doesn't display a configured dbcc named cache (but **sp_dbcc_configreport** does).

(12.5.0.3) sp_dbcc_exclusions [*db_name* [, *action* [, *type* [, *exclusion_list*]]]]
Without parameters or with only *db_name*, displays tables and/or faults that may be excluded from processing by **dbcc checkverify** and **sp_dbcc_faultreport**. When *action* is **'add'** or **'drop'**, adds/drops one or more items (as defined in the comma-separated *exclusion_list*) to be excluded, for *db_name* or for all databases (*db_name* = **NULL**). When *action* = **'listall'**, displays all defined items of the specified *type*. The item *type* can be **'faults'**, **'tables'**, **'combo'** (a combined table+fault) or **NULL**.
Example: **sp_dbcc_exclusions my_db, 'add', 'combo', 'tab1:100004, tab2:100005'**

sp_dbcc_faultreport [*report_type* [, *db_name* [, *object_name* [, **'***date***'** [**(12.5.1),** *hard_only* [**(12.5.0.3),** *exclusion_mode* [, *exclusion_faults* [, *exclusion_tables* [, *exclusion_combo* [, *display_recommendations* [**(15.0),** *operationID* [, *fault_type*]]]]]]]]]]]
Displays faults found by **dbcc checkstorage** for all databases, or only for *db_name*. *report_type* can be **'short'** (brief output; =default) or **'long'**. With *object_name*, only displays faults for that object. With *date*, displays results for that date; otherwise displays most recent results. In 12.5.0.3, *exclusion_faults/_tables/_combo* are comma-separated lists of faults, tables, or both, to exclude from reporting. *exclusion_mode* must be **'ignore'** or **'extend'**, to ignore or apply exclusions defined with **sp_dbcc_exclusions**. When *display_recommendations* = 1, also recommends repair actions. In 12.5.1, with *hard_only* = 1, reports hard faults only. In 15.0, with *operationID*, reports only for the checkstorage run with that ID; with *fault_type*, reports only for faults of that type (default=all faults).

sp_dbcc_fullreport [*db_name* [, *object_name* [, **'***date***'**]]]
Runs the following reports for all databases, or only for *db_name*: **sp_dbcc_summaryreport**, **sp_dbcc_configreport**, **sp_dbcc_statisticsreport**, and **sp_dbcc_faultreport 'short'**. With *object_name*, displays information for that object. With *date*, displays results for that date; otherwise displays most recent results.

(12.5.0.3) sp_dbcc_help_fault [*fault_number*]
Displays a description of a fault, or of all faults, and the recommended repair action.

(12.5.0.3) sp_dbcc_patch_finishtime *db_name*, *opid* [,*type* [,*seq_no* [, **'***finish_time***'**]]]
Marks an aborted run (*type* = **'checkstorage'** or **'checkverify')** for the specified database as completed at the specified time, so that reporting procedures can be run for it. *opid* is the aborted run's ID number; *seq_no* is the **checkverify** sequence number.

(12.5.0.3) sp_dbcc_recommendations *db_name* [, **'***date***'** [, *run_id* [, **'***object_name***'**]]]
Displays recommended repair actions for faults found in the specified database. Without further parameters, do so for all faults in the most recent **dbcc checkstorage** run. With *date* or *run_id*, only for faults in the run on that date, or with that run ID. With *object_name*, only for faults for that object.

sp_dbcc_runcheck *db_name* [, *final_procedure*]
Runs **dbcc checkstorage** and **dbcc checkverify** for *db_name*. After completion, runs *final_procedure* when specified; otherwise runs **sp_dbcc_summaryreport**.

sp_dbcc_statisticsreport [*db_name* [, *object_name* [, '*date*']]]
Displays allocation statistics from **dbcc checkstorage** results for all databases, or only for *db_name*. With *object_name*, displays results for that object. With *date*, displays results for that date; otherwise displays most recent results.

sp_dbcc_summaryreport [*db_name* [, '*datetime*' [, **'checkstorage'** | **'checkverify'** [**(12.5.0.3),** *display_recommendations*]]]]
Displays a summary of **dbcc checkstorage** or **checkverify** results (default=both) for all databases, or for *db_name*. With *datetime*, shows results before that date/time. In 12.5.0.3, when *display_recommendations* = 1, also recommendeds repair actions.

sp_dbcc_updateconfig *db_name*, *config_option*, '*value_1*' [, '*value_2*']
Updates the **dbccdb** configuration settings to be used by **dbcc checkstorage** for checking database *db_name*. In 12.5.0.3, with *db_name* = **NULL**, sets a default value to be used for all databases without a database-specific setting. *config_option* can be:

- **'dbcc named cache'** - *value_1* is the cache name (like **'default data cache'**); *value_2* is the cache size as **'***size***P|K|M|G'** (**P**=pages; **K**=Kb(=default); **M**=Mb; **G**=Gb). Note: any size seems fine, regardless of the actual cache size.
- **'max worker processes'** - the number of worker processes
- **'scan workspace'** - the name for the scan workspace
- **'text workspace'** - the name for the text workspace
- **'IO error abort'** - the max. number of I/O errors on a page
- **'linkage error abort'** - the max. number of page linkage errors for an object
- **'OAM count threshold'** - max. percentage of OAM count difference
- **(12.5.0.3) 'enable automatic workspace expansion'** - either **1** (enabled, =default) or 0 (disabled).

In 12.5.0.3, an existing setting is deleted by specifying **'delete'** for '*value_1*'.

67. Supported DBCC commands

For most **dbcc** commands, traceflag 3604 must be enabled to see any output on the client. In pre-12.5, most **dbcc** commands require **sa_role** and/or **sybase_ts_role**. In 12.5, execute permission on most (not all) **dbcc** commands in this section can be granted (➢p.70).

dbcc checkalloc [**(** *db_name* [, **'fix'** | **'nofix'**] **)**]
Checks and/or fixes corruptions in *db_name* (default = current database). Default is **'nofix'** mode; for **'fix'**, the database must be in single-user mode. **dbcc checkalloc** is equivalent to **dbcc tablealloc** + **dbcc indexalloc** on all tables in the database.

dbcc checkcatalog [**(** *db_name* [**(12.5.2), 'fix'** | **'fixall'** | **'all'**] **)**]
Checks consistency of system table contents in the specified database (default = current database). In pre-12.5.2, does not fix any errors; in 12.5.2 with **'fix'**, fixes certain errors related to user tables; **'fixall'** also fixes errors for system tables; **'all'** also does checks (but no fixes) for system tables. **'fixall'** and **'all'** are undocumented.

dbcc checktable (*table_name* | *table_id* [, **'skip_ncindex'** | **'fix_spacebits'**
[, **(15.0)** *ptn_name* | *ptn_id*]] **)**
Checks (but does not fix) consistency of data and index pages in the specified table. or partition. One of the checks verifies that, for all indexes, a data row exists for each index row. To skip nonclustered indexes on user tables, specify **'skip_ncindex'**. To fix hard faults with code **100035** (from **dbcc checkstorage)**, use **'fix_spacebits'**.

(12.5.3) dbcc checkindex (*table_name* | *table_id* , *index_id* [, **'bottom_up'** | **NULL**
[, **(15.0)** *ix_ptn_name* | *ix_ptn_id*]] **)**
For the specified index or index partition, verifies that for each index row, a data row exists (like **dbcc checktable**). With **'bottom_up'** (only for DOL tables), the check is performed the other way around: an index row must exist for each data row.

dbcc checkdb [**(** *db_name* [, **'skip_ncindex'** | **'fix_spacebits'**] **)**]
As **dbcc checktable**, for all tables in the specified database.

dbcc checkstorage (*db_name* **)**
Checks database consistence more efficiently than the 'classic' dbcc commands like dbcc **checkalloc/checkdb**. Requires that the **dbccdb** database be set up and configured. After completing **dbcc checkstorage**, always run **dbcc checkverify**.

dbcc checkverify (*db_name* [**(12.5.0.3),** *table_name* [, *ignore_exclusions*]] **)**
Reclassifies soft faults found by **dbcc checkstorage**. In 12.5.0.3, this can be limited to a specific table. If *ignore_exclusions* = 0 (=default), tables and/or faults defined with **sp_dbcc_exclusions** are excluded from processing; if 1, these exclusions are ignored. In 12.5.1, after **set command_status_reporting on**, displays progress info.

dbcc dbrepair(*db_id* | *db_name*, **'dropdb')**
Drops a database marked suspect (when **drop database** can't); bits 256 and 64 must be set in **sysdatabases.status**. For more **dbcc dbrepair** options, ➢p.89.

dbcc dbrepair(*db_name*, **'remap'** [, **'fixalloc'**] **)**
Refreshes the in-memory copy of **master..sysusages** (**sp_dbremap** *db_name* is equivalent). With **'fixalloc'**, checks/corrects segment mapping and database ID in all allocation pages (avoids **dbcc checkstorage** 100005 errors).

(pre-12.5) dbcc engine ('online' | **'offline'** [, *engine_nr*] **)**
Dynamically starts (**'online'**) or stops (**'offline'**) the specified server engine. Without *engine_nr*, these commands apply to the highest-numbered engine. **dbcc engine** can be used with traceflag 1608. In 12.5, use **sp_engine** instead (➢p.82).
To display engine status, use this query: **select * from master..sysengines**.

dbcc engine ('net', 'showall')
Displays connection-to-engine mapping (may not work on some platforms).

dbcc fix_text (*table_name* | *table_id* **)**
After changing to a multibyte character set, run this for all tables with **text** columns.

dbcc complete_xact (*transaction_name*, { **'commit'** | **'rollback'** } [**(12.5.2), '1pc'**] **)**
Heuristically completes (i.e. commits or rolls back) a distributed transaction. Use **'1pc'** for transactions under a 1-phase commit protocol, which are in a 'done' state.

dbcc forget_xact (*transaction_name* **)**
Removes a heuristically completed distributed transaction from **systransactions**.

dbcc gettrunc
(Replication) Displays the secondary log truncation point.

dbcc indexalloc (*table_name* | *table_id*, *index_id* [, *report_type* [, **'fix'** | **'nofix'** | **NULL** [, **(15.0)** *ix_ptn_name* | *ix_ptn_id*]]] **)**
Checks and/or fixes corruptions in the specified index or index partition. *report_type* is **'full'**, **'optimized'** (=default) or **'fast'**. Default=**'fix'**, except for system tables.

(12.5.2) dbcc prsqlcache [**(** *ssql_id* [, *printopt*] **)**]
Without parameters, displays the contents of the statement cache (➢p.54). With *ssql_id*, displays only the cached statement with that **ssql_id** value. When *printopt* = **1** (default = **0**), also displays the showplan output for the cached statement.

(12.5.2) dbcc purgesqlcache
Clear the statement cache (➢p.54), except for statements that are currently in use.

dbcc rebuild_text (*table_name* | *table_id* [, *col_name* | *col_id* [, *page_nr* [, **(15.0)** *ptn_name* | *ptn_id*]]] **)**
(12.5) dbcc rebuild_text ('all') (= **sp_rebuild_text** *current_db_name*)
(Re)creates the 12.0+, direct-access structure for **text/image** data, either for a table or for the specified partition, for a specific **text/image** column, or for the **text/image** page chain starting at *page_nr*. This operation is fully logged. With **'all'**, recreates all **text/image** data for all tables in the current database, but in 'minimally logged' mode. This is identical to **sp_rebuild_text** *current_db_name*.

dbcc reindex (*table_name* | *table_id* **)**
Rebuilds a table's indexes (if necessary) after the changing the server sort order.

dbcc settrunc (ltm, { **valid** | **ignore** } **)**
dbcc settrunc (ltm, gen_id, *db_generation* **)**
(Replication) Modifies the secondary truncation point in the current database (the ReAgent should be stopped first). The subcommands are:

- **valid** - activates the secondary truncation point. This should be used in combination with **rs_zeroltm** in the RSSD (see the RepServer documentation).
- **ignore** - removes the secondary truncation point, which will stop all replication from this database. ***Warning:*** ***this is a drastic, last-resort measure that may put your replication system in jeopardy. Use this command only when you***

fully understand the implications!

- **gen_id** - sets the database generation number for a primary database.

dbcc tablealloc (*table_name* | *table_id* [**,** *report_type* [**,** **'fix'** | **'nofix'**]] **)**
Checks and/or fixes corruptions in the specified table and its indexes. *report_type* is **'full'**, **'optimized'** (=default) or **'fast'**. Default=**'fix'**, except for system tables.

dbcc textalloc (*table_name* | *table_id* [**,** *report_type* [**,'fix'** | **'nofix'**]] **)**
Checks and/or fixes corruptions in the **text** and **image** columns for the specified table. *report_type* is **'full'**, **'optimized'** or **'fast'** (default = **'optimized'**). Default is **'fix'**.

dbcc traceon [**(** *traceflag* [**,** *traceflag*...] **)**]
dbcc traceoff [**(** *traceflag* [**,** *traceflag*...] **)**]
Enable / disable server traceflags. If no traceflags are specified in **dbcc traceoff**, all previously enabled flags are disabled.

dbcc tune (*option***,** *value_1***,** *value_2*...**)**
Modify certain run-time configuration settings. These settings are not persistent (i.e. not maintained after an ASE restart) unless specified otherwise. Possible options are:

- **('ascinserts',** *value***,** *table_name***)** - reduces page splits in a composite clustered index on an APL table for ascending key inserts; if *value* = 0, this optimization is disabled (=default) for the specified table; if *value* = 1, enabled. This setting is persistent (stored in bit 64 of **sysindexes.status2**).
- **('cleanup',** *value***)** - if *value* = 0, memory cleanup checking is enabled (=default); if *value* = 1, disabled.
- **('cpuaffinity',** *firstcpu***,** { **'on'** | **'off'** } **)** - enables/disables CPU affinity, provided this is supported by the platform; starting with engine 0, engines are bound to CPU *firstcpu.* Run **('cpuaffinity', -1)** to write current setting to server errorlog.
- **('des_bind',** *db_id***,** *table_name* **)** - Binds a table to an object descriptor so that it won't be pushed out of the metadata cache. Specify **'des_unbind'** to remove.
- **('des_greedyalloc',** *db_id***,** *table_name***,** { **'on'** | **'off'** } **)** - enables (**on**) or disables (**off**, =default) a 'greedy allocation' scheme for the table (to reduce latch contention).
- **('deviochar',** *vdevno***,** *value***)** - sets max. outstanding I/Os by housekeeper for device *vdevno* to *value* (1..255; default=3); if *vdevno* = -1; applies to all devices.
- **(pre-12.5.1) ('doneinproc',** { **0** | **1** } **)** - enables (**1**,=default) or disables (**0**) most (but not all) *done-in-proc* network packets. To disable all *done-in-proc* packets, enable traceflag 292 and run **dbcc tune('doneinproc', 0)** (note: disabling all *done-in-proc* packets may cause certain client apps to fail). In 12.5.1, this command is replaced by the config option **'send doneinproc tokens'**.
- **(pre-12.5.1) ('maxwritedes',** *value***)** - sets maximum number of outstanding disk writes; default=10. In pre-12.0, the max. value is 50; in 12.0+, this is unlimited. In 12.5.1, this option is replaced by **sp_configure 'i/o batch size'** (dynamic).

68. Unsupported DBCC commands

***WARNING!* These (arbitrarily selected) DBCC commands represent unsupported functionality which may have unexpected side effects, may cause irreversible damage to your databases and/or lead to loss of data. Use entirely at your own risk. Do *not* contact Sybase Technical Support for assistance !**
Many **dbcc** commands require that the role **sybase_ts_role** be enabled for the executing session. This can be done as follows (assuming the login is 'sa'):

grant role sybase_ts_role to sa
set role sybase_ts_role on

dbcc help (*command* **)**
Displays syntax info for the specified **dbcc** command.

(12.5.0.3) dbcc addtempdb (*db_id* | *db_name* **)**
Adds a temporary database to the global list of temporary databases.

dbcc allocdump (*db_id* |*db_name***,** *alloc_page_nr* **)**
Lists extents in an allocation unit, identified by the allocation page number.

dbcc bytes (*address***,** *length* **)** / **dbcc bytes (** *address***,** *printopt***,** *structure_name* **)**
Dumps *length* bytes, starting at *address* (e.g. a physical page address), in hex & ASCII. **dbcc bytes(0,0,'showlist')** displays all structures that can be specified as masks in **dbcc bytes(***address***,** *printopt***,** *structure_name***)**. Specify -1 for *printopt*.

dbcc cacheremove (*db_id* | *db_name*, *object_id* | *object_name* **)**
Deallocates the object descriptor (DES) for the specified table.

dbcc cis (*subcommand* **)**
Displays CIS-related information. Subcommands are:

- **'remcon'** displays all CIS remote connections
- **'showcaps'** [, '*server_name*'] - displays the capabilities of the remote server
- **'srvdes'** [, *server_id*] - without argument, displays all SRVDES structures. With *server_id*, syncs the in-memory SRVDES with **master..sysservers**
- **(pre-12.5) 'rusage'** - displays CIS shared memory usage

dbcc connection_hangup (*remote_server_name* **)**
Closes a site handler connection to the specified remote server (like a Backup Server).

dbcc corrupt (*table_name* | *table_id*, *index_id*, *error_nr* **)**
Creates a corruption of the specified *error_nr* in the specified table or index. The table must reside in, and this command must be issued from, a database named **victimdb**. *error_nr* is an error number as used in **dbccdb** (i.e. 100000 and higher).
This command is intended to help testing software for detecting database corruptions.

(12.5.3) dbcc dbcacheremove (*db_id* | *db_name* **)**
Clears the DBTABLE information for the specified database, for use when commands fail with a 'keep count' reported as > 0 although no users are active in the database.

dbcc dbinfo (*db_name* **)**
Displays the DBINFO structure for the specified database.

dbcc dbrecover (*db_id* | *db_name* **)**
Performs recovery for the specified database (without restarting the ASE server); works only when bit 64 in **sysdatabases.status** is set.

dbcc dbrepair (*db_id* | *db_name*, *option* [, *table_name*, *index_id*] **)**
Performs various maintenance actions. Possible *option* values:

- **'dropdb'** - drops a database marked suspect (when **drop database** can't); bits 256 and 64 must be set in **sysdatabases.status**.
- **'findstranded'** - displays data extents located ('stranded') on the logsegment'
- **(12.5) 'fixlogfreespace'** - recalculates amount of free space in **syslogs**.
- **'ltmignore'** - like **dbcc settrunc(ltm, ignore)**, but works for an offline database: can be issued from outside the target database.
- **'repairindex'** - rebuilds a system table index (dangerous!!); best use **sp_fixindex** instead: **sp_fixindex** *db_name*, *table_name*, *index_id ;* the database should be in single-user mode before running this.

dbcc dbtable (*db_id* | *db_name* **)**
Displays the DBTABLE structure for the specified database (includes 'keep count').

(12.5.4) dbcc delete_dol_page (*db_id*, *object_id*, *page_nr [*, **'noblock'** *]* **)**
Deallocates a data page (typically, a corrupt page) from a DOL table. Without **'noblock'**, takes an exclusive-table lock.

dbcc des [**(** *db_id* | *db_name* [, *object_name* | *object_id*] **)**]
Displays the DES structure for the specified object, or for all objects.

dbcc extentcheck (*db_id*, *table_id*, *index_id*, *sort_bit* **)**
Displays all extents of the specified table or index with the 'sort bit' specified (0 or 1).

dbcc extentdump (*db_id*, *page_nr* **)**
Displays the extent on which the specified page is located.

dbcc extentzap (*db_id*, *object_id*, *index_id*, *sort_bit* **)**
Delete extents for the specified object and index with the 'sort bit' specified (0 or 1). To delete an object completely, run once with *sort_bit* = 0 and once with *sort_bit* = 1.

dbcc findnotfullextents (*db_id*, *object_id*, *index_id*, *sort_bit* **)**
Finds extents for the table or index which contain unused pages; *sort_bit* is 0 or 1.

dbcc fix_al [**(** *db_name* **)**]
Fixes allocation errors within the specified database (default = current database).

dbcc gam (*db_id* | *db_name***,** *start_alloc_page***,** *nr_alloc_pages***,** *action* **)**
Checks, modifies or fixes the GAM bits of the specified database. *action* can be: **'check'**, **'fix'** (=default), **'set'** (=set to **1**, indicating no free pages on this allocation unit), or **'clear'** (set to **0**). Starts at the GAM bit for allocation page *start_alloc_page*, and affects the next *nr_alloc_pages* (**0**=all subsequent pages).
Example: **dbcc gam (my_db, 0, 0, fix)**

dbcc istraceon (*traceflag* **)**
Tests if the specified traceflag is enabled; if so, **@@error** will be 0; otherwise <> 0.

dbcc listoam (*db_id* | *db_name***,** *object_name* | *object_id***,** *index_id* **)**
Displays the OAM pages for the specified object or index.

dbcc locateindexpgs (*db_id***,** *object_id***,** *page_nr***,** *index_id***,** *level* **)**
Within the specified index on the specified index *level*, finds all references to the specified *page_nr* (*level* should be 0 when *page_nr* is a data page).

dbcc lock
Displays currently active locks, including types of locks not shown by **sp_lock**.

dbcc log (*db_name* | *db_id* [**,** *object_id*] [**,** *page_nr*] [**,** *row_nr*] [**,** *nr_recs*] [**,** *rec_type*] [**,** *printopt*] [**, (15.0)** *index_id*] [**, (15.0)** *ptn_id*] **)**
Displays the contents of the transaction log for the specified database (note that the output of **dbcc log** may be large!). *object_id* is an object ID to which the operations in the log records apply; *page_nr* is a log page number; *row_nr* is the row ID on a log page (set to 0 if not used). However, the combination of *object_id*, *page_nr* and *row_nr* determines which log records are displayed:

- if *object_id* = 0 and *page_nr* = *row_nr* = 0 log records are displayed from the start of the log; in 15.0, if *ptn_id* > 0, displays only log records for this partition.
- if *object_id* < 0, log records are displayed starting at the log record identified by *page_nr* and *row_nr*;
- if *object_id* > 0 and *page_nr* = *row_nr* = 0, log records for modifications to object *object_id* are displayed;
- if *object_id* = 0 and *page_nr* > 0, log records for modifications to page *page_nr* are displayed;
- if *object_id* < 0 and *page_nr* = -3, log records for a particular spid (=session) are displayed; the spid is the absolute value of *object_id*; only 'begin transaction' log records can be displayed.
- if *object_id* > 0 and *page_nr* > 0, log records for the transaction-ID formed by concatenating *page_nr* and *row_nr* are displayed;
- in 15.0, if *object_id* > 0 and *index_id* >= 0 , log records for this index are displayed, irrespective of *ptn_id*.

The other parameters can be used to specify further filtering:

- if *nr_recs* = 0, shows all log records; if *nr_recs* > 0, shows the first *nr_recs* log records. If *nr_recs* < 0, shows the last *nr_recs* log records in reverse order.
- if *rec_type* = -1, shows all log records; If *rec_type* ≥ 0, shows only log records of the specified type. Some types are: 0=begin transaction; 30=end transaction (i.e. commit or rollback); 17=checkpoint; 26=CLR.
- if *printopt* = 1, shows only log record headers. If *printopt* = 0, shows complete log records (=default).

Examples:

- display all log records in database 9: **dbcc log(9)**
- find the last checkpoint in database 9: **dbcc log(9,0,0,0,-1,17,0)**
- dump the last 1000 log records in backward order: **dbcc log(9,0,0,0,-1000,-1,0)**

dbcc logprint ('*string***'** [**, '***string***'** ...] **)**
Writes the specified text strings to the server errorlog. Ignore the message 'background task error -1:' that shows up in the errorlog in pre-12.5.1.

dbcc printolog ('*string***')**
Prints the specified text string to the server errorlog.

dbcc logtransfer (...**)**
(Replication) Used by LTM or RepAgent. Not for manual use.

(12.5.1) dbcc memdump ('*comment***')**
Creates a shared memory dump as configured with **sp_shmdumpconfig**. Do not use this command unless instructed by Sybase Technical Support!

dbcc memusage
Displays information about internal ASE memory usage.

dbcc monitor (...**)**
Used by **sp_sysmon** to fill the **sysmonitors** table. Not for manual use.

dbcc object_atts (*table_name*, *0*, *subcommand* [, *new_value*] **)**
Displays or patches identity values on the OAM page of the specified table. *subcommand* can be **'get'** (displays the current value in hex), or **'put'** (writes *new_value* (in hexadecimal !)). When using **'put'**, the server must be shut down **with nowait** afterwards. Note: **dbcc object_atts** is difficult to use! (See **www.sypron.nl/idfix.html**)

dbcc object_stats (*action* [,*db_id* | *db_name* [,*object_id* | *object_name*]] **)**
Displays lock wait times for a specific database and/or table (default = all tables in all databases). **sp_object_stats** (➤p.44) is a wrapper around **dbcc object_stats**.

(12.5.0.3, 12.0.0.7) dbcc orphantables [**('drop'** [, **'#***table_name***'**] **)**]
Without parameters, lists all 'orphan' #temp tables (i.e. #temp tables without a parent session; these do not normally occur) in a temporary database. With only **'drop'**, drops all orphan #temp tables; with also **#***table_name*, drops only that table.

dbcc page (*db_id* |*db_name*, *page_nr* [, *printopt* [, *cache* [, *vdevno* [, *cache_name*]]]]**)**
Dumps page *page_nr* in the specified database. *printopt* can be 0 (=default; print page header), 1 (print page header, data rows and row offset table), 2 (print page header and hex dump of data page) or 3 (print the control page for table partition). In 15.0, adding 16 to *printopt* supresses the buffer info. When *cache* = 1, the page is read from cache (default); if 0, it's read from disk. If *cache_name* is -1, searches in all caches; if **NULL** (=default), searches in cache bound to object; otherwise searches in *cache_name*.
(pre-15) If *vdevno* =1, *page_nr* is a logical page; if 0, a virtual page (*cache* must be 0).
(15.0) If *vdevno* = -1, *page_nr* is a logical page; if ≥ 0, *page_nr* is a virtual page on the device with *vdevno* (*cache* must be 0).

dbcc pglinkage (*db_id* | *db_name*, *start_pg_nr*, *nr_pgs*, *printopt*, *srch_pg_nr*, *order***)**
Walks down a page chain (for APL data pages, OAM pages and some DOL pages), starting at page *start_pg_nr*, for *nr_pgs* pages. If *nr_pgs* = 0, walks until the end or until *srch_pg_nr* is found (to search until end, set *srch_pg_nr* = 0). *printopt* can be 0 (shows total number of pages accessed), 1 (displays page nrs. of last 16 pages), or 2 (shows all pages nrs. accessed). If *order* = 0, walks backward; if 1, walks forward.

(12.5.0.3) dbcc pravailabletempdbs
Displays a list of all temporary databases, including those which are not in a group.

dbcc procbuf ([*db_id* | *db_name* [,*object_id* | *object_name* [, *nr_entries* [, *printopt*]]
Displays (in binary, non-readable format) query plans existing in the procedure cache. By default, the entire procedure cache is displayed; specify a database and/or object as a search filter. When *nr_entries* > 0, the first *nr_entries* matching entries are displayed in MRU-LRU order; when < 0, in LRU-MRU order. When *printopt* = 0 (default), only headers are displayed; when 1, displays details. Note: the output can be large.

dbcc prtipage (*db_name*, *object_name*, *index_id*, *index_page_nr* **)**
Prints all index or data pages pointed to by the index rows on index page *index_page_nr* of the specified index.

dbcc pss [**(** [*suid* [, *spid* [, *printopt*]] **)**]
Prints PSS info for selected sessions; specify *suid* = 0 to indicate a specific *spid*. *printopt* can be 0 (displays basic PSS structures), 1 (displays more details), 2 (locks), 3 (cursors, incl. their query plans), 4 (active transactions) or 5 (worktables, incl. size). Part of the session's currently executing SQL may be displayed with **dbcc pss,** but **dbcc sqltext** is recommended instead.

dbcc rebuild_log (*db_id* | *db_name*, *rebuild_flag*, *delete_flag* **)**
Creates a new, empty (containing only a checkpoint) transaction log for the database. Requires **sysdatabases.status** = -32768 (= 'bypass recovery' mode). Specify **1** for *rebuild_flag* and *delete_flag*. ***Note: do not run this command unless it is understood and absolutely needed; it may corrupt your database!***

dbcc rebuildextents (*db_id*, *object_id*, *index_id* **)**
Rebuilds the extents and OAM pages for the specified object and index.

dbcc refreshides (*db_id* | *db_name*, *object_id*, *index_id* **)**
For the specified index, refreshes the in-memory index descriptor (IDES) with the current contents of **sysindexes**.

dbcc resource
Displays internal settings. Most of this output is unusable; the ASE errorlog pathname is shown at the keyword **'rerrfile'**, and the **interfaces** file used by ASE at **'rinterfpath'**.

dbcc save_rebuild_log (*db_id* | *db_name* **)**
Same as **dbcc rebuild_log** but also saves the old log extents with object_id = -1.

(12.5) dbcc serverlimits
Displays various server-, database-, and object-related limits.

(12.5.1) dbcc set_identity_burn_max (*db_name*, *object_name*, **'***identity_value***')**
Resets the identity counter for the specified table to *identity_value*. **sp_chgattribute...identity_burn_max** can be used instead (➢p.38).

(12.5.3) dbcc showrecovery [**(** *db_id* | *db_name* **)**]
Displays information about the recovery status of the specified database, or about all unrecovered databases.

dbcc sqltext (*spid* **)**
Displays (part of) the T-SQL command text of the currently executing, or most recently executed command for the specified session (like **dbcc pss**, but brief). Note: you can also use **sp_showplan** to display a *spid*'s currently executing query's plan.

dbcc sqtprint ([**'descriptors'** | **'pages'**] **)**
Displays info on 'lightweight' procedures (for OpenClient-generated dynamic SQL).

dbcc stacktrace (*spid* | *-kpid* **)**
Prints a stacktrace for the specified *spid* (positive value) or *kpid* (negative value). This command may not always work.

(12.5.2) dbcc stackused
Prints the amount of stack space used by any process since ASE startup.

dbcc traceflags [**(** *printopt* **)**]
Display traceflags currently enabled in the server, when *printopt* is 1 or omitted. When *printopt* is 2, also displays which sessions have enabled any traceflags.

dbcc traceprint [**('***string***', '***string***', '***string***', ...)**]
Writes the strings, each on a separate line, to the client (with 3604) or errorlog (3605).

dbcc thresholds (*db_id* | *db_name* **)**
Displays a database's threshold cache.

dbcc usedextents (*db_name* | *db_id*, *type*, *printopt*, [*fragment*] *)*
Displays extents used by the entire database (*type*=0) or just the log devices (*type*=1). When *printopt*=0, displays extent details; when 1, displays count. When *fragment*=1, output is by device fragment; when 0, it's not (=default)

dbcc upgrade_object (*db_id* | *db_name* [, *object_name* | *object_type*] [, **'force'** | **(12.5.0.2) 'check'**]] **)**
(Only to be used during an ASE upgrade or downgrade) Upgrades a specific compiled object (or an entire category) from its source text in **syscomments**. *object_type* can be **'procedure'**, **'view'**, **'trigger'**, **'rule'** or **'default'**. With **'force'**, forces the upgrade. With **'check'**, checks for **syscomments** corruption -- if errors are reported, the object(s) concerned must be dropped and recreated.

dbcc user_stats (*action*, *spid* **)**
Displays how long a specific spid had to wait for locks. When action = **'init_locks'**, counters are cleared; when action = **'locks'**, displays results. If *spid* = 0, show results for all *spids*. Before running this command, enable traceflag 1213 first.

dbcc xls ('plcstate' | **'plcflush'**, *spid* **)**
Operates on the User Log Cache (also known as 'Private Log Cache' or PLC) of session *spid*; when *spid*=0, applies to all sessions. **'plcstate'** displays the contents of the ULC; **'plcflush'** flushes the ULC to the transaction log.

69. ASE Traceflags

***WARNING!* These (arbitrarily selected) traceflags represent unsupported functionality which may have unexpected side effects, cause irreversible damage to your databases and/or lead to loss of data. Use entirely at your own risk. Do not contact Sybase Technical Support for assistance !**
Traceflags can be set with **dbcc traceon/traceoff** or added to the **RUN_***servername* file (i.e. '**-T3609**'), depending on their function and the desired effect. Traceflags marked 'boot-time' can only be specified in the **RUN_***servername* file. For output to be displayed on the client, traceflag **3604** must usually be enabled as well.

In 12.5.4esd1, traceflags can also be set with **set switch** [**serverwide**] { **on** | **off** } *traceflag* [, ...*traceflag*...] [**with override**]. This enables (**on**) or disables (**off**) a traceflag for the current session only, unless **serverwide** is specified. **with override** is required for enabling internal traceflags. **show switch** displays the currently active traceflags. *traceflag* can be a number or a name.
Examples: **set switch on 302 / set switch on print_plan_index_selection**

208 - print info about the locking strategy for each statement
(12.5, 12.0.0.4) 243 - in compiled objects, don't expand **select *** to the full column list
(pre-15) 291 - reverse datatype conversion rules for predicates with functions
292 - reduces network traffic by suppressing server-to-client 'done-in-proc' network packets, combined with **'send doneinproc tokens'** or **dbcc tune('doneinproc', 0)** (➢p.107 and 88, respectively)
299 - don't recompile stored procedures inheriting a temp. table from a parent proc.
(pre-15) 302 - print info about the optimizer's index selection (for 15.0, see p.55)
(pre-15) 310 - print info about the optimizer's join selection (shows better join orders)
(pre-15) 311 - print estimated number of logical and physical I/Os before execution
(pre-15) 317 - print info about the optimizer's join selection(show rejected join orders)
(pre-15) 319 - print info on table reformatting during query processing
(pre-15) 321 - like traceflag **319**, but brief
(pre-15) 334 (boot-time) - enables JTC server-wide (➢p.54)
(pre-15) 384 (boot-time) - enables merge joins server-wide (➢p.54)
(15.0esd2) 450 - use classic sorting for **group by**, giving predictable result set order when **order by** is not specified
(15.0) 526 - **set showplan** also prints part of the **set statistics plancost** output
693 - disables concurrency optimizations on DOL tables (non-blocking uncommitted inserts and certain updates).
694 - print (cryptic) info about concurrency optimizations on DOL tables(also see **693**)
1116 - suppress runtime 115x errors raised by **data_pgs()**, **used_pgs()** etc.
1202 - includes blocked lock requests in **master..syslocks** (and therefore in **sp_lock**)
1204 - replaced by configuration option **'print deadlock information'** since 11.0
1212 - prints all acquired & released locks (this can be a lot of output; also see **1212**)
1213 - used by **dbcc object_stats** (➢p.91)
1217 - same as **1212**, but only for locks on user tables
(15.0) 1223 - all deadlock info in the errorlog is prefixed with date/time/engine/spid
(pre-12.5) 1608 (boot-time) - starts only engine 0; use with **dbcc engine('online')**
1622 (boot-time) - allows more engines to be configured and started than there are physical CPUs (for testing purposes).
1623 - (boot-time) all disk write I/O to file system devices with **dsync=on** will be unbuffered (like **dsync=off**) instead. *Do not use this trace flag in production systems!*
1624 - (boot-time) same as **1623**, but only for **master** device I/O.
(12.5) 1634 (NT only) - when NT shuts down, ASE attempts a normal **shutdown** instead of a **shutdown with nowait** (=default).
(12.5.4esd1) 1648 - (boot-time; Linux only) allows **directio** for block devices
2201 (boot-time) - emulates OS-level HA subsystem (for testing of ASE_HA)
2512 - **dbcc checkalloc** will skip **syslogs** to suppress spurious allocation errors
3100 - allow loading a master database dump with a non-default char.set or sort order
3300 (boot-time) - prints detailed info when performing recovery (can be voluminous)
(12.5.2) 3477 (boot-time) - ignores & clears the 'bypass recovery' setting for **master** db
3502 - logs each automatic checkpoint to the console (with **3605**, to the errorlog)
3602 - error messages sent to the client are also written to the server errorlog
3604 - redirect output from dbcc commands to the client session
3605 - redirect output from dbcc commands to the server errorlog
3607 (boot-time) - opens only **master** dev.; **master** db is accessible but not recovered
3608 (boot-time) - recovers only the **master** db; other databases are accessible but not recovered; to avoid 'log suicide', **shutdown with nowait** and *do not checkpoint*. To set 'bypass recovery' for a specific database, set **sysdatabases.status** = -32768 and **shutdown with nowait**. Don't allow users into the server while booted with 3608!
3609 (boot-time) - all databases are recovered, but **tempdb** is not re-initialised
3610 - divide-by-zero results in **NULL** (as in version 4.x), instead of an error

(12.5) 3631 (boot-time) - disables most **sp_monitorconfig** sampling (➢p.73)
(12.5.3) 3662 - when violating a resource limit, the SQL text is written to the errorlog
(12.5.0.3-12.5.4) 3706 (boot-time) - when dropping #temp tables, locks are released quicker; this is default behaviour as of 12.5.4
4001 (boot-time)- write the login record to the console for successful & failed logins
4013 (boot-time)- write login name, spid, kpid to the errorlog for successful logins only
4044 (boot-time)- allows to log into server as 'sa' when this login is locked
(12.5.4) 4072 - disables execution of the global login trigger, if configured
(12.5.4) 4073 - allows exporting some **set** options from a login trigger to the session
4413 - raises a warning message (message 11046) for outer joins that may produce different results in pre-12.0; **@@error** is not affected.
7703 - the left-hand side of a variable assignment in a select list is evaluated for every matching row (can be used for accumulating values from different rows in a variable)
(12.5.0.3, 12.0.0.7) 7838 - when enabled, allows killing a RepAgent (disable again!)
8003 - prints info on outgoing RPC calls
(pre-12.5.2) 8399 - used by **sp_sysmon** (by **dbcc monitor** to fill **sysmonitors**)
(15.0) 9500 - displays query tree operators & associated optimizer estimates/actuals
11201 - logs CIS client connect- / disconnect- and attention events to the errorlog
11202 - logs CIS client language, cursor declare, dynamic prepare, and dynamic execute-immediate text to the errorlog, as well as the T-SQL text for all sessions.
11203 - logs info about CIS RPC events to the errorlog
11204 - logs all CIS messages coming back from the remote server, to the errorlog
11205 - logs all CIS interaction with remote servers to the errorlog
(12.5) 11206 - logs diagnostics about file system access (ASE_XFS) to the errorlog
11208 - **create index** and **drop table** statements will not be sent to the remote server
11209 - for **update statistics** on proxy tables, gets only row counts (not the full stats)
11218 - cursors involving proxy tables will be 'read only' by default
(12.5) 11223 - disables index creation on proxy tables by **create existing table** and **create proxy_table**
(12.5.3esd3) 11231 - close the CIS connection once the remote command completes; in 15.0.1, **'cis idle connection timeout'** (➢p.95) is a fully supported alternative.

70. Configuring remote access with RPCs

Server-to-server RPCs (Remote Procedure Calls), also called 'site handler RPCs/ connections', require the following setup steps:

1. In both the local server (where the RPC is initiated from) and the remote server (where the executed RPC resides), define the **@@servername** with **sp_addserver MY_SERVER_NAME, 'local'** ; then shutdown & restart the ASE server and check **@@servername** is set correctly.
2. Set the config option **'allow remote access'** to **1** in both servers (dynamic).
3. In the local server, add the remote server name with **sp_addserver REMOTE_SERVER_NAME** ; ensure the **interfaces** file (NT: **SQL.INI** file) used by the local server contains the correct interfaces definition for this remote server.
4. In the remote server, set up a remote login to accept incoming RPC connections, using **sp_addremotelogin** (see below).
5. Finally, test the configuration by executing an RPC from the local server, such as: **exec REMOTE_SERVER_NAME...sp_who** .

Note: to use site handler RPCs, CIS must be disabled by running **set cis_rpc_handling off** (or by **sp_configure 'cis rpc handling', 0** (dynamic)). When either of these options is enabled, RPCs are performed by CIS. In that case, remote logins (see below) are not relevant, as external logins (➢p.96) are used instead.

sp_addserver *local_name* [**,** *class* [**,** *remote_name*]]
Defines or modifies a server name mapping so that remote server *remote_name* can be accessed as *local_name* from the current ASE server. *remote_name* must be defined in the **interfaces** file (NT: **SQL.INI**). Without *remote_name*, it defaults to *local_name*. With *class* = **'local'**, the current server's **@@servername** is set to *local_name* (effective after ASE restart). Otherwise, specify **NULL** for *class* (see the *ASE Reference Manual* for more values). In 12.5.1, and for CIS connections only, *remote_name* can also be specified as **'***hostname***:***port_no*[**:ssl**]**'** (➢p.96).
Examples: **sp_addserver PROD, 'local'** -- sets **@@servername** as 'PROD'
sp_addserver SYB_BACKUP, NULL, PROD_BS -- sets Backup Server
sp_addserver PROD2 -- defines access for PROD2 as PROD2

sp_dropserver *local_name* [**, 'droplogins'**]
Drops the server name mapping for the server *local_name*. With **'droplogins'**, all associated remote logins are also dropped (by default, these are not dropped).

sp_helpserver [*local_name*]
Displays servername mapping (**master..sysservers**) for *local_name*, or for all servers.

sp_addremotelogin *remote_server* [, *login_name* [, *remote_name*]]
Allows RPCs coming from *remote_server* to login into the current server. With only *remote_server*, all remote logins are mapped to identically named local logins. With *login_name*, all remote logins are mapped to the local login *login_name*. With *remote_name*, that remote login is mapped to the local *login_name*. Note that the passwords for the logins must match in both servers.

sp_dropremotelogin *remote_server* [, *login_name* [, *remote_name*]]
Drops remote user login mappings created by **sp_addremotelogin.**

sp_helpremotelogin [*remote_server* [, *remote_name*]]
Displays remote user login mappings created by **sp_addremotelogin.**

sp_remoteoption [*remote_server* [, *login_name* [, *remote_name* [, *option* [, **'true'** | **'false'**]]]]]
Displays or defines options for remote server logins. The only available option is **'trusted'** - when **'true'** (default is **'false'**), login passwords are not checked for the remote login mapping specified (note: this could result in a security problem!)

sp_serveroption [*remote_server*, *option*, **'true'** | **'false'**]
Displays or modifies options for remote server connections. Possible *option* values:

- **'net password encryption'** - if **'true'** (default is **'false'**), RPC connections to a remote server will use login password encryption. As of 12.5.3, this setting also applies to CIS connections initiated from this ASE server.
- **'readonly'** - if **'true'**, access to the remote server is read-only (option only available with Component Integration Services)
- **'timeouts'** - when **'false'** (default: in pre-12.5.4 **'true'**; else **false**), the site handler won't drop the physical connection after 1 minute with no logical connection
- **'rpc security model A'** - the default security model for handling RPCs, which does not support the features of security model B
- **'rpc security model B'** - a more advanced security model, supporting security mechanisms and features for authentication, confidentiality and integrity.
- **'mutual authentication'** / **'use message confidentiality'** / **'use message integrity'** - additional network security features (only with security model B)

sp_serveroption [*remote_server*, **'security mechanism'**, **'***mechanism_name***'**]
Sets the security mechanism for connections to this remote server (security model B only). For available security mechanisms, run: **select * from master..syssecmechs**.

sp_configure 'remote server pre-read packets', *value* (static)
For site handler connections, sets the number of buffered network packets. Default=**3**.

71. Configuring remote access with CIS

Server-to-server access with CIS (see next section) requires these setup steps:

1. If not already set, run **sp_configure 'enable cis', 1** (static).
2. In pre-12.5, set **sp_configure 'max cis remote connections'** to a value greater than 0 (static). In 12.5+, this parameter isn't needed anymore.
3. In the local server, add the remote server name with **sp_addserver REMOTE_SERVER_NAME** ; ensure the **interfaces** file (NT: **SQL.INI** file) used by the local server contains the correct interfaces definition for this remote server.
4. With **sp_addexternlogin**, set up external logins to connect to the remote server.
5. Test the configuration with a query like **sp_remotesql REMOTE_SERVER_NAME, 'select @@servername'**

By default, CIS creates an OpenClient connection to the remote server. This connection is maintained until the parent session disconnects from the local ASE server.
In 15.0.1, the CIS connection is closed (by the housekeeper, which checks periodically) when it has been idle for more seconds than defined by the config option **'cis idle connection timeout'** (**0**=never times out).
With the **'server logins'** option of **sp_serveroption** enabled (see below), a 'server connection' is created instead (this requires configuration with **sp_addremotelogin**, like an RPC).

72. Component Integration Services (CIS) features

CIS is a connectivity feature (sometimes referred to as 'OmniConnect' or 'Omni'). ASE-to-ASE connectivity is included in ASE; connectivity to other DBMSs (such as

Oracle, DB2, etc.) must be licensed separately. Before using CIS features, some setup is necessary (see previous section). The CIS version is stored in the global variable **@@cis_version**.

sp_addserver *local_name* [, *class* [, *remote_name* | **(12.5.1)** '*hostname*:*port_no*']]
Defines or modifies a server name mapping so that a remote server can be accessed as *local_name* from this ASE server. *remote_name* must be defined in the **interfaces** file (NT: **SQL.INI**). The '*hostname*:*port_no*[**:ssl**]' syntax is for CIS only. Also ➢p.94.
Example: **sp_addserver REMOTE_ASE, NULL, 'pluto:5010'**

sp_dropserver *local_name*
Drops the server name mapping for the server *local_name*.

sp_helpserver [*local_name*]
Displays servername mapping (**master..sysservers**) for *local_name*, or for all servers.

sp_serveroption [*remote_server*, *option*, **'true'** | **'false'**]
Displays or modifies options for CIS connections. Possible *option* values:

- **'server logins'** - allows CIS to connect to this remote server using 'server connections', which are validated against **master..sysremotelogins** instead of against external logins (=default).
- **(12.5.0.3) 'cis hafailover'** - allows CIS connections to use ASE HA failover
- **(12.5.1) 'negotiated logins'** - allows CIS RPC calls to Backup & XP Server
- **(12.5.3) 'net password encryption'** - if **'true'** (default is **'false'**), CIS connections to a remote server will use login password encryption.

(12.5) sp_serveroption [*remote_server*, **'server cost'**, '*nr_of_milliseconds*']
Specifies the turnaround time (in milliseconds) to this remote server (used by the query optimizer for optimizing CIS queries).

sp_addexternlogin *server_name*, *local_login*, *extern_login_name* [, *extern_passwd*]
(12.5) sp_addexternlogin *server_name*, **NULL**, *extern_login_name* [, *extern_passwd*] [, *role_name*]
Defines (or modifies) the external login/password to be used for CIS connections to the remote server *server_name*. Without *extern_passwd*, the current password of the login making the CIS connection will be used. In the first form (all ASE versions), the login *local_login* will use the specified external login/password. If specified, this 1-to-1 mapping takes precedence. In 12.5, with **NULL** for *local_login*, and with *role_name* specified, all logins having that role will use the specified external login/password; without *role_name*, all logins <u>not</u> having this role will use that login/password. Finally (all ASE versions), if no external login is defined for a local login, it connects to the remote server as itself, using its own current password.

sp_dropexternlogin *server_name* [, *local_login*]
(12.5) sp_dropexternlogin *server_name*, **NULL** [, *role_name*]
Drops the external login(s) for CIS connections to *server_name*. With only *server_name*, *local_login* is the current session's login.

sp_helpexternlogin [*server_name* [, *local_login*]]
(12.5) sp_helpexternlogin [*server_name*, **NULL** [, *role_name*]]
Displays existing external logins. Without parameters, displays all external logins. With only *server_name*, display all external logins for that remote server. With only *local_login* (i.e. *server_name* = **NULL**), displays all external logins for this login.

create database *db_name* [...*regular-options*...] [**with default_location** = '*remote-_server_name*.[*db_name*].[*owner*].'] [**for proxy_update**]
With **with default_location**, creates a new database *db_name* as a proxy database, i.e. newly created tables in *db_name* will be proxy tables for tables in the remote location. With **for proxy_update**, proxy tables are automatically created for all tables currently existing at the remote location. **for proxy_update** cannot be used without **with default_location**. For the regular **create database** options, see page 58.
Example: **create database my_proxydb with default_location = 'REMOTE_SRVR.otherdb.dbo.' for proxy_update**

alter database *db_name* **for proxy_update**
Creates proxy tables for all tables at the default location for this database; this location must have been defined with **create database...with default_location** or with **sp_defaultloc**. If proxy tables already existed, they are dropped and recreated.

sp_defaultloc *db_name*, { '*server_name*.[*db_name*].[*owner*].' | **NULL** } [, *remote_type*]
Defines a default remote location for proxy tables in *db_name*. *remote_type* specifies the default type of remote objects for proxy tables created with **create existing table** or **create table**; this default may be overridden with **sp_addobjectdef**. *remote_type* can be **'table'** (the remote object is a table), **'view'** (remote object is a view) or **'rpc'** (remote object is a stored procedure; the result set appears as a read-only table). **sp_defaultloc** *db_name*, **NULL** removes the current default location for *db_name*.

sp_remotesql *server_name*, *string_1* [, *string_2*, ..., *string_254*]
Concatenates the specified string parameters (max. 254; each can be max. 255 characters) into a query and executes this query in the remote server *server_name*.
Example: **sp_remotesql REMOTE_SERVER, 'sp_who exec sp_helpdb'**

connect to *server_name*
Opens a passthrough connection to the remote server *server_name*: all subsequent SQL commands are passed directly to the remote server without processing by the local ASE server. The connection will be active until the first **disconnect** command.

disc[onnect]
Closes a passthrough connection to a remote server which was previously established by a **connect to** command, or as a result of **sp_autoconnect**.

sp_autoconnect *server_name*, { **true** | **false** } [, *login_name*]
Enables (**true**) or disables (**false**) whether *login_name* will automatically be connected to remote server *server_name* in passthrough mode when this login logs in to ASE. Without *login_name*, this applies to the current session's login.
Note: be careful when using **sp_autoconnect** for logins with **sa_role** or **sso_role**.

sp_passthru *server_name*, *cmd_string*, *@error_code* **output**, *@error_msg* **output**, *@nr_rows* **output** [,*@result_1* **output** [, *@result_2* **output** [,... *@result_250* **output**]]]
Executes the contents of *cmd_string* (max. 255 characters) in a remote server. The other parameters are returned by the remote server: when *@error_code* = 0, the query executed successfully; when <> 0, *@error_msg* contains an error message; *@nr_rows* is the number of rows affected by the last command executed; the optional *@result_nnn* parameters may contain column values for the last row in the result set.

create existing table [**#**]*proxy_table_name* **(** *column_list* **)** [**on** *segment_name*] [[**external** { **table** | [**(15.0.1) transactional** | **non_transactional**] **procedure** }]
at '*server_name*.[*db_name*].[*owner*].*object_name*']
Creates a proxy table, mapping it to the remote table/view/stored procedure specified in the **at** clause. Without **at**, settings by **sp_addobjectdef** or **sp_defaultloc** define the remote mapping. **external** { **table** | **procedure** } overrides any default remote object type setting by **sp_defaultloc**. *column_list* are column names, datatypes and optional constraints as in a regular **create table** statement, matching the remote table or view. In 12.5.3, a #temp table name may be specified. In 15.0.1, when mapping to a remote procedure, **transactional** (=default) specifies that the procedure can participate in a transaction and is executed in the current connection; with **non_transactional**, the procedure is executed through a separate connection.
Examples: **create existing table my_proxy (a int) at 'MY_SRVR.my_db..my_tab'**

sp_addobjectdef my_proxy_2, 'MY_SRVR.my_db..my_tab', 'table'
create existing table my_proxy_2 (a int)

create proxy_table *proxy_table_name* [**external table**] **at**
'*server_name*.[*db_name*].[*owner*].*object_name*'
Creates a proxy table. Similar to **create existing table**, but **create proxy_table** determines the column names/datatypes of the remote table/view itself (it cannot map to a remote procedure). **external table** is the default, and may be omitted.
Example: **create proxy_table my_proxy at 'MY_SRVR.my_db..my_tab'**

(12.5) create proxy_table *proxy_table_name*
external directory at '*directory-pathname*[**;R**]'
(12.5) create proxy_table *proxy_table_name* **external file at** '*file-pathname*'
(12.5) create [**existing**] **table** [**#**]*proxy_table_name* **(** *column_list* **) external file at** '*file-path-name*' [**column delimiter** '*delimiter_string*']
(12.5) select *select_list* **into** [**#**]*proxy_table_name* **external file at** '*file-path-name*' [**column delimiter** '*delimiter_string*'] [*…rest of* **select** *query…*]
(12.5) select *select_list* **into existing table** [**#**]*proxy_table_name* [*…rest of query…*]
Creates a proxy table, mapping it to a file or a file system directory. This requires enabling (=**1**) the config option **'enable file access'** (dynamic) and -in pre-15 only- licensing ASE_XFS.

For a directory, each file appears as a row in the proxy table; with **;R**, also includes all subdirectories. Allowed DML is **select** (reads directory contents), **insert** (creates a new file or directory), **update** (renames a file or directory), **delete** (deletes a file or directory), **readtext** (retrieves file contents) and **writetext** (modifies file contents). In 12.5.3, a **#**temp table name may be specified.
For a file (assumed to contain text), each line in the file appears as a row in the proxy table. If the file does not exist, it is created. Allowed DML is **select** (reads all lines), **insert** (appends a line) and **truncate table** (truncates the file). With **create proxy_table**, the proxy table has only one column called **record**; with **create [existing] table** or **select**...**into**...**external file**, all columns must be specified. By default, the column delimiter is a tab, but **column delimiter** can specify a different string (max. 16 bytes). **select**...**into existing table** inserts rows into an already existing proxy table. Note that multiple concurrent users accessing the same underlying file may interfere, since access is not transactional.
Examples: **create table t (a char(5), b varchar(20), c int) external file at '/tmp/x.txt'**
insert t values ('abcde', 'this is a line', 12345) -- add a line to the file

create proxy_table d external directory at '/opt/import_dir;R'
insert d (filename, filetype) values ('subdir1', 'DIR') -- create directory
insert d (filename, filetype, content)
values ('file1.txt', '', 'this is a line') -- create a file and add a line

create table [#]*proxy_table_name* **(** *column_list* **)** [**on** *segment_name*] [[**external table**] **at '***server_name*.[*db_name*].[*owner*].*object_name***'**]
Creates a proxy table; also creates the remote table *server_name*.[*db_name*].[*owner*].*object_name*, to which the proxy table is mapped. The **at** clause overrides default settings by **sp_defaultloc**. Without **at**, **sp_addobjectdef** or **sp_defaultloc** define the remote mapping. **external table** overrides defaults by **sp_defaultloc**. *column_list* are column names, datatypes and optional constraints as in a regular **create table**. In 12.5.3, a **#**temp table name may be specified.
Example: **create table my_proxy (a int) at 'MY_SERVER.my_db..my_tab'**

drop table *proxy_table_name* [**,** *...more tables...*]
Drops the specified proxy table(s). Only for proxy tables created with **create table**, the remote table is also dropped.

sp_addobjectdef *proxy_table_name***, '***server_name*.[*db_name*].[*owner*].*object_name***'** [**,** *remote_type*]
Maps a proxy table to the remote object specified. *remote_type* can be **'table'** (the remote object is a table), **'view'** (it's a view) or **'rpc'** (it's a stored procedure; the result set appears as a read-only table); this overrides any default setting by **sp_defaultloc**. **sp_addobjectdef** should be followed by **create table** *table_name* or **create existing table** *table_name* to actually create the proxy table.

sp_dropobjectdef *proxy_table_name*
Drops the remote object mapping for the proxy table.

sp_helpobjectdef [*proxy_table_name*]
Displays remote object mapping for one, or for all, proxy tables in this database.

sp_configure 'cis packet size', *value* (dynamic)
Defines the network packet size when creating a CIS connection (default = **512**).

Note: all **set** commands below affect the current session only.

(12.5.0.3) set bulk array size *value*
Defines the number of rows buffered in memory before transferred through the bulk interface. **@@bulkarraysize** contains the current setting for a session.
In 12.0, **sp_configure 'cis bulk insert array size'** defines the server-wide default.

(12.5.0.3) set bulk batch size *value*
Defines the number of rows transferred through the bulk interface by a **select**...**into** a proxy table. **@@bulkbatchsize** contains the current setting for a session.
In 12.0, **sp_configure 'cis bulk insert batch size'** defines the server-wide default.

set cis_rpc_handling { **on** | **off** }
Enables (**on**) or disables (**off**, =default) whether outbound RPCs are handled by CIS.
sp_configure 'cis rpc handling', { **1** | **0** (=default) } has the same effect server-wide.

set transactional_rpc { **on** | **off** }
Enables (**on**) or disables (**off**, =default) whether RPCs are transactional (those RPCs

will be handled by CIS). **@@transactional_rpc** contains the current setting.

set raw_object_serialization { **on** | **off** }
Enables (**on**) or disables (**off**, =default) CIS handling of remote Java objects.

(12.5) set remote_indexes { **on** | **off** }
Enables (**on**,=default) or disables (**off**) whether **drop/create index** statements are applied to, and index information is retrieved from, remote tables.

set textptr_parameters { **on** | **off** }
Affects how **text** or **image** parameters are handled by CIS RPC calls (➢p.21).

73. XP Server

XP Server is a utility running outside ASE (not a certain Microsoft product with a similar name) to perform actions outside ASE (like executing OS commands) from T-SQL code executed inside ASE. Those actions are performed by the XP Server process, which is started and stopped by ASE as needed. Communication with XP Server goes through so-called 'Extended Stored Procedures' (ESPs), whose names start with '**xp_**' (located in the **sybsystemprocs** database by default). Each ASE server has its own dedicated XP Server, named *ASE_servername*_**XP**.
The following steps are required to configure XP Server:

1. The **interfaces** file (NT: **SQL.INI** file) must contain the XP Server's name.
2. Add the XP Server to the ASE server with **sp_addserver**; i.e. **sp_addserver PROD_XP** (for an ASE server named **PROD**).
3. Determine the setting for the config option **'xp_cmdshell context'** (see below).
4. Test the setup: run a command like **dir** (NT) or **ls** (Unix) with **xp_cmdshell**.

xp_cmdshell '*OS_command***'** [, { **no_output** | **return_status** | **(12.5.2) no_wait** }]
Executes the specified OS-command on the system where ASE (actually, its XP Server) runs. The command output appears as a result set; with **no_output**, all output is suppressed. By default, **xp_cmdshell** returns 1 for failure and 0 for success. With the **return_status** option, **xp_cmdshell** returns the result status of the executed OS command. In 12.5.2, **no_wait** does not wait until the OS command returns.
Example: **xp_cmdshell 'pwd'** (Unix) or **xp_cmdshell 'dir'** (NT).

xp_deletemail, **xp_enumgroups**, **xp_logevent**, **xp_findnextmsg**, **xp_readmail**, **xp_sendmail**, **xp_startmail**, **xp_stopmail**
These extended stored procedures (available on Windows NT only) perform special functions; see the *ASE Reference Manual* for details.

sp_configure 'xp_cmdshell context', { **0** | **1** } (dynamic)
Defines security settings for executing commands with **xp_cmdshell**. When set to **1** (=default), these execute under the OS account with the same name as the ASE login executing **xp_cmdshell**; if this account doesn't exist, **xp_cmdshell** fails. When set to **0**, **xp_cmdshell** commands execute under the OS account running the ASE server.

sp_addextendedproc *xp_proc_name*, *dll_file_name*
Only in the **master** database, creates an extended stored procedure *xp_proc_name*, which must be an existing entry point in the DLL file *dll_file_name*.
Example: **sp_addextendedproc xp_my_esp, 'my_esp.dll'**

create proc[**edure**] *xp_proc_name* **as external name** *dll_file_name*
As **sp_addextendedproc**, but works in any database.
Example: **create procedure xp_my_esp as external name 'my_esp.dll'**

sp_dropextendedproc *xp_proc_name*
Drops the extended stored procedure *xp_proc_name* from the current database.

sp_freedll *dll_file_name*
Unloads (releases) a DLL used by XP Server for executing extended stored procs.

sp_helpextendedproc [*xp_proc_name*]
Displays information about all extended stored procedures in the current database. With *xp_proc_name*, displays only that procedure.

74. Lock promotion

Lock promotion is an optimization attempted by the server and involves changing a number of page locks or row locks on a table to a table lock on that same table. Lock promotion decisions involve these configurable thresholds (note: the following refers to page locks for **allpages/datapages** tables and to row locks for **datarows** tables):

- **LWM** (Low Water Mark; must be ≥2; default=200) - when the number of locks on a table is below the LWM, no promotion to a table lock will occur
- **HWM** (High Water Mark; default=200) - when the number of locks on a table exceeds the HWM, promotion to a table lock will be attempted
- **PCT** (PerCentage of Table; must be 1≤PCT≤100; default=100) - when the number of locks on a table is between LWM and HWM, table lock promotion is attempted only when the nr. of locks is > *(PCT*number-of-pages-in-table)/100*

sp_setpglockpromote { **'database',** *db_name* | **'table',** *table_name* }, *lwm*, *hwm*, *pct*
sp_setpglockpromote 'server', NULL, *lwm*, *hwm*, *pct*
Defines or modifies page lock promotion thresholds for a specific database or table (with **'database'** or **'table'**), or for the entire server (with **'server'**). When no value should be set for LWM, HWM or PCT, specify **NULL** for the corresponding parameter.

sp_dropglockpromote { **'database',** *db_name* | **'table',** *table_name* }
Removes page lock promotion thresholds for a specific table or database. Server-wide thresholds cannot be dropped, but only modified.

sp_configure { **'page lock promotion LWM'** | **'page lock promotion HWM'** | **'page lock promotion PCT'** }, *value* (dynamic)
Equivalent to settings by **sp_setpglockpromote 'server', NULL,** *lwm*, *hwm*, *pct*

sp_setrowlockpromote { **'database'** | **'table'** }, *object_name*, *lwm*, *hwm*, *pct*
sp_setrowlockpromote 'server', NULL, *lwm*, *hwm*, *pct*
sp_droprowlockpromote { **'database'** | **'table'** }, *object_name*
sp_configure { **'row lock promotion LWM'** | **'row lock promotion HWM'** | **'row lock promotion PCT'** }, *value* (dynamic)
Defines/modifies/drops row lock promotion thresholds for DOL tables. Otherwise identical to the above APL-table page lock promotion commands.

75. Auditing

On Unix, auditing can be installed with the **auditinit** utility, but this can also be done manually as follows (on NT, only manual installation is possible):

1. Create a database named **sybsecurity** with separate data (>10Mb) and log (>2Mb). Do not use the same device for data+log with **with override**: this will cause errors in **installsecurity**.
2. Using **isql**, execute the script **scripts/installsecurity** (on NT: **scripts\instsecu**), located in the **$SYBASE/$SYBASE_ASE** directory tree.
3. Shutdown and restart the ASE server.
4. Enable auditing with **sp_configure 'auditing', 1**
5. (optional) Add additional audit tables with **sp_addaudittable** (see below)
6. Configure auditing settings with **sp_audit** (see below)
7. Query the system tables **sybsecurity..sysaudits_01..08** to view collected auditing records (see the *ASE System Administration Guide* for details).

sp_configure 'auditing', { **0** | **1** } (dynamic)
Enables (**1**) or disables (**0**) auditing.

sp_configure 'audit queue size', *size* (static; 12.5:semi-dynamic)
Sets the audit queue size (the max. number of audit records buffered in memory).

sp_configure 'current audit table', *n* [, **'with truncate'**] (dynamic)
Sets the current audit table. *n* can be **1**..**8** indicating **sysaudits_01**..**08**; **0** means the next in sequence. Default=**1**. **'with truncate'** truncates the new table first.

sp_configure 'suspend audit when device full', { **0** | **1** } (dynamic)
Controls the behaviour of the audit process: when an audit device gets full: **0** switches to the next audit table (which is truncated first); **1** (=default) suspends all audited actions (except those by **sso_role** logins) until space becomes available.

sp_addauditrecord [*comment* [, *db_name* [, *object_name* [, *owner_name* [, *db_id* [, *object_id*]]]]]]
Adds an ad-hoc audit record to **sybsecurity**. *comment* is free text; *db_name*, *db_id* can specify a database; *object_name*, *owner_name*, *object_id* can specify an object.

sp_addaudittable { *device_name* | **'default'** }
Adds a system audit table named **sysaudits_0*x*** (***x***=1..8). It will be placed on its own segment which is created on *device_name*. With **'default',** the new audit table and its

segment are created on the first device of **sybsecurity**.

sp_displayaudit ['procedure' | 'object' | 'login' | 'database' | 'global' | 'default_object' | 'default_procedure' [, *name* **]]**
Displays the status of auditing options set with **sp_audit**, optionally filtering for an object or database specified by *name*.

sp_audit *option*, *login_name*, *object_name* [, *setting*]
Configure auditing options (requires **sso_role**). *login_name* is a specific login to be audited. To audit an option for all logins, specify **'all'** (incl. quotes) for *login_name*. To audit all actions by users with a particular active system role (not a user-defined role), set *login_name* to that role. *object_name* represents a database name for various options. For values for *setting*, see page 102. To display current settings, use **sp_displayaudit**.
Possible values for *option* are listed below (evt=nnn indicates the corresponding event ID code in the **sysaudits_0**x**.event** column (also see **audit_event_name()**;➢p.102).

- **'adhoc'** - allows adding ad-hoc audit records by **sp_addauditrecord** (evt=1)
- **'all'** - all actions by a user, or users with a certain role (excl. ad-hoc audit records)
- **'alter'** - execution of the **alter table** (evt=3) or **alter database** (evt=2)
- **'bcp'** - execution of the **bcp**-in utility (evt=4)
- **'bind'** - **sp_bindefault** (evt=6), **sp_bindmsg** (evt=7), **sp_bindrule** (evt=8)
- **'cmdtext'** - the T-SQL commands sent to the server by the client (evt=92)
- **'create'** - **create** commands: **database** (evt=9), **table** (also: **select**...**into**) (evt=10), **procedure** (evt=11), **trigger** (evt=12), **rule** (evt=13), **default** (evt=14), **sp_addmessage** (evt=15), **view** (evt=16), **(12.5) function** (evt=97), **(12.5.1) index** (evt=104)
- **'dbaccess'** - access to the current database from another database (evt=17)
- **'dbcc'** - execution of **dbcc** commands (evt=81)
- **'delete'** - deleting rows from a table (evt=18) or view (evt=19)
- **'disk'** - execution of **disk** commands: **init** (evt=20), **refit** (evt=21), **reinit** (evt=22), **mirror** (evt=23), **unmirror** (evt=24), **remirror** (evt=25), **release** (evt=87), **resize** (evt=100)
- **'drop'** - **drop** commands: **database** (evt=26), **table** (evt=27), **procedure** (evt=28), **trigger** (evt=29), **rule** (evt=30), **default** (evt=31), **sp_dropmessage** (evt=32), **view** (evt=33), **(12.5) function** (evt=98), **(12.5.1) index** (evt=105)
- **'dump'** - execution of **dump database** (evt=34), **dump transaction** (evt=35)
- **(12.5.3a) 'encryption_key'** - execution of **sp_encryption** (evt=106), **create/alter/drop encryption key**(evt=107/108/109)
- **'errors'** - fatal (evt=36) and non-fatal errors (evt=37)
- **'exec_procedure'** - execution of an (extended) stored procedure (evt=38)
- **'exec_trigger'** - execution of a trigger (evt=39)
- **'func_dbaccess'**, **'func_obj_access'** - access to a database or database object via a T-SQL function (evt=86)
- **'grant'** - execution of the **grant** command (evt=40)
- **'insert'** - inserting rows into a table (evt=41) or view (evt=42)
- **'install'** - installing (evt=93) or removing (evt=94) a Java class in a database
- **'load'** - execution of **load database** (evt=43), **load transaction** (evt=44)
- **'login'** - all login attempts into ASE (evt=45)
- **'logout'** - all logout attempts from ASE (evt=46)
- **(12.5.1) 'mount'** - execution of **mount database** (evt=101)
- **'quiesce'** - execution of **quiesce database** (evt=96)
- **'reference'** - creation of **references** constraints between tables (evt=91)
- **'revoke'** - execution of the **revoke** command (evt=47)
- **'rpc'** - execution of RPC from (evt=48) or to another server (evt=49)
- **'security'** - covers the following security-relevant events:
  - starting up (evt=50) or shutting down the ASE server (evt=51)
  - enabling or disabling a role (evt=55)
  - regenerating a password with **dataserver -p** by an **sso_role** user (evt=76)
  - unlocking a role or login with **dataserver -u** (evt=95)
  - execution of function **proc_role()** or **has_role()** (evt=80)
  - **create/drop/alter/grant/revoke role** (evt=85)
  - various actions by **sp_configure** and **sp_cacheconfig** (evt=82)
  - **online database** (evt=83)
  - running the commands **set proxy**, **set session authorization** (evt=88)
  - running the commands **connect to** (evt=90), **kill** (evt=89)
  - accessing the auditing tables in the **sybsecurity** database (evt=61)
  - **(12.5)** running **sp_ssladmin 'addcert'** and **'dropcert'** (evt=99)
  - **(15.0)** running **sp_webservices 'deploy'** (110) and **'undeploy'** (111)
- **'select'** - selecting rows from a table (evt=62) or view (evt=63)

- **'setuser'** - execution of the **setuser** command (evt=84)
- **'table_access'** - access to any table by a specific user: **select** (evt=62), **delete** (evt=18), **insert** (evt=41), **update** (evt=70)
- **'truncate'** - execution of the **truncate table** command (evt=64).
- **'unbind'** - **sp_unbindefault** (evt=67), **sp_unbindrule** (68), **sp_unbindmsg** (69)
- **(12.5.1) 'unmount'** - execution of **unmount database** (evt=102)
- **'update'** - updating rows in a table (evt=70) or view (evt=71)
- **'view_access'** - access to any view by a specific user: **select** (evt=63), **delete** (evt=19), **insert** (evt=42), **update** (evt=71)

Events 73 (**sp_configure 'auditing', 1**) and 74 (**sp_configure 'auditing', 0**) are always recorded regardless of any **sp_audit** settings.
In 12.5, **sp_audit 'restart'** restarts the auditing thread (use only when it's terminated).

object_name is the name of the object to be audited. Valid values are:

- in most cases, the name of the object being audited (may include owner name)
- **'all'** for all objects
- **default table**, **default view** (when *option* is **delete**, **insert**, **select**, or **update)** for new tables or views
- **default procedure** (when *option* is **exec_procedure)** for new procedures
- **default trigger** (when *option* is **exec_trigger)** for new triggers
- when *option* is **'alter'**, **'bcp'**, **'bind'**, **'create'**, **'dbaccess'**, **'drop'**, **'dump'**, **'func_dbaccess'**, **'grant'**, **'install'**, **'remove'**, **'load'**, **'revoke'**, **'setuser'**, **'truncate'**, **'unbind'**: *object_name* is a database name; *login_name* = **'all'**.

setting can be **'on'** (activates auditing for option), **'off'** - (deactivates), **'pass'** (activates auditing for events passing permission checks) or **'fail'** (activates auditing for events failing permission checks). **on** and **off** apply to all options; **pass** and **fail** apply to all except **errors** and **adhoc**. Both **pass** and **fail** for an option is identical to **on**.

(12.5.1) audit_event_name (*audit_event_id* **)**
For an audit event ID (as stored in **sysaudits_0**x**.event**), returns the description of the audit event. Example: **select audit_event_name(27)** returns **'Drop Table'**

76. Database recovery

sp_dbrecovery_order [*db_name* [, *order_nr* [, **'force'** [, **(12.5.1) 'strict'** | **'relax'**]]]]
Displays (without parameters or with just *db_name*) or defines the database recovery order for non-system databases. Values for *order_nr* must start at 1 and form a range without gaps. To assign an already used *order_nr* to a database, specify **'force'**. To remove a database from the list, specify *order_nr* = **-1**.
With parallel recovery in 12.5.1, **'strict'** specifies the database must be onlined in strict recovery order; with **'relax'** (=default), it is onlined once recovery is complete.

(12.5.1) sp_configure 'max concurrently recovered db', *value* (dynamic)
Defines the maximum number of databases that can be recovered in parallel during ASE startup. When set to 0 (=default), ASE will determine this maximum itself. During startup, **@@recovery_state** indicates whether recovery is still in progress.

(12.5.1) sp_configure 'number of checkpoint tasks', *value* (dynamic)
Defines the maximum number of checkpoint threads (default = 1; maximum = 8).

sp_listsuspect_db
Displays all databases containing any offline pages (corrupted or suspect).

sp_listsuspect_object [*db_name*]
Displays all indexes in database *db_name* (if omitted, in all databases) that are offline due to corrupted or suspect pages. DOL indexes are always taken offline completely when a corrupted page is found; APL indexes can have individual offline pages.

sp_listsuspect_page [*db_name*]
Displays all offline pages in database *db_name* (if omitted, in all databases).

sp_forceonline_page *db_name*, *page_nr*, **'sa_on'** | **'sa_off'** | **'all_users'**
Forces online the offline (corrupted or suspect) page *page_nr* in database *db_name*, which must have its recovery fault isolation mode set to **'page'**.

- **'sa_on'** - forces the page online, but only for access by users having **sa_role**
- **'sa_off'** - forces the page offline again; it must previously have been forced online with **'sa_on'**
- **'all_users'** - forces the page online for access by all users; the page cannot be forced offline anymore after this.

sp_forceonline_db *db_name*, **'sa_on'** | **'sa_off'** | **'all_users'**
Forces online all offline (corrupted or suspect) pages in database *db_name*. See **sp_forceonline_page** for a description of the command options.

sp_forceonline_object *db_name*, *table_id*, *index_id*, **'sa_on'** | **'sa_off'** | **'all_users'** [, **'no_print'**]
Forces online all offline (corrupted or suspect) pages in the index *index_id* of table *table_id* in database *db_name*, which must have its recovery fault isolation mode set to **'page'**. **'no_print'** suppresses output on further offline indexes. See **sp_forceonline_page** for a description of the command options.

sp_makesuspect_obj [*db_name* [, *table_name* [, *index_id*]]]
Simulates a corrupted/suspect page in the specified table and/or index. This is for testing database recovery configuration only: not to be used on production servers.

sp_setsuspect_granularity *db_name*, { **'database'** | **'page'** } [, **'read_only'**]
From the **master** database, modifies the recovery fault isolation mode for a user database; with only *db_name*, displays the current setting. This setting defines what happens when suspect or corrupted pages are found during recovery:

- **'database'** - the entire database will be marked suspect and offline (default)
- **'page'** - only the corrupt / suspect pages will be offline; the rest is accessible
- **'read_only'** - the database will be online but in read-only mode

sp_setsuspect_threshold [*db_name* [, *threshold_nr_pages*]]
Defines the number of corrupt/suspect pages (default=20) above which the database will be marked as suspect; without *threshold_nr_pages*, displays the current settings.

77. Resource limits ('Resource Governor')

Resource Governor can be used to place limits on certain programs and/or logins, such as a maximum amount of I/O usage, execution time, or result set size.

sp_configure 'allow resource limits', { **0** | **1** } (static)
Enables (**1**) or disables (**0**) resource limits being enforced.

sp_add_time_range *timerange_name*, *startday*, *endday*, *starttime*, *endtime*
Creates a new time range, running from *starttime* to *endtime* on each of the days between *startday* and *endday* (inclusive). Times are specified as **'***hh:mm***'**; to match an entire day, specify **'00:00'** as both start and end time. A default time range named **'at all times'** exists by default, covering 24*7. Note that the day and time are those on the ASE host; ASE itself is not aware of any time zones.
Example: **sp_add_time_range '9_to_5', Monday, Friday, '09:00', '17:00'**
To display existing time ranges: **select * from master..systimeranges**

sp_drop_time_range *timerange_name*
Drops the specified time range.

sp_modify_time_range *timerange_name*, *startday*, *endday*, *starttime*, *endtime*
Modifies the specified time range. See **sp_add_time_range** for parameter details.

sp_add_resource_limit *login_name*, *program_name*, *timerange_name*, *limit_type*, *limit_value* [, *enforced_code* [, *action_code* [, *scope_code*]]]
Creates a new resource limit, which applies to the specified *login_name* (when **NULL**, applies to all logins), in combination with *program_name* (when **NULL**, applies to all programs), during the specified *timerange_name*. Possible values for *limit_type*:

- **'row_count'** - *limit_value* is the maximum number of rows that a query can return to the client; *enforced_code* must be **2** (=during execution) or omitted.
- **'elapsed_time'** - *limit_value* is the maximum number of elapsed seconds allowed for a transaction or query batch (note: this limit does not apply to individual queries!); *enforced_code* must be **2** (=during execution) or omitted.
- **'io_cost'** - when *enforced_code* = **1**, *limit_value* is the optimizer's estimated I/O cost of a query (before execution); when *enforced_code* = **2**, the actual I/O cost (during execution); when *enforced_code* = **3** (=default), it applies to both.
- **(12.5) 'tempdb_space'** - *limit_value* is the max. number of data pages a session can allocate in a temporary database; this includes space used by worktables. *enforced_code* must be **2** (=during execution) or omitted.

action_code is a number specifying what happens when exceeding the limit: **1**: warning is issued; **2**: batch is aborted (=default); **3**: transaction is aborted; **4**: session is killed. *scope_code* is a number specifying what the limit applies to: **1**: applies only to **'row_count'**, **'io_cost'**, **'tempdb_space'**; **2**,**4**,**6**: applies to a batch, a transaction, or

both, respectively (only for **'elapsed_time'**) (defaults are **1** and **6**).
In 12.5.3, with traceflag 3662 enabled, when a resource limit is violated, the SQL text of the offending batch is written to the ASE errorlog.
Example: **sp_add_resource_limit jsmith, NULL, 'at all times', 'row_count', 1000, 2, 4, 1** -- stops login 'jsmith' from returning more than 1000 rows

sp_drop_resource_limit *login_name*, *program_name* [, *timerange_name*, *limit_type*, *enforced_code*, *action_code*, *scope_code*]
Drops one or more resource limits for the combination of the specified login and program name, optionally combined with the other parameters. Specifying **NULL** for any parameter matches all possible values. See **sp_add_resource_limit** for details.

sp_modify_resource_limit *login_name*, *program_name*, *timerange_name*, *limit_type*, *limit_value*, **NULL**, *action_code*, **NULL**
Modifies *limit_value* or *action_code* for an existing resource limit, identified by the other parameters. See **sp_add_resource_limit** for parameter details.

sp_help_resource_limit [*login_name* [, *program_name* [, *limit_time* [, *limit_weekday* [, *scope_code* [, *action_code* [**(12.5.3)**, *verbose*]]]]]]]
Displays existing resource limits; optionally those existing at a specified time ('*hh:mm*') and/or day (e.g. **'Sunday'**). By default, the limit type, action etc. are shown as numeric codes whose description is in **master..spt_limit_types**. In 12.5.3, by specifying **1** for the *verbose* parameter, descriptive output is produced. See **sp_add_resource_limit** for details.
Example: **sp_help_resource_limit @verbose=1**

78. Logical Process Manager ('Execution Classes')

Logical Process Manager (LPM) is a resource tuning feature intended for large, multi-engine servers with a high workload, typically running on powerful hardware. On servers with a single or only a few engines, LPM is not likely to deliver any gain.

sp_addengine *engine_nr*, *engine_group_name*
Adds engine *engine_nr* to engine group *engine_group_name*. If the engine group doesn't exist, it is created.

sp_dropengine *engine_nr*, *engine_group_name*
Drops engine *engine_nr* from engine group *engine_group_name*. If *engine_nr* is the last engine in the engine group, the engine group is dropped.

sp_addexeclass *class_name*, *base_priority*, **0**, *engine_group_name*
Creates an execution class. *base_priority* can be **'HIGH'**, **'MEDIUM'** or **'LOW'**. *engine_group_name* is an existing engine group, or **'ANYENGINE'**, or **'LASTONLINE'**.

sp_dropexeclass *class_name*
Drops execution class *class_name*, which must not be bound to any objects.

sp_showexeclass [*class_name*]
Displays attributes of all execution classes; with *class_name*, displays only this class.

sp_bindexeclass *object_name*, *object_type*, *scope*, *class_name*
Binds the execution class to *object_name* and an optional further object specified by *scope*. The type of *object_name* is defined by *object_type* : **'LG'** = login; **'AP'** = application; **'PR'** = stored procedure. For a login or application, *scope* can specify an application or a login, respectively; for a procedure, it can specify the owner name.

sp_unbindexeclass *object_name*, *object_type*, *scope*
Unbinds the execution class *class_name* from the specified execution object and scope. See **sp_bindexeclass** for details on the parameters.

sp_setpsexe *spid*, *exec_attribute*, *attribute_value*
Sets a specific execution attribute for session *spid*. When *exec_attribute* is **'priority'**, *attribute_value* can be **'HIGH'**, **'MEDIUM'** or **'LOW'**. When *exec_attribute* is **'enginegroup'**, *attribute_value* is the name of an engine group.

sp_clearpsexe *spid*, *exec_attribute*
Removes the execution attribute previously set with **sp_setpsexe.**

sp_showpsexe [*spid*]
Displays execution attributes for all sessions; with *spid*, displays only this session.

sp_showcontrolinfo [*object_type*, *object_name*, *spid*]
Displays execution object bindings and engine groups. With *object_type*, displays only this type: **'LG'** = login; **'AP'** = application; **'PR'** = stored procedure; **'EG'** = engine group; **'PS'** = session. With also *object_name*, displays only this object. Only for **'PS'**, *object_name* must be **NULL**. *spid* can only be specified for **'PS'**.

79. Abstract Query Plans

Abstract Query Plans (AQPs) specify a complete or partial query plan for a query. AQPs can be used for **select**, **update** and **delete** statements. **if**, **while** and **return** statements which include a query can also have an AQP. For full details on the AQP language, see the *ASE Performance and Tuning Guide*. Examples:

select * from my_table plan '(i_scan ix1 my_table)' -- force index ix1

select * from t1,t2 where t1.key = t2.key plan '(g_join (scan t2) (i_scan ix1 t1))' -- force join order, and force index for **t1**

select * from t1,t2 where t1.key = t2.key
plan '(m_g_join (scan t2) (scan t1))' -- force a merge join (**m_join** in 15.0+)

(15.0) select * from t1,t2 where t1.key = t2.key
plan '(h_join (scan t2) (scan t1))' -- force a hash join

(15.0) select * from t1,t2 where t1.key = t2.key -- force a merge join,
plan '(use (m_join on) (nl_join off) (h_join off))' -- but not the join order

(15.0) select * from t1,t2 where t1.key = t2.key
plan '(use optgoal allrows_dss)' -- force the optimization goal

To find the AQP for a query, use **set option show_abstract_plan on** in 15.0 (➢p.55); in pre-15, use abstract plan dump (see below).

create plan '*T-SQL-query***' '(** *AQP-language* **)'** [**into** *aqp_group*] [**and set @***var*]
Creates an AQP for the specified T-SQL query. With **into** *aqp_group*, the AQP is stored in this AQP group, otherwise in the currently active AQP group. With **and set** *@var*, the plan ID for the new AQP is stored in the specified local variable.

set plan dump [*aqp_group*] { **on** | **off** }
sp_configure 'abstract plan dump', { **0** | **1** } (dynamic)
Enables/disables capturing of AQPs from executing queries, on session level (**set plan**) or server-wide (**sp_configure**, **0**=off=default, **1**=on). Captured AQPs are stored in the system table **sysqueryplans** in the database from where the query is executed. By default, AQPs are stored in the AQP group **ap_stdout**, unless a different group is specified by **set plan dump**. The session-level setting applies only in the current database: when changing databases with **use**, session-level AQP capture is disabled.

set plan load [*aqp_group*] { **on** | **off** }
sp_configure 'abstract plan load', { **0** | **1** } (dynamic)
Enables/disables association of stored AQPs with executing queries. By default, AQPs are loaded from the AQP group **ap_stdin**, unless a different group is specified. Otherwise similar to **set plan dump**.

set plan replace { **on** | **off** }
sp_configure 'abstract plan replace', { **0** | **1** } (dynamic)
During AQP capture, replaces saved plans with newly captured plans for identical queries, using the AQP group for plan capture. Otherwise similar to **set plan dump**.

set plan exists check { **on** | **off** }
sp_configure 'abstract plan cache', { **0** | **1** } (dynamic)
When AQP association is enabled, speed up plan association processing on session level (**set plan**) or server-wide (**sp_configure**). This works only when the source AQP group contains ≤ 20 queries; otherwise, the option is automatically disabled.

Note: The stored procedures below, which operate on individual AQPs, can only access AQPs owned by the executing user (except for **dbo** users or **sa_role**).
sp_help_qplan *plan_id* [**, full** | **brief** | **list**]
Displays information about an individual AQP. Default display option is **brief**.

sp_drop_qplan *plan_id*
Drops the specified AQP.

sp_drop_all_qplans *aqp_group*
Drops all AQPs from the specified group.

sp_find_qplan *search_pattern* [, *aqp_group*]
Searches the specified AQP group, or all groups, for an AQP, matching the specified search pattern. Example: **sp_find_qplan '%my_table%'**.

sp_copy_qplan *plan_id*, *destination_aqp_group*
Copies the specified AQP to the AQP group *destination_aqp_group.*

sp_copy_all_qplans *source_aqp_group*, *destination_aqp_group*
Copies all AQPs in the AQP group *source_aqp_group* to *destination_aqp_group.*

sp_cmp_qplans *plan_id_1*, *plan_id_2*
Compares the specified AQPs and prints a message indicating whether the AQPs are identical. The return status is the sum of these values and indicates the result: **0** - original query text and AQPs both are identical; **1** - original query text and hash keys both are different; **2** - original query text is different, hash keys are identical; **10** - AQPs are different; **100** - one or both of the AQP IDs does not exist.

sp_cmp_all_qplans *aqp_group_1*, *aqp_group_2* [, **counts** | **brief** | **same** | **diff** | **first** | **second** | **offending** | **full**]
Displays differences in AQPs between the two specified AQP groups. Default display option is **counts**; other options display more details on any differences found.

sp_set_qplan *plan_id*, '*new-AQP-text*'
Replaces the AQP text for the specified existing AQP; the original query text remains unchanged. Example: **sp_set_qplan 123456789, '(i_scan new_nc_ix authors)'**

sp_help_qpgroup [*aqp_group* [, **full** | **stats** | **hash** | **list** | **queries** | **plans** | **counts**]
Displays information about an AQP group. Default option is **full**, displaying overall totals; to display (part of) existing individual AQPs, use option **list**.

sp_add_qpgroup *aqp_group*
Creates a new AQP group.

sp_drop_qpgroup *aqp_group*
Drops an existing AQP group, which must be empty.

sp_rename_qpgroup *old_aqp_group*, *new_aqp_group*
Renames the existing AQP group *old_aqp_group* to *new_aqp_group.*

sp_export_qpgroup *user_name*, *aqp_group*, [*db_name*..]*table_name*
Exports all AQPs in *aqp_group* which are owned by *user_name*, to *table_name*, which will be created in the current database.

sp_import_qpgroup [*db_name*..]*table_name*, *user_name*, *aqp_group*
Imports AQPs from *table_name* (which must exist in the current database) into AQP group *aqp_group.* The imported AQPs will be owned by *user_name.*

80. Query metrics capture (15.0)

Captured metrics about executed queries, such as elapsed time and I/O count, are accessible through **sysquerymetrics** (a view on top of **sysqueryplans**) in the database from where the query is executed. Warning: enabling metrics capture without filtering can quickly accumulate large volumes of metrics data on busy servers.

sp_configure 'enable metrics capture', { **0** | **1** } (dynamic)
Enables (**1**) or disables (**0**, =default) query metrics capture server-wide.

sp_configure *condition*, *value* (dynamic)
Specifies a filter condition; metrics below this threshold are not captured (this is to avoid capturing a large volume of uninteresting metrics). *condition* can be:

- **'metrics elap max'** - *value* is the number of milliseconds of elapsed time
- **'metrics exec max'** - *value* is the number of milliseconds of CPU time
- **'metrics lio max'** - *value* is the number of logical I/Os
- **'metrics pio max'** - *value* is the number of physical I/Os

set metrics_capture { **on** | **off** }
Overrides server-wide query metrics capture for the current session.

sp_metrics *subcommand* [, *value1* [, *value2*]]
Manages captured query metrics. *subcommand* and subsequent parameters can be:

- **'help'** [, '*subcommand*'] - displays usage information for all subcommands or for the specified subcommand only.
- **'flush'** - writes accumulated captured query metrics from memory to disk.
- **'backup'**, '*group_id*' - moves the captured metrics from group **'1'** to a group with the specified *group_id* (a number >1, must be quoted; the group is created if it doesn't exist). Captured metrics are always written to group **'1'**.
- **(15.0.1esd1) 'show'** - displays the number of captured metrics in each group. In earlier releases, use this query instead:
  select gid, count(*) from sysquerymetrics group by gid order by 1
- **'drop'**, '*group_id*' [, '*id*'] - with '*id*', deletes the specified metric from the specified group; without '*id*', deletes the entire group.
- **'filter'**, '*group_id*', '*filter_predicate*' - deletes captured metrics from the specified group according to the predicate (used in a **delete** statement). Example:
  sp_metrics 'filter', '2', 'lio_max < 10'

81. MDA tables / monitoring tables (12.5.0.3)

The MDA tables (often called 'monitoring tables') are proxy tables in the **master** database, named **mon**... (e.g. **monSysSQLText**, **monCachedObject**). These tables are mapped to native RPCs inside ASE, and provide low-level monitoring details about the ASE server when queried (with regular SQL).
The MDA tables are not installed by default. To install them, run the script **scripts/installmontables** (in **$SYBASE/$SYBASE_ASE**); some additional setup steps are also needed. For more information about setup and use, see **www.sypron.nl/mda**.

82. Advanced configuration parameters

The configuration parameters in this section affect ASE's internal resource usage and scheduling behaviour. Unless there is a good reason to change (like a recommendation by Sybase Technical Support), leave these parameters at their default settings.

(12.5.1) sp_configure 'send doneinproc tokens', { **0** | **1** } (dynamic)
When **1** (=default), the server sends all *done-in-proc* network packets; when **0**, sends only those packets for **select** statements; when **0**, and with traceflag 292 enabled, no *done-in-proc* packets are sent at all (note: this may cause certain client apps to fail).

sp_configure 'runnable process search count', *value* (dynamic)
Defines the number of times an ASE engine will execute a dummy loop when there are no tasks to be executed, before yielding the CPU to the OS (default = **2000**). With more ASE engines than CPUs (e.g. with multiple ASE servers), reducing this setting (e.g. to **3**) may reduce CPU consumption (though throughput may also be reduced).

sp_configure 'i/o polling process count', *value* (dynamic)
Defines the maximum number of internal tasks that can be executed without checking for completed disk I/O or network I/O (default = **10**).

sp_configure 'time slice', *value* (static; 12.5:dynamic)
Max. nr. of milliseconds (default = **100**) an internal task may run before it should yield.

sp_configure 'cpu grace time', *value* (static; 12.5:dynamic)
Defines the maximum number of ASE clock ticks (default = **500**) an ASE task can run without yielding before it is considered a runaway process, and will be terminated by ASE (this is known as a 'timeslice' error and usually indicates an ASE bug).

sp_configure 'sql server clock tick length', *value* (static)
Defines the internal ASE clock tick length, in microseconds (default = **100000** = 0.1 sec). **@@timeticks** also reflects the current ASE clock tick length.

sp_configure 'allow sql server async i/o', { **0** | **1** } (static)
Enables (**1**, =default) or disables (**0**) asynchronous disk I/O.

(12.5.1) sp_configure 'i/o batch size', *value* (dynamic)
Defines the maximum number of outstanding disk writes (default = **100**). This parameter replaces **dbcc tune(maxwritedes,...)** in pre-12.5.1.

sp_configure 'lock shared memory', { **0** | **1** } (static)
Disallows (**1**) or allows (**0**, =default) swapping of ASE shared memory to disk. This

setting is platform-specific and should be changed in special cases only.

sp_configure 'shared memory starting address' , *address* (static)
Start address of ASE's shared memory. Default=**0**; change in special cases only.

sp_configure 'stack size' , *nr_of_bytes* (static)
sp_configure 'stack guard size' , *nr_of_bytes* (static)
Server-wide size of the stack and stack guard area (in bytes) for each ASE process.

sp_configure 'disk i/o structures', *value* (static; 12.5:semi-dynamic)
Defines the maximum number of concurrently outstanding disk I/Os (default = **256**). Increase this setting when **sp_sysmon** or **sp_monitorconfig** (in 12.5.2) indicate that insufficient disk i/o structures are available.

(12.5.3) sp_configure 'max native threads per engine', *value* (dynamic)
Defines the maximum number of native OS threads (**50**(=default)..**1000**) that can be used per ASE engine.

(12.5.3) sp_configure 'rtm thread idle wait period', *nr_of_seconds* (dynamic)
Defines the number of seconds a native thread waits before exiting when it is idle; default and minimum = **600** (= 10 minutes).

83. Replication Server

Sybase Replication Server is a complex product to administrate, and only some basic ASE-related commands are mentioned briefly here. See my book *'The Complete Sybase Replication Server Quick Reference Guide'* (**www.sypron.nl/repqr**), for a full quick reference guide covering all replication-related commands.

sp_configure 'enable rep agent threads', { **0** | **1** } (dynamic)
Enables (**1**) or disables (**0**, =default) the internal ASE Replication Agent threads.

sp_config_rep_agent *db_name***,** *options* - configures the RepAgent for *db_name*
sp_help_rep_agent *db_name***,** *options* - displays information about RepAgents
sp_start_rep_agent *db_name* - starts the RepAgent for *db_name*
sp_stop_rep_agent *db_name* - stops the RepAgent for *db_name*

set replication { **on** | **off** }
When **off** (default=**on**), all subsequent activity in this ASE session is not replicated.

84. ASE Replicator (12.5)

ASE Replicator is an ASE feature for 'lightweight' data replication (for enterprise-level replication, use Sybase Replication Server instead). ASE Replicator provides log-based, publish/subscribe replication, and also supports procedure replication. ASE Replicator is located in **$SYBASE/RPL-12_5**. See **www.sypron.nl/aserep.html**.

85. Job Scheduler (12.5.1)

The job scheduler allows jobs to be scheduled and executed inside ASE. It consists of a database named **sybmgmtdb**, a collection of stored procedures and an external program **jsagent** (in **$SYBASE/$SYBASE_ASE/bin**). The job scheduler is not installed by default. To install it, run the script **scripts/installjsdb** (in **$SYBASE/$SYBASE_ASE**); some additional setup steps are also needed (see the documentation for details).
Jobs can be managed either with the stored procedures in **sybmgmtdb**, or through the Sybase Central GUI. See the *Job Scheduler User's Guide* for full details about setup and use of the job scheduler. Note: for some platforms (e.g. NT), the job scheduler was not released in 12.5.1, but in later ASE releases.

86. Enterprise Java Beans (12.5 only)

Enterprise Java Beans are not supported in 15.0.

sp_configure 'enable enterprise java beans', { **0** | **1** } (dynamic)
Enables (**1**) or disables (**0**) Enterprise Java Beans; this requires the **ASE_EJB** option to be licensed. EJBs run on a separate, 'external' server engine.

sp_extengine SYB_EJB, { **start** | **stop** | **status** }
Starts, stops or displays the status of the external engine for Enterprise Java Beans.

sp_serveroption SYB_EJB, 'external engine auto start', { **true** | **false** }
Enables or disables automatic start of the EJB external engine when ASE starts.

87. Shared memory dumps

Warning: ***this undocumented and unsupported feature dumps the ASE shared memory to a file; this is for special troubleshooting purposes only. Only Sybase TechSupport can read the dump file; it contains no useful information for a DBA. Use this feature only when instructed by Sybase TechSupport or when regularly encountering serious errors. Avoid using this feature routinely or frequently, as it may temporarily delay or suspend other activity in the server.***

sp_shmdumpconfig [*action*, *type*, *value*, *max_nr_dumps*, *directory*, *file_name*, *option_1*, *option_2*, *option_3*, **(12.5.2)** *option_4*]
Displays or modifies configured dump conditions. A dump condition is a specific event, like a certain error, upon which ASE will dump its shared memory to a file (for troubleshooting purposes by Sybase TechSupport only). *action* can be:

- **'add'**, **'drop'**, **'update'** - adds/drops/changes a dump condition, respectively
- **'reset'** - resets the counter (counting the number of times a dump has been made) for a dump condition
- **'display'** - displays currently configured dump conditions (=default)

The actual dump condition is specified by a *type* and (usually) a *value*. *type* can be:

- **'error'** - *value* is an ASE error number (example: 605)
- **'module'** - *value* is the first of a block of 100 ASE error numbers (example: 1100 corresponds to error numbers 1100-1199)
- **'signal'** - *value* is an OS signal number (example: 11)
- **'severity'** - *value* is a severity level (example: 17); the dump condition applies to errors with a severity ≥ *value*.
- **'timeslice'** - a timeslice error (*value* = **NULL**)
- **'panic'** - a server 'panic' (which crashes the server) (*value* = **NULL**)
- **(12.5.0.3, 12.0.0.5) 'message'** - *value* is an ASE kernel error number
- **'defaults'** - updates default settings (*value* = **NULL**; to restore the default generated file name specify **''** for *file_name*); these defaults will be used when no value is specified for a dump condition
- **(12.5.1) 'dbcc'** - allows making a shared memory dump with **dbcc memdump**.

max_nr_dumps is the max. number of times a memory dump will be performed for this dump condition (this counter is reset at ASE startup). *directory* and *file_name* specify the pathname of the memory dump file. Use **sp_shmdumpsize** to check whether there's a risk of exceeding the maximum file size on your platform.

option_1, *option_2*, *option_3*, *option_4* - These options determine which sections are included in the memory dump. Possible values are **'include_page'**, **'omit_page'**, **'default_page'**, **'include_proc'**, **'omit_proc'**, **'default_proc'**, **'include_unused'**, **'omit_unused'**, **'default_unused'**. Legend: **'include_...'** or **'omit_...'** means a section is included or omitted, respectively; **'default_...'** means the default setting is used. Possible sections are **'..._page'** (data cache), **'..._proc'** (procedure cache), or **'..._unused'** (unused memory). In 12.5.2, also **'halt'** (halts the ASE engines during the dump) **'no_halt'** (doesn't halt ASE) and **'default_halt'** (uses the default setting) can be specified. Examples:

sp_shmdumpconfig 'add', 'timeslice'
(12.5.2) sp_shmdumpconfig 'add', 'error', 691, 1, NULL, 'err691.dmp','no_halt'

sp_shmdumpsize *data_cache_option*, *proc_cache_option*, *size_in_Mb* **output**
Calculates the expected size (in Mb) of the shared memory dump file for this ASE server; this value is returned as an output parameter of datatype **int**. *data_cache_option* and *proc_cache_option* specify whether the size of the data cache and procedure cache should be included. To exclude, specify **'Omit'**; to use the current default setting as configured through **sp_shmdumpconfig**, specify **'Default'**; to include, specify any other string (note: **'Omit'** and **'Default'** are case-sensitive).

sp_configure 'dump on conditions', { **0** | **1** } (dynamic)
Enables (**1**) or disables (**0**, =default) shared memory dumps.

sp_configure 'maximum dump conditions', *max_nr_conditions* (static)
Defines the max. number of dump conditions that can be configured (default = **10**).

(12.5.2) sp_configure 'number of dump threads', *value* (dynamic)
Defines the number of parallel threads (**1**..**8**; default=**1**) for creating a memory dump.

Miscellaneous Topics

88. The interfaces file

Assuming LDAP is not used (=default), the **interfaces** file is an essential part of the Sybase client-server environment. For client applications, it must contain the network address for every server the client application should connect to. To start a server, it must be able to find its own network address in the interfaces file. By default, the **interfaces** file is located in **$SYBASE/interfaces** (on NT: **%SYBASE%\INI\SQL.INI**). It may also be named or located differently, which must then be specified with a command-line parameter for the client or server program (see the following sections). Best use the **dsedit** or **dscp** utilities to edit the **interfaces** file. Note that the **interfaces** file (for Unix) and the **SQL.INI** file (for NT) use incompatible formatting.

dscp (Unix only) - an ASCII-interface utility to view/edit the **interfaces** file. **dscp** has its own command set. At the prompt, type **help** for on-line help.

dsedit - a GUI utility to view/edit the **interfaces** file.

89. Server programs

For all programs, the option **-v** displays the software version.

backupserver (NT: **bcksrvr**) - Backup Server

[**-C** *nr_connections*]	max. # Backup Server connections (default=30)
[**-S** *server_name*]	server name (default=**$DSLISTEN**, otherwise **SYB_BACKUP**)
[**-I** *interfaces_file*]	**interfaces** file pathname (default=**$SYBASE/interfaces**)
[**-e** *errorlog_file*]	Backup Server errorlog (default=**backup.log**)
[**-M** *sybmultbuf*]	pathname of the **sybmultbuf** binary file
[**-N** *net_connections*]	max. # of Backup Server network connections (default=25)
[**-L** *language*]	language used by Backup Server
[**-J** *character_set*]	character set used by Backup Server
[**-P** *active_threads*]	max. # active stripes (for multiple dump/load sessions)
[**-c** *tape_config_file*]	tape configuration file (default=**$SYBASE/backup_tape.cfg**)
[**-V0** | **-V1** | **-V2** | **-V3**]	level of detail for error logging (lower = more detail).
[**-T** *traceflag*]	boot-time traceflags (multiple options are allowed)
[**-m** *max_Mb*]	max. amount of memory (Mb) to be used by Backup Server (default= (number of active stripes)*1Mb)
[**-p** *packet_size*]	TDS packet size (in bytes; default=2048) requested by a local Backup Server from a remote Backup Server for a remote dump/load. Both servers must allow the requested value.

(pre-12.5) buildmaster (NT: **bldmastr**) - Buildmaster (for (re)building a new master device). In 12.5, **buildmaster** is removed; its functionality is merged into **dataserver**.

[**-d** *master_device*]	master device pathname
[**-c** *controller_nr*]	controller number; always specify 0 (=default)
[**-s** *size*]	size of master device in 2Kb pages
[**-m**]	rewrites only **master** database (doesn't rebuild master device)
[**-q**]	doesn't clear unallocated pages in **master** & **model** databases
[**-x**]	rewrites only **model** database (overrides **-q**)

dataserver (NT: **sqlsrvr**) - ASE server. In 12.5, this is also used for building a new ASE server (see the options marked '(build)' below).

[**-d** *master_device*]	master device pathname
[**-r** *master_mirror*]	master device mirror pathname (when master is mirrored)
[**-s** *server_name*]	server name (default= **$DSLISTEN**, otherwise **SYBASE**)
[**-c** *config_file*]	server config. file (default= **$SYBASE/***server_name***.cfg**)
[**-e** *errorlog_file*]	ASE server errorlog (default=**errorlog**)
[**-m**]	boot server in standalone (single-user) mode
[**-M** *sharedmem_dir*]	shared memory directory
[**-i** *interfaces_file_dir*]	directory containing **interfaces** file (default=**$SYBASE**)
[**-T** *traceflag*]	boot-time traceflags (multiple **-T** options can be specified)
[**-a** *keytab_file*]	CAPs directive filename
[**-G** *logserver_name*]	specifies a server name for event logging
[**-g**]	disables event logging
[**-H**]	specified when using the High Availability feature (ASE_HA)
[**-h**] **(12.5)**	'help' function; displays all possible parameters
[**-K** *keytab_file*]	keytab filename (when using DCE)
[**-k** *principal_name*] **(12.5.4)**	the server's principal name (used with Kerberos)

[**-P**]	(NT only) start ASE server with high priority (default=medium)
[**-p** *login_name*]	generates a new random password (printed on the console) for the specified login (which must have been granted **sso_role**)
[-q] **(12.5)**	databases 'created' via **quiesce database for external dump** remain offline (so **standby_access** log dumps can be loaded)
[**-u** *role_or_login*]	unlocks the specified role or login (which must have **sa_role** and/or **sso_role**)
[-y] **(12.5)**	prompts for SSL certificate password (use with **sp_ssladmin**)

[**-b** *size***k**|**K**|**m**|**M**|**g**|**G**] **(12.5)** (build) master device size to create(**15.0**: **t**|**T** also allowed)
[-f[**orcebuild**]] **(12.5)** (build) use with **-b**, **-w** and -**z** to override an existing situation
[**-w** *db_name*] **(12.5)** (build) rewrites specified database (only **master** or **model**)
[**-z** *page_size***k**|**K**] **(12.5)** (build) server page size (**2k**, **4k**, **8k**, or **16k**)
[**-D** *size***k**|**K**|**m**|**M**|**g**|**G**] **(12.5.1)** (build) default database size (for model and tempdb)
[**-Z** *size***k**|**K**|**m**|**M**|**g**|**G**] **(12.5.1)** (build) size of master database

diagserver (NT: **diagsrvr**) - a diagnostic, but otherwise identical, version of the **dataserver** executable. This should be run only when instructed to do so by Sybase Technical Support.

monserver (NT: **monsrvr**) - Monitor Server

-M *Mon_server_name*	name of the Monitor Server
-S *ASE_server_name*	name of the ASE server to monitor
-U *login_name*	login into the ASE server; also a login into Monitor Server
[**-P** *password*]	password for *login_name*
[**-E**]	don't overwrite an exiting *.mrg* file
[**-O**]	overwrite an exiting *.mrg* file
[**-i** *interfaces_file*]	**interfaces** file pathname (default=**$SYBASE/interfaces**)
[**-l** *errorlog_file*]	Monitor Server errorlog (default=**ms.log**)
[**-L** *config_file*]	Monitor Server configuration file
[**-m** *sharedmem_dir*]	ASE server shared memory directory
[**-n** *max_connections*]	max. number of client connections to Monitor Server
[**-p**]	(NT only) sets Monitor Server execution priority to high
[**-T0**]	Monitor Server does not print ASE error messages
[**-T1**]	Monitor Server will not shut down when ASE shuts down

histserver (NT: **histsrvr**) - Historical Server

-D *home_directory*	directory containing control file and recorded data files
[**-S** *Hist_server_name*]	name of the Historical Server
[**-U** *login_name*]	Historical Server super-user login (to execute **hs_** commands)
[**-P** *password*]	password for super-user login
[**-i** *interfaces_file*]	**interfaces** file pathname (default=**$SYBASE/interfaces**)
[**-l** *errorlog_file*]	Historical Server errorlog (default=**hs.log**)
[**-n** *max_connections*]	max. number of client connections to Historical Server

startserver (Unix only) - starts one ore more ASE-, Backup-, or other servers

[**-f** *RUN_server_file*	file name of the **RUN_***servername* file
[**-m**]]	start ASE server in single user mode
[**-f** … [**-m**]]…	additional servers to be started

Example: **startserver -f RUN_PROD**

xpserver - XP Server (➢p.99)
ASE starts/stops XP Server when needed; do not start XP Server explicitly.

asecfg (Unix only) - a GUI utility to create/configure a server

srvbuild (Unix only) - a GUI utility to create/configure a server.

srvbuildres (Unix only) - a non-interactive utility to create/configure a server. For details on the resource file format, see the Installation Guide for your Unix platform (note: **sybinit4ever**, a free tool, is easier to use; see **www.sypron.nl/si4evr.html**).
[**-r** *file_name*] executes a resource file (the log file is in …**/init/logs**)

sybatch (NT only) - a non-interactive utility to create/configure a server, located in **%SYBASE%\%SYBASE_ASE%\bin**. See the *Installation Guide for Windows NT.*
[**-r** *file_name*] executes a resource file (the log file is in …**\init\logs**)

syconfig (NT only) - a GUI utility to create/configure a server; named 'Server Config' in the Start Menu->Programs->Sybase.

90. Client programs

All client programs (except **auditinit**) can have the following command-line options:

[**-S** *server_name*] server to connect to
[**-U** *login_name*] login name
[**-P** *password*] login password (if omitted, it will be prompted for)
[**-I** *interfaces_file*] **interfaces** file to be used
[**-A** *packet_size*] network packet size
[**-X**] use login password encryption
[**-J** [*client_charset*]] performs the specified character set conversion. **-J** alone suppresses character set conversion
[**-a** *display_charset*] display character set used
[**-z** *language*] language used for error messages and prompting
[**-R** *principal*] the server's principal name (used with Kerberos)
[**-K** *keytab_file*] keytab file (for use with DCE only)
[**-V** [*security_options*]] use network user authentication before logging into ASE
[**-Z** *security_mech*] a security mechanism (must be defined in the **libctl.cfg** file)
[**-v**] displays software version

auditinit (Unix only) - An interactive utility to install auditing. When used interactively, hit **CTRL+W** to create a resource file (which can later be executed with **-r**).
[**-a**] validates a resource file (must be combined with **-r**)
[**-r** *resource_file*] executes a resource file
[**-e**] only writes environment info in a log file
[**-v**] displays software version
[**-l** *language*] language to be used in the dialog screens
[**-log** *log_filename*] non-default pathname for log file (by default, it's in **./init/logs**)
[**-s** *release_directory*] ASE release directory (default = **$SYBASE**)
[**-c** *character_set*] character set
[**-h**] displays command-line parameters

bcp - Bulk copy data between a table or view, and a file
[[*db_name.*]*owner.*][*view_name* | *table_name*[**:***ptn_id*]]
the table or view from/to which to copy; *ptn_id* can only be specified when copying into a round-robin partitioned table.
[**partition** *ptn_name*[,...]] **(15.0)** the partition(s) to be copied to/from
{ **in** | **out** } **in**: copy from file to table; **out**: from table to file
file_name [,...] file to be copied to/from; with **partition** (15.0), this can be a list
[Common options: **-S -U -P -I -A -X -a -J -z -R -K -V -Z -v** -- see list on page 112]
[**-c**] copy in character mode (platform-independent)
[**-C**] **(12.5.3a)** for encrypted columns, copies ciphertext instead of plaintext
[**-n**] copy in native (binary) mode (platform-specific)
[**-f** *format_file*] format file to be used
[**-r** *row_delimiter*] (**-c** only) row delimiter character string (default=**\n**)
[**-t** *field_delimiter*] (**-c** only) column delimiter character string (default=**\t**)
[**-N**] does not copy the identity column
[**-E**] (**in** only) takes identity column values from the input file
[**-g** *identity_start*] (**in** only) starting value for the identity column
[**-b** *batch_size*] (**in** only) nr. of rows after which **bcp** commits; without **-b**, and with **-b** but without *batch_size*, inserts all rows in 1 transaction
[**-e** *error_file_name*] (**in** only) file to log error rows into
[**-m** *max_errors*] (**in** only) max. nr. of errors before **bcp** aborts (default=10)
[**-F** *first_row*] row at which to start copying (inclusive)
[**-L** *last_row*] row at which to end copying (inclusive)
[**-q** *datafile_charset*] character set used by *file_name*
[**-T** *max_text_image*] max. #bytes copied for **text** or **image** columns (default=32 Kb)
[**-Q**] handles fixed-length nullable columns as in OpenClient 10.0.4
[**--sho-fi**] **(15.0)** copy hidden columns for function indexes (default: don't copy)
[**--hide-vcc**] **(15.0)** do not copy virtual (non-materialized) computed columns
[**--maxconn** *nr_conns*] **(15.0)** the maximum number of parallel connections to ASE
Example: **bcp my_db..my_table out my_file.dat -Usa -Pmypasswd -SMYSERVER**

charset - Installs an additional sort order for an existing character set, or install a new character set, including a sort order.
[Common options: **-S -U -P -I -v** -- see list on page 112]
sort_order name of the sort order to be installed
[*character_set*] name of the character set to be installed
Example: **charset -Usa -Pmypasswd -SMYSERVER binary.srt utf8**

(15.0) dbisql (NT: **dbisql.bat**) - a GUI query tool, including graphical query plan viewer, located in **$SYBASE/DBISQL/bin**. Can also be invoked from Sybase Central.

(12.5) ddlgen (NT: **ddlgen.bat**) - Reverse-engineers (i.e. generates DDL for) database objects in ASE 12.0+ databases (in 12.5.3, also for 11.9). Depending on the ASE version, **ddlgen** is located in **$SYBASE/ASEP/bin**, **$SYBASE/sybcent**** or **$SYBASE/shared/sybcentral****; on NT, **ddlgen.bat** is located in **%SYBASE%\ASEP\bin**, **%SYBASE%\Sybase Central****** or **%SYBASE%\shared\Sybase Central******.
Note: do <u>not</u> put any spaces between a command parameter flag and its value.
Common options: **-U -P -v -J** -- see list on page 112
-S*hostname***:***port_nr* hostname and port number of the ASE server
(12.5.1) -S*servername* name of ASE server
[**-D***db_name*] database name (default= executing login's default database)
[**-T***object_type*] object type to be reverse-engineered (see below; default=**DB**)
[**-N***object_name*] used with **-T**: specifies object name, may contain wildcards or may be fully qualified (*db_name***.***owner***.***table_name*[**.***index*])
[**-X** {**OU**|**OD**|**OA**} additional filtering: with **-TU**: **OU** = user tables; **OD** = proxy tables (just **-TU**, without **-X** = both user and proxy tables) In 12.5.1, with **-TDB**: **OU** = non-temporary DBs; **OD** = temporary DBs; with **-TP**: **OU** = stored procedures; **OD** = SQLJ procedures. In 12.5.4: with **-TDB**: **OA** = archive databases.
[**-F**{*type*,*type*,…|**%**}] with **-TU**, excludes DDL for objects types **TR**, **I**, **KC**, **RI** for those table(s); in 12.5.1, with **-TDB**, excludes DDL for all database-related objects (**SGM**, **GRP**, **P**, **U**, **UDD**, etc). Different object types may be combined with commas. **%** excludes DDL for all these object types; **-F** alone has no effect.
[**-O***output_file*] output file name
[**-E***error_file*] file to log errors into
[**-L***progress_file*] **(12.5.1)** file to log progress info into

Object types that can be specified with the **-T** option (default=**DB**):

C - cache	**I** - index	**SGM** - segment
DB - database	**KC** - primary/unique key constraints	**TR** - trigger
D - default		**U** - table (see **-X** option above)
DBD - database device	**L** - login	**UDD** - user-defined datatype
DPD - dump device	**P** - stored procedure	**USR** - user
EC - execution class	**R** - rule	**V** - view
EG - engine group	**RI** - RI constraints	**XP** - extended stored procedure
EK - encryption key **(12.5.3a)**	**RO** - role	**WS** - web service **(15.0)**
GRP - user group	**RS** - remote server	

Examples: **ddlgen -Ulogin1 -Ppswd -Spluto:5001** -- default database of 'login1'
ddlgen -Ulogin1 -Ppswd -Spluto:5001 -TDB -N% -- all databases
(12.5.1) ddlgen -Ulogin1 -Ppswd -SPROD -Dprod -- database 'prod'

defncopy - Generates (**out**) or executes (**in**) DDL for rules, defaults, views, triggers and stored procedures to/from a file, respectively (to generate DDL for tables, use Sybase Central or **ddlgen**).
[Common options: **-S -U -P -I -A -X -a -J -z -R -K -V -Z -v** -- see list on page 112]
{ **in** | **out** } **in**: executes DDL from a file; **out**: generates DDL to a file
file_name file containing DDL
db_name database containing object(s)
[*owner.*]*object_name* [*…more objects…*] (**out** only) object(s) to generate DDL for
Example: **defncopy -Usa -Pmypasswd -SMYSERVER out trig.sql my_db my_trig**

extractjava (NT: **extrjava**) - Extracts Java classes from ASE into a JAR file
-f *file_name* client file to extract JAR into
-j *jar_name* JAR to be extracted (with all Java classes it contains)
[Common options: **-S -U -P -I -a -J -z -v** -- see list on page 112]
[**-D** *db_name*] database in which the JAR resides
[**-t** *exec_timeout*] command execution timeout (in seconds; default = indefinite)

isql - Interactive (ASCII, non-GUI) T-SQL query tool. Note that **isql** is rather rudimentary; you may want to consider using **sqsh** instead (see **www.sqsh.org**).
[Common options: **-S -U -P -I -A -X -a -J -z -R -K -V -Z -v** -- see list on page 112]
[**-b**] suppresses column headers
[**-e**] echoes T-SQL commands to output
[**-F**] signals non-ANSI SQL (equivalent to **set fipsflagger on**)
[**-n**] suppresses **isql** prompt and line numbering

[**-p**] prints elapsed execution times for each statement
[**-Y**] use chained transaction mode (equivalent to **set chained on**)
[**-c** *cmd_string*] command terminator (in lowercase; default = 'go')
[**-D** *db_name*] the default database after connecting to the server
[**-E** *editor*] editor used for command editing (default=vi (NT: EDIT.COM)
[**-h** *headers_rows*] nr. of result set rows printed before headers are repeated
[**-H** *hostname*] specifies a value for **sysprocesses.hostname**
[**-i** *input_file_name*] input file containing T-SQL commands
[**-o** *output_file_name*] output file
[**-m** *severity_level*] suppresses error messages of lower severity than specified
[**-s** *column_separator*] single character used as column separator (default = space)
[**-l** *login_timeout*] login timeout (in seconds; default = 60)
[**-t** *exec_timeout*] command execution timeout (in seconds; default = indefinite)
[**-w** *output_width*] width of output lines (default = 80)
[**-Q**] create a HA connection (allowing connection failover)

isql subcommands:

exit, **quit**, **CTRL+D** - exit session	**!!***command* - execute *command* in shell
go - send command batch to ASE	**:r** *filename* - read text from *filename*
reset - discard command batch	**vi** - edit command batch (see **-E** option)
up-/down-arrow keys - scroll through previous commands (NT only)	

installjava (NT: **instjava**) - Installs Java classes from a JAR file into an ASE database. Note: **tempdb** must be large enough to (temporarily) contain the JAR.
-f *file_name* uncompressed JAR file containing Java classes to be installed
[**-new** | specifies that installation should fail if any class already exists
-update] specifies to overwrite existing classes
[**-j** *jar_name*] indicates JAR should be retained (default = not retained)
[Common options: **-S -U -P -I -a -J -z -v** -- see list on page 112]
[**-D** *db_name*] database in which the classes will be installed
[**-t** *exec_timeout*] command execution timeout (in seconds; default = indefinite)

jisql - A Java-based GUI T-SQL query tool, located in **$SYBASE/jutils-2_0/jisql**. Note: there must be a space between a command parameter flag and its value.[Common options: **-U -P -v** -- see list on page 112]
[**-S** *hostname***:***port_nr*[**?***jdbc_properties*]] network address of ASE server
[**-Z** *language_name*] Language to be used ('french', 'spanish', etc.); default=english
[**-C** [*login_pathname*]] File with login values; with only **-C**, creates a file in the home dir
[**-d**] Prints diagnostic messages
[**-L** *look_n_feel*] 'Look & Feel': **metal** =Java; **system** = Motif, Windows or Mac

langinstall (NT: **langinst**) - Installs a new language in an ASE server.
[Common options: **-S -U -P -I** - see list on page 112]
[**-R** *release_number*] release number. Normally, do not specify this option.
language_name the language name to be installed, for example: **spanish**
character_set the character set used by the server
Example: **langinstall -Usa -Pmypasswd -SMYSERVER spanish cp850**
Note: installation of a language inserts rows in **master..sysmessages** and could therefore fill up the master database.

optdiag - Display and edit table statistics (see **www.sypron.nl/optdiag.html** for Kevin Sherlock's handy **sp__optdiag** stored procedure)
[**binary**] (display only) display binary values for full precision
[**simulate**] (edit only) load simulated statistics
statistics mandatory keyword
[**-i** *input_file*] (edit only) client input file to load statistics from
[*db.owner.*]*table_name*[*.column_name*]]]] (display only) table or column to display statistics for
[Common options: **-S -U -P -I -a -J -z -v** -- see list on page 112]
[**-o** *output_file*] (display only) client output file
[**-h**] displays **optdiag** command help info
[**-s**] also displays info about system tables
[**-T** *traceflag*] **optdiag** traceflag (flag values are 1, 2, 4 or 6)

preupgrade (NT: **preupgrd**)
Checks whether a server can be upgraded. **preupgrade** is located in **$SYBASE/$SYBASE_ASE/upgrade**.
[Common options: **-S -U -P -I -v** -- see list on page 112]
[**-h**] print help text and exit
[**-N**] run in non-interactive mode

[**-p** [**skip_sybprocs**]]	**-p**: don't check that **syscomments** text exists for compiled objects (default: do this check); **-p skip_sybprocs**: do this check for all databases except **sybsystemprocs**
[**-D** *db_name*] (15.0)	checks only the specified database (default: all databases)
[**-X** *option-list*] (15.0)	specified a list of checks ; use **-h** to display options

Ribo (NT: **Ribo.bat**) - Intercepts/logs TDS packets by sitting between the client and ASE server; Ribo is transparent for clients. To use Ribo, define the environment variables **$JAVA_HOME** (e.g. **$SYBASE/_jvm**) and **$RIBO_HOME** (= **$SYBASE/jutils-2_0/ribo**), add an entry to the **interfaces** file with a free port *ribo_port*, and start Ribo as follows: **Ribo -l** *ribo_port* **-s** *ASE_hostname* **-p** *ASE_port* . Clients should then connect to Ribo, not to ASE directly. Command options are (there must be a space between a parameter flag and its value):

-l	the port on which Ribo listens for client connections
-s	the host name of the ASE server
-p	the port number of the ASE server
[**-c** *prefix*]	a prefix for the TDS capture files (default=**cap***nnn***.tds**)
[**-x** *charset*]	specifies the character set to use when dumping TDS packets to a file
[**-t** [*prefix*]]	translates captured data to a file with *prefix* (default= **cap***nnn***.txt**)
[**-d**]	displays translated data while it is captured
[**-gui**]	start Ribo as a GUI
[**-f** *file*]	specifies a filter (located in *file*) to be applied
[**-h**]	displays usage information

See **$SYBASE/jutils-2_0/ribo/doc** for additional documentation.

sqladv.exe (Windows only) - SQL Advantage, a GUI ASE query tool. Located in %SYBASE%\sqladv-12_5 (12.5). SQL Advantage was not distributed with ASE 12.0 (but the 11.9 or 12.5 executables work fine with 12.0).

(12.5) sqldbgr (NT: **sqldbgr.bat**) - A command line-oriented SQL debugger utility (located in **$SYBASE/$SYBASE_ASE/bin**), to debug T-SQL code executed by ASE sessions. Warning: be very careful to use this on production servers! To display available **sqldbgr** commands, enter **help**, **help all** or **help** *command* at the prompt. See the ASE *Utility Guide* for further command details.

Note: there must be a space between a command parameter flag and its value.

-U *login_name*	login name
-P *password*	login password
-S *hostname*:*port_nr*	hostname and port number of the ASE server
[**?**]	prints the required command-line options

(12.5) sybmigrate (NT: **sybmigrate.bat**) - Migration tool to migrate both the schema and the data of database objects between ASE 12.5 servers (which may have different server page sizes). Without the **-r** option, **sybmigrate** runs as a GUI. Note: there must be a space between a command parameter flag and its value.

[Common options: **-I -J -z -v** -- see list on page 112]

[**-f**]	forces execution (overrides 'locks' left by previous sessions)
[**-h**]	'help' function; displays all possible parameters
[**-l** *log_file*]	log file containing session log
[**-D** *debug_level*]	sets debug level (*debug_level* =1, 2, 3 or 4; default = 2)
[**-m** *action*]	action to perform: **setup**, **migrate**, **validate** or **report**
[**-rn** *report*]	(with **-m report**) type of report: **status**, **space_est**, **repl**, **(12.5.0.3) diff** or **password**.
[**-r** *resource_file_name*]	executes a resource file (non-interactively)
[**-t** *resource_file_name*]	generates a resource file (for use with **-r**)
[**-T** *traceflag*, ...]	traceflags for **sybmigrate**
[**-Tase** *traceflag*, ...]	ASE traceflags to be enabled for all **sybmigrate** connections

sqlupgrade, **sqlupgraderes** (Unix only)

Upgrades the ASE installation; **sqlupgrade** is a GUI, **sqlupgraderes** is not. The utilities are located in **$SYBASE/ $SYBASE_ASE/bin**.

[Common options: **-v** -- see list on page 112]

[**-s** *sybase_dir*]	(**sqlupgradesres**) points to **$SYBASE** for the new version
[**-r** *resource_file*]	(**sqlupgradesres**) the resource file for the upgrade

91. ASE environment variables

The following Unix environment variables are used by ASE. The variables $SYBASE_*xxx* should not contain full pathnames, but only a single directory name which is located below $SYBASE. In pre-12.0, the variables (and directories) $SYBASE_*xxx* did not exist. On NT, read %VARIABLE% instead of $VARIABLE.

Environment variable	Function
$SYBASE	Pathname of installation directory of all Sybase software
$PATH	Points to $SYBASE, .../$SYBASE_ASE/bin and .../$SYBASE_OCS/bin; on Unix, also points to .../$SYBASE_ASE/install; on NT, also points to .../$SYBASE_ASE/dll and .../$SYBASE_OCS/dll
$DSQUERY (optional)	Default server name used by client utilities (like **isql**)
$DSLISTEN (optional)	Default server name used by ASE when server starts
$DISPLAY (optional)	only required for X-based GUI tools (**hostname:0.0**)
$LD_LIBRARY_PATH	(All Unix flavours except AIX, HP-UX and MacOS X) Points to .../$SYBASE_ASE/lib
$LD_LIBRARY_PATH_64	(Solaris 64-bit) Points to .../$SYBASE_ASE/lib
$LIBPATH	(AIX only) Points to .../$SYBASE_OCS/lib
$SHLIB_PATH	(HP-UX only) Points to .../$SYBASE_OCS/lib
(12.5) $DYLD_LIBRARY_PATH	(MacOS X only) Points to .../$SYBASE_OCS/lib
%LIB%	(NT only) Points to ...\%SYBASE_OCS%\lib
$SYBASE_ASE	ASE installation directory
$SYBASE_OCS	OpenClient installation directory (with **isql, bcp**, etc.)
$SYBASE_FTS	Full-text search installation directory
$SYBASE_SYSAM	License manager installation directory
$LM_LICENSE_FILE	License file pathname (used by the license manager)
$CLASSPATH	List of Java libraries (for Java-based tools)
$JAVA_HOME	JDK installation directory (for Java-based tools)
$SYBASE_JRE	Java run-time environment (for Java-based tools)
(12.5) $SYBASE_EJB	Enterprise Java Beans installation directory
(12.5.4) $SYBASE_PRINCIPAL	Kerberos principal name of the ASE server (overridden by the **-k** boottime option)
(15.0) $SYBOCS_CFG	Location of CT-Lib config file; default= **$SYBASE_OCS/config/libtcl.cfg** or **%SYBASE%\ini\libtcl.cfg**
(15.0) $SYBASE_UA	Unified Agent Framework directory, e.g. **ua**
(15.0) $SYBASE_WS	WebServices directory, e.g. **WS-15_0**
(15.0) $SCROOT	Directory where SybaseCentral is installed
(15.0) $SYBROOT	Parent of $SCROOT; typically the same as $SYBASE; also used for other tools like **dbisql** and **ddlgen**

The following variables are only relevant when using Replication Server 12.0+:

$SYBASE_REP	RepServer installation directory
$SYBASE_RSM	RepServer Manager installation directory
$SYBASE_RSP	RepServer plug-in (for Sybase Central) install. directory

92. Running servers as Windows NT services

On Windows NT, Sybase servers are installed as NT services. The name of the NT service is composed of a server type prefix, followed by the server name:

Server type	Name of NT service
ASE (also known as SQL Server)	SYBSQL_*server_name*
Backup Server	SYBBCK_*server_name*
Historical server	not automatically installed as a service
Monitor Server	SYBMON_*server_name*
Replication Server	SYBREP_*server_name*
RepServer Manager Server	SYBRSM_*server_name*

To start/stop an ASE server named 'PROD' on the local NT host, use this DOS command: **net** [**start** | **stop**] **SYBSQL_PROD** (but note that the preferred way of stopping a server is with the **shutdown** command).
Servers can also be started and stopped from Sybase Central when running on the same system as the servers. A server can also be started by executing the corresponding **RUN_***server_name***.BAT** file (located in the **install** subdirectory), but the server will then run in the foreground in a DOS box.

To start/stop a backup server named 'PROD_BS' on a remote NT host named '\\otherhost', use the commands **sc** or **netsvc** (which are part of the NT resource kit):

sc \\otherhost [**start** | **stop**] **SYBBCK_PROD_BS**
netsvc SYBBCK_PROD_BS \\otherhost [**start** | **stop**]

The command-line parameters used when a server is started as an NT service, are stored in the NT registry. These can modified with the 'Server Config' utility (**syconfig.exe**), or by directly editing the NT registry key:
HKEY_LOCAL_MACHINE\SOFTWARE\SYBASE\Server\<*servername*>\Parameters

93. Global variables: Session-specific

(12.5.2) @@authmech
Indicates the security mechanism with which this session was authenticated.

(12.5.0.3) @@bulkarraysize / @@bulkbatchsize
Contains the number of buffered rows for CIS bulk inserts, and the number of bulk-copied rows for **select**...**into** proxy table, respectively; ➢p.98.

@@char_convert
Contains **1** if character set conversion is currently in effect; **0** if not.

@@client_csexpansion
Contains the expansion factor for conversion from server- to client character set.

@@client_csname / @@client_csid
Contain the name and ID of the client's most recently used character set. Contain **NULL** and **-1**, respectively, if the client character set has not been initialised.

@@curloid
Contains the current session's LOID (Lock Owner ID).

(12.5.0.3) @@datefirst
For the current session, contains the first day of the week, as set by **set datefirst**.

@@cis_rpc_handling
For the current session, indicates whether outbound RPCs are handled by CIS (**0**=off=default; **1**=on). Set with **set cis_rpc_handling**. **@@cis_rpc_handling** is not affected by changing the configuration option **'cis rpc handling'**.

(15.0) @@cursor_rows
For scrollable cursors only, contains the total number of rows in the result set; ➢p.41.

@@error
Contains the error status of the most recently executed statement in the current session. A value of **0** means successful completion; other values may indicate errors. Note: **@@error** is reset by commands that don't return rows, such as **if** statements, so **@@error** should be checked or saved before executing any other statements.

(15.0) @@fetch_status
Contains the result status of the last **fetch** statement in a scrollable cursor; ➢p.41.

@@identity
Contains the last value inserted into an identity column in the current session; ➢p.38.

@@isolation
Contains the session's current transaction isolation level (**0**, **1**, **2** or **3**). Level **2** applies to DOL tables only; for APL tables, level **3** will be used instead. Also ➢p.45.

@@langid / @@language
Contain the language ID and name of the current session's language.

(12.5.0.3) @@lock_timeout
Contains the session's current lock timeout setting, as set by **set lock [no]wait**.

@@maxcharlen / @@ncharsize
Contain the maximum length and average length (both in bytes) of a character in the default character set.

@@nestlevel
Contains the procedure nesting level in the current session. This is initially **0**, and is incremented when entering a stored procedure or trigger; when exiting a stored procedure or trigger, it is decremented. The maximum allowed nesting level is **16**.

(15.0) @@optgoal
Contains the current session's optimization goal (➢p.53).

@@options
Contains a bitmap for the current status of some (not all) session-specific **set** commands. In 12.5.4, **sp_show_options** displays those that are currently set.

(15.0) @@opttimeoutlimit
Contains the current session's optimization timeout limit (➢p.54).

@@parallel_degree / @@scan_parallel_degree
Contain the current session's maximum parallel degree settings for partition scans and hash scans, repectively.

@@procid
In a stored procedure, contains the object ID of the currently executing stored procedure. In a trigger, ➢p.36.

(15.0) @@repartition_degree.
Contains the current session's maximum repartitioning degree (➢p.54).

(15.0) @@resource_granularity
Contains the current session's maximum resource granularity (➢p.54).

@@rowcount
Contains the number of rows affected by the last query. **@@rowcount** is reset by commands that don't access rows, such as **if**-statements, so it should be checked or saved before executing any other statements. For a cursor, after a fetch, contains the total number of rows fetched from the cursor result set since the cursor was opened. **@@rowcount** has a special meaning in a trigger; ➢p.36.

(15.0) @@setrowcount
Contains the current **set rowcount** setting for the current session.

@@spid
Contains the server process ID number of the current session.

@@sqlstatus
Contains the result status of the last cursor **fetch** statement; ➢p.41.

(12.5.3) @@ssl_ciphersuite
If not **NULL**, indicates this is an SSL connection, and the cipher suite used.

(12.5) @@stringsize
Contains the max. number of characters returned by Java method **toString();** ➢p.47.

(12.5.0.3) @@tempdbid
Contains the ID of the session's temporary DB. Equivalent to **tempdb_id(@@spid)**.

@@textptr_parameters
For the current session, indicates whether **text** or **image** data is passed 'by value' with CIS RPC calls (**0**=off=default; **1**=on). Set by **set textptr_parameters**.

@@transactional_rpc
For the current session, indicates whether RPCs are transactional (**0**=off=default; **1**=on). Set by **set transactional_rpc** (requires CIS).

@@tranchained
The session's current transaction mode: **0**=unchained;**1**=chained. Set by **set chained**.

@@trancount
Contains the nesting level of transactions in the current session; ➢p.43.

@@transtate
Contains the state of the current transaction in the current session. Possible values are: **0** - transaction in progress; **1** - transaction committed; **2** - previous statement aborted; transaction still in progress; **3** - transaction aborted and rolled back.

@@textsize / @@textdbid / @@textobjid / @@textcolid / @@textptr / @@textts
Contains text/image-related information for the current session; ➢p.21.

(12.5) @@unicharsize
Contains the length (in bytes) of a unicode character; this value is always 2.

94. Global variables: Server-wide, non-static

@@connections
Contains the number of successful and attempted logins since ASE was last started.

@@dbts
The value of the current database's 'timestamp', which is assigned to columns of the **timestamp** datatype. This is an internal counter that is incremented for each inserted, updated or deleted row, and for other reasons. Note: the **@@dbts** value is not directly related to real-life clock time (only indirectly, and with an error margin, at best).

@@cpu_busy / @@io_busy / @@idle
Contains the CPU / IO / idle time spent (in ticks) since ASE was last started. The length of a tick is stored in **@@timeticks**.

(12.5) @@heapmemsize
Contains the size (in bytes) of the server's heap memory pool.

(12.5) @@logintrigger
Contains the name of the global login trigger (➢p.66).

(12.5.2) @@monitors_active
Indicates whether applications like **sp_sysmon** and Monitor Server, which modify the internal monitor counters, are currently running (>**0**) or not (**0**).

(12.5.1) @@recovery_state
Indicates whether ASE is currently doing recovery. Values: **NOT_IN_RECOVERY**, **RECOVERY_TUNING**, **BOOTIME_RECOVERY**, or **FAILOVER_RECOVERY**.

@@pack_received / @@pack_sent / @@packet_errors
Contains the number of network packets received/sent/in error since ASE was started.

@@total_read / @@total_write / @@total_errors
Contains the number of disk reads / writes / errors since ASE was started.

95. Global variables: Server-wide, static

(12.5) @@boottime
Contains the date and time when the server was last started.

(12.5.0.3) @@bootcount
Contains the number of times this ASE server has been started.

@@cis_version
Contains the version ID of CIS in this ASE server, provided CIS is enabled.

@@errorlog
Contains the server errorlog pathname.

@@max_connections
Contains the maximum number of concurrent connections that this ASE server can support with the current host computer configuration.

@@nodeid
Contains the server-specific node ID, used for DTM (undocumented).

(12.5) @@guestuserid
Constant value of the database user ID for the **guest** user: 2.

(12.5) @@invaliduserid
Constant value of an invalid database user ID: -1 (used in **sp_adduser**, among others).

(12.5) @@mingroupid / @@maxgroupid
Constant values of the lowest (16384) and highest (1048576) possible user group ID.

(12.5) @@minsuid / @@maxsuid
Constant values of the lowest (-32768) or highest (2147483647) possible login ID.

(12.5) @@minuserid / @@maxuserid
Constant values of the lowest (-32768) or highest (2147483647) possible DB user ID.

(12.5) @@probesuid
Constant value of the server login ID of the **probe** login: 2 (used for 2-phase commit).

(12.5.0.3) @@max_precision
Constant value of the maximum precision for **numeric** and **decimal** datatypes: 38.

(12.5) @@maxpagesize
Contains the server page size (in bytes) for this server (2048, 4096, 8192 or 16384).

@@pagesize
(undocumented) Contains the disk page size, which is always 2048 (bytes). This is independent of the server page size in 12.5, indicated by **@@maxpagesize**.

@@servername
Contains the current ASE server name. To define **@@servername** as 'MYSERVER', run **exec sp_addserver 'MYSERVER', 'local'**, then shutdown & restart ASE.

@@thresh_hysteresis
Related to the amount of free space before thresholds are activated; ➢p.64.

@@timeticks
Contains the number of microseconds per tick, as defined by the config option **'sql server clock tick length'**. It is usually set to 100000 (i.e. 100 milliseconds).

@@version
Contains the full software version ID of this ASE server.

(12.5) @@version_as_integer
Contains the major, and sometimes the minor, software version ID of this ASE server.

(12.5.2) @@version_number
Contains the major and minor software version ID of this ASE server.

96. Logical keys

The following stored procedures can be used to describe data model keys; this information is stored in the **syskeys** table. This is for documentation purposes only and does not affect any SQL functionality. See the ASE manuals for full details.

- **sp_commonkey** *table_A*, *table_B*, *column_1A*, *column_1B* [, *column_2A*, *column_2B*, ..., *column_8A*, *column_8B*] - defines pairs of columns which may be used to join *table_A* and *table_B*
- **sp_dropkey** { **'primary'** | **'common'** | **'foreign'** } , *table_A* [, *table_B*] - drops info about keys on *table_A*
- **sp_foreignkey** *table_A*, *table_B*, *column_1* [, *column_2*, ..., *column_8*] - defines a foreign key on the specified columns of *table_A*, mapping to *table_B*.
- **sp_primarykey** *table_name*, *column1* [, *column2*, ..., *column8*] - defines the columns making up the primary key of the specified table.
- **sp_helpjoins** *table_A*, *table_B* - displays columns which could possibly be used to join the two specified tables.
- **sp_helpkey** [*table_name*] - displays information stored by these procedures.

97. Catalog stored procedures

The stored procedures below, collectively known as 'Catalog stored procedures', are typically used by applications to retrieve schema ('catalog') information about database objects. Unlike many other **sp_** procedures, these return a single result set. Pattern matching characters ('**%**' and '**_**'; ➢p.9) may be used for some names, except *db_name* (this must either match the current database, or be **NULL**). See the ASE manuals for further details.

- **sp_column_privileges** *table_or_view* [, *owner_name* [, *db_name* [, *col_name*]]] - displays information about permissions on table or view columns
- **sp_columns** *table_or_view* [,*owner_name* [,*db_name* [,*column_name*]]] - displays information about columns in a table or view
- **sp_databases** - lists all databases in the server
- **sp_datatype_info** [*odbc_datatype*] - display info about ODBC datatypes
- **sp_fkeys** *table_A* [, *owner_A* [, *db_name_A* [, *table_B* [, *owner_B* [, *db_name_B*]]]]] - displays foreign key constraints on *table_A*
- **sp_pkeys** *table_name* [, *table_owner* [, *db_name*]] - displays primary keys
- **sp_server_info** [*attribute_id*] - displays a list of attributes of the current server
- **sp_special_columns** *table_or_view* [, *object_owner* [, *db_name* [, **V** | **R**]]] - displays columns uniquely identifying a row in a table or a view
- **sp_sproc_columns** *procedure_name* [, *owner_name* [, *db_name* [, *param_name*]]] - displays info about one or more stored procedure parameters
- **sp_statistics** *table_name* [, *owner_name* [, *db_name* [, *index_name* [, **Y** | **N**]]]] - displays information about indexes on the specified table
- **sp_stored_procedures** *procedure_name* [, *owner_name* [, *db_name*]] -

displays information about stored procedures

- **sp_tables** *table_or_view_name* [, *owner_name* [, *db_name* [, '*type_list*']] - displays a list of user tables, system tables or views, depending on *type_list*
- **sp_table_privileges** *table_or_view_name* [, *owner_name* [, *db_name*]] - display permission info for all columns in a table or view

98. Issues with BCP-in

To **bcp** data into a table, 'fast' (minimally logged) mode **bcp** will be used automatically when all of the following are true:

- the table has no indexes
- the table has no enabled triggers; when triggers exist, they must have been disabled with **alter table** *table_name* **disable trigger**
- the database option **select into/bulkcopy/pllsort** is enabled

In all other cases, 'slow' mode (fully logged) will be used. When **bcp**-ing into a table in either mode, rules, triggers and RI constraints are not executed, but defaults are. This can lead to problems when the table has first been **bcp**'d out and is then **bcp**'d back in: for columns with a default, rows originally having **NULL** values in such columns will not be **NULL** anymore after being **bcp**'d back in, but will have the default value instead (solution: drop the default before **bcp**-in and restore it afterwards).
bcp-in performance is affected by the config option **'number of pre-allocated extents'** (static, 12.5:dynamic), which defines the number of extents allocated by **bcp** for each transaction, and when additional space is needed (default=2). Setting this option too high can result in a lot of unused space in the database.

99. Minimally logged operations

The following operations are 'minimally logged' (sometimes incorrectly referred to as 'unlogged'), meaning that only page (de)allocations, but no actual data row modifications, are written to the transaction log:

- ➢ **select**…**into**
- ➢ **(15.0) select**…**into existing table** (for regular, non-indexed user tables)
- ➢ fast **bcp**-in (for tables without indexes or triggers)
- ➢ **writetext** (when the '**with log**' option is not used)
- ➢ **create index** (when executed in parallel mode)
- ➢ **reorg rebuild** *table_name*
- ➢ **alter table**…{ **add** | **modify** | **drop** } *column* (when data copying is required)
- ➢ **alter table** … **lock** … (when changing from APL to DOL schemes or vice versa)
- ➢ **(12.5) dbcc rebuild_text ('all')** (= **sp_rebuild_text** *current_db_name*)
- **truncate table** (read note below!)
- **dump transaction** … **with truncate_only** (also: **'trunc log on chkpt'** option)
- **dump transaction** … **with no_log** (this command really logs nothing at all)

With the exception of **truncate table**, when any of these commands has been executed, the transaction log of the database can not be dumped anymore as it doesn't contain all data required to fully recover these operations. Therefore, a database dump should normally be made after executing any of these commands. Note: the commands marked '➢' above require the database option **select into/bulkcopy/pllsort** to be enabled.

100. Monitor Server & Historical Server

Monitor Server is a utility to obtains real-time performance data for an ASE server. Historical Server can collect this data (optionally for multiple Monitor Servers) and store it for later analysis. To display the data gathered by Monitor Server, a client is needed, such as the ASE plug-in for Sybase Central. Avoid running **sp_sysmon** and Monitor Server concurrently, as this may lead to incorrect data being reported.

Installing and configuring Monitor Server

To install Monitor Server, run **srvbuild** (Unix; ➢p.111) or **syconfig.exe** (NT, ➢p.111). See page 111 for Monitor Server command-line options. For configuration issues, see the *Monitor Server User's Guide* for details.
The following commands can be issued through **isql** (default: login 'sa', no password):

- **sms_shutdown** [**no_wait**] - stops Monitor Server; with **no_wait**, does not wait for active sessions to complete.
- **sms_status** { **server** | **numeventbuf** | **scan_interval** } - displays status info: with **server**, displays the name of the ASE server being monitored.

Installing and configuring Historical Server

To install and configure Historical Server, see the *Monitor Historical Server User's*

Guide. Historical Server command-line options are on page 111. A quick reference guide with all commands can be downloaded from **www.sypron.nl/hs_qref.html**. Historical Server commands can be issued through **isql** (default: login 'sa', no password). **hs_shutdown** [**no_wait**] stops Historical Server.

101. ASE limits

ASE property	Max. value in ASE version:		
	12.0	**12.5**	**15.0**
length (bytes) of object, column, index, variable, parameter name	30	30	255
length (bytes) of a #temp table name (incl. '#')	13	13	238
length (bytes) of character expressions	255	16384	16384
server page size	2Kb	16Kb [1]	16Kb [1]
objects (tables, views, etc) per database	2 billion	2 billion	2 billion
variable-length columns per table (APL)	250	254	254
variable-length columns per table (DOL)	250	1024	1024
nr. of columns per table or view	250	1024	1024
length (bytes) of a row (APL table)	1960	≥1960 [2]	≥1960 [2]
length (bytes) of a row (DOL table)	1958	≥1958 [2]	≥1958 [2]
length (bytes) of a **(var)char/binary** column	255	≥1948 [2]	≥1948 [2]
parameters per stored procedure	255	2048	2048
clustered indexes per table	1	1	1
nonclustered indexes per APL table	249	249	249
nonclustered indexes per DOL table	248	248	248
columns per index	31	31	31
index key length (bytes)	600	≥ 600 [2]	≥ 600 [2]
user tables per statement	50	50	50
worktables per statement	14	14	46
subqueries per statement (per side of a **union**)	16	16 / 50 [8]	50
RI **references** constraint checks per statement	192	192	192
expressions in a **group by** or **having** clause	31	31	>31 [10]
number of items in an **in()** - list	1024	1024	>1024 [11]
user tables on all sides of a union	256	256	256
databases per server	32767	32767	32767
temporary databases per server	1	1 / 512 [9]	512
database devices per server (incl. **master** dev.)	256	256	2 billion
size of a database device	32 Gb	32 Gb	4 Tb
device fragments per database	>1000	>1000	>1000
database size	4 Tb	4Tb-8Tb [5]	4Tb-32Tb [6]
server size (all databases)	8 Tb	8 Tb	1 Exabyte
databases involved in one transaction	16	[7]	[7]
stripes in a **dump** or **load** command	> 500 [3]	> 500 [3]	> 500 [3]
max. memory per server (32-bit platform)	1.4 Gb - 4 Gb [3]		
max. memory per server (64-bit platform)	> 4 Gb (limited by OS/hardware)		
logins per server	65535	2 billion	2 billion
engines per server	128	128	128

[1] possible server page sizes are 2Kb, 4Kb, 8Kb and 16Kb
[2] depends on server page size; see **dbcc serverlimits** (➢p.92)
[3] platform-dependent; see platform-specific ASE documentation
[4] depends on the platform-specific maximum size of a database device
[5] 4Tb for a server page size of 2Kb; 8Tb for all page sizes > 2Kb
[6] 4Tb for a server page size of 2Kb; 32Tb for a page size of 16Kb
[7] limited by the setting of the config option **'number of open databases'**
[8] in 12.5.2, this limit has been increased to 50
[9] in 12.5.0.3 (in pre-12.5.0.3, the maximum is 1)
[10] the total size of all expression values must be ≤ 16Kb
[11] limited only by the amount of available procedure cache

102. ASE licensing

Starting with 12.0, some areas of ASE functionality are enabled only under a separate license. This is based on encrypted license keys, managed by the license manager, which resides in the **$SYBASE/$SYBASE_SYSAM** directory; in pre-15, **$SYBASE_SYSAM** should be **SYSAM-1_0**; in 15.0, **SYSAM-2_0**.
In pre-15, the environment variable **$LM_LICENSE_FILE** contains the pathname of the license file read by the license manager (typically, **$SYBASE_SYSAM/licenses/license.dat**). In 15.0, all files in **$SYBASE_SYSAM/licenses** whose names end in

.lic are automatically read.
In pre-15, when buying a license you'll receive an encrypted key from Sybase to enable the option in your ASE server, which must be entered in your license file. In 15.0, license keys must be generated by the customer himself, by logging into **http://sybase.subscribenet.com**.

lmutil
An OS-level command for starting/stopping the license manager daemon. This is located in **$SYBASE/$SYBASE_SYSAM/bin**. Where a 'vendor name' is needed, specify **SYBASE.**

(15.0) sp_lmconfig [*property* [, *value*]]
Manages license configuration. Without parameters or with only the first, displays the current configuration. *property* and *value* can be:

- **'edition'** - *value* is the ASE 'edition': **'EE'** (Enterprise Edition), **'SE'** (Small Business Edition), **'DE'** (Delevoper's Edition) or **'XE'** (Express Edition); when set to **'null'**, a license for any edition is valid.
- **'license type'** - *value* is the license type, e.g. **'CP'** (CPU license), **'DV'** (development)
- **'email recipients'** - *value* is a comma-separated list of email addresses to reeive license-related warnings/notifications by email
- **'email sender'** - *value* is the sender's email address
- **'email severity'** - *value* is the email severity: **'INFORMATIONAL'**, **'ERROR'** (=default), **'WARNING'**.
- **'smtp host'** - *value* is the hostname for SMTP server (for email notifications)
- **'smtp port'** - *value* is the port no. for SMTP server (for email notifications)

The license manager must be running when an ASE server is started; if not, ASE will still start, but in pre-15 all licensable options will be disabled; in 15.0, the options work during a grace period only.
Existing license options are:

- **ASE_SERVER** - in pre-12.5, this is not an option, but just refers to the basic ASE product. In 12.5, this is the license for the 'Enterprise Edition' of ASE: no limitation on user connections, engines, or parallelism. Replaced by **ASE_CORE** in 15.0.
- **(12.5) ASE_SBE** - 'Small Business Edition' of ASE: limited to 256 user connections, 4 engines, and parallelism is disabled
- **(12.5) ASE_DEV** - the free 'Developer's Edition' of ASE: limited to 25 user connections (5 in pre-12.5.2) and 1 engine, but most license options below enabled
- **ASE_ASM** - 'Advanced Security Mechanisms' (network-based authentication and encryption, row-level access control in 12.5)
- **ASE_DTM** - 'Distributed Transaction Management'
- **ASE_JAVA** - use of Java in ASE (➢p.46)
- **ASE_HA** - 'High Availability' (fast ASE-to-ASE failover)
- **(12.5) ASE_EFTS** - 'Full Text Search' (a specialty data store for text-indexing)
- **(12.5) ASE_EJB** - 'Enterprise Java Beans' (not supported on all platforms)
- **(12.5) ASE_DIRS** (pre-12.5.0.2: **ASE_DIR**) - use LDAP instead of **interfaces** file
- **(12.5) ASE_XFS** - file system access (access files as proxy tables; ➢p.97)
- **(12.5.0.3) ASE_XRAY** - required for BMC's 'DB X-Ray' product
- **(12.5.1) ASE_XML** - native XML/XPath/SQLX in ASE (➢p.47)
- **(12.5.1) ASE_WEBSERVICES** - ASE Web Services features (➢p.49)
- **(12.5.2) ASE_MESSAGING** - ASE Real-Time Database features (messaging from T-SQL). In 15.0 esd2, replaced by **ASE_MESSAGING_TIBJMS** (for Tibco JMS) and **ASE_MESSAGING_IBMMQ** (for MQ Series).
- **(12.5.3a) ASE_ENCRYPTION** - column encryption (➢p.28)
- **(15.0) ASE_CORE** - the basic ASE server license
- **(15.0) ASE_PARTITIONS** - semantic partitioning (range-, list-, hash-partitions)
- **(15.0) ASE_EXPRESS** - the free-for-deployment ASE Express Edition (limited database and data cache size, 1 engine only)
- **(15.0esd2) ASE_RLAC** - required for row-level access control (access rules; ➢p.71), replaces **ASE_ASM** for this purpose.

Notes:

- Use the built-in function **license_enabled()** to test if a license option is enabled (returns **1**) or not (returns **0**). Returns **NULL** if the license option does not exist. Example: **select license_enabled('ASE_PARTITIONS')**.
- In 15.0, the options **ASE_JAVA**, **ASE_XFS**, **ASE_XML**, **ASE_WEBSERVICES** need no longer be licensed separately, but are included in the base product.
- In 15.0, the active license options are also visible in the MDA table **monLicense** (➢p.107)

sp_configure 'license information', *nr_of_licenses* (dynamic)
When set to a value > **0** (and **'housekeeper free write percent'** is also > **0**), logs the highest number of active 'licenses' (=distinct combinations of host name & login name) during each 24-hour period, into **master..syblicenseslog**. This is purely informational; it is unrelated to, and does not restrict functionality like, the license options described above.

103. *Essential DBA tasks*

The below overview lists the most essential, as well as some optional, DBA tasks that need to be performed regularly in any ASE environment. As a rough guideline, a typical frequency is suggested for each task. See the *ASE System Administration Guide* for details and additional guidelines.

Essential DBA Tasks	Frequency (typical)
Perform database and transaction log dumps	daily / hourly
Run **dbcc checkstorage** for all databases and follow up any problems found	weekly
Run **update [index] statistics** on user tables	weekly
Run **reorg rebuild** *table_name index_name* for indexes on DOL tables with heavy insert/delete activity	weekly / monthly
Regular preventive stop and restart of the ASE server	monthly / quarterly
Monitor server errorlog for anomalies	daily
Troubleshoot unforeseen emergencies	when necessary
Attend to (end)user/developer needs	when necessary

Additional / Optional DBA Tasks	Frequency (typical)
Monitor growth of data volume and log space usage	daily / weekly
Monitor/tune resource usage with **sp_monitorconfig**	daily / weekly
Monitor/tune resource usage with **sp_sysmon**	when possible
Defragment tables (**reorg** or (re)build clustered index)	monthly / quarterly
Report problems to Sybase Technical Support	when necessary
Install EBFs or upgrades for ASE	when necessary
Set up the **dbccdb** database for **dbcc checkstorage**	once (➢p.84)
Set up the **sybsyntax** database	once (➢p.80)

104. ASE resources on the Internet

Here's an arbitrary selection of some ASE-related Internet resources:

All ASE product manuals (PDF, searchable)	**manuals.sybase.com/as.html**
The Sybase FAQ	**www.isug.com/Sybase_FAQ**
ISUG (International Sybase User Group)	**www.isug.com**
Ed Barlow's 'sp__' Stored Procedures	**www.edbarlow.com**
sqsh, a great **isql** replacement by Scott Gray	**www.sqsh.org**
Michael Peppler's SybPerl & ASE-for-Linux FAQ	**www.peppler.org**
Sybase-related public Usenet newsgroup	**comp.databases.sybase**
Sybase's own newsgroup server	**forums.sybase.com**
Sybase, Inc. corporate website	**www.sybase.com**
Rob Verschoor's web site, with ASE tools & docs	**www.sypron.nl**

Index

Legend

- Keywords followed by **', sp_'** are stored procedures where the **sp**prefix has been chopped off to make a better reference; for example, **addserver, sp_** refers to **sp_addserver**. This is done for other commands as well; for example **checkdb, dbcc** refers to **dbcc checkdb**, and **showplan, set** to **set showplan**.
- Keywords followed by **(config)** are server configuration options, settable with **sp_configure**. Keywords followed by **(DB option)** are database options, settable with **sp_dboption**.

@

@@authmech ... 117
@@bootcount ... 119
@@boottime ... 119
@@bulkarraysize ... 117
@@bulkbatchsize ... 117
@@char_convert ... 117
@@cis_rpc_handling ... 117
@@cis_version ... 96, **119**
@@client_csexpansion ... 117
@@client_csid ... 117
@@client_csname ... 117
@@connections ... 118
@@cpu_busy ... 119
@@curloid ... 117
@@cursor_rows ... **41**, 117
@@datefirst ... 12, **117**
@@dbts ... 119
@@error ... 117
@@errorlog ... 119
@@fetch_status ... **41**, 117
@@guestuserid ... 119
@@heapmemsize ... 119
@@identity ... **38**, 117
@@idle ... 119
@@invaliduserid ... 119
@@io_busy ... 119
@@isolation ... 46, **117**
@@langauge ... 117
@@langid ... 117
@@language ... 117
@@lock_timeout ... **45**, 117
@@logintrigger ... **66**, 119
@@max_connections ... 119
@@max_precision ... 119
@@maxcharlen ... 117
@@maxgroupid ... 119
@@maxpagesize ... 120
@@maxsuid ... 119
@@maxuserid ... 119
@@mingroupid ... 119
@@minsuid ... 119
@@minuserid ... 119
@@monitors_active ... 119
@@ncharsize ... 117
@@nestlevel ... 35, 37, **117**
@@nodeid ... 119
@@optgoal ... **53**, 117
@@options ... 117
@@opttimeoutlimit ... **54**, 118
@@pack_received ... 119
@@pack_sent ... 119
@@packet_errors ... 119
@@pagesize ... 120
@@parallel_degree ... 81, 118
@@probesuid ... 119
@@procid ... 35, **118**
  in a trigger ... 36
@@recovery_state ... **102**, 119
@@repartition_degree ... **54**, 118
@@resource_granularity ... **54**, 118
@@rowcount ... 118
  in a cursor ... 41
  in a trigger ... 36
@@scan_parallel_degree ... 81, 118
@@servername ... 120
@@setrowcount ... **53**, 118
@@spid ... 118
@@sqlstatus ... **41**, 118
@@ssl_ciphersuite ... 118
@@stringsize ... **47**, 118
@@tempdbid ... **60**, 118
@@textcolid ... **21**, 118
@@textdbid ... **21**, 118
@@textobjid ... **21**, 118
@@textptr ... **21**, 118
@@textptr_parameters ... 118
@@textsize ... 118
@@textts ... **21**, 118
@@thresh_hysteresis ... **64**, 120
@@timeticks ... **107**, 120
@@total_errors ... 119
@@total_read ... 119
@@total_write ... 119
@@tranchained ... 118
@@trancount ... **43**, 118
@@transactional_rpc ... 118
@@transtate ... **43**, 118
@@unicharsize ... 118
@@version ... 120
@@version_as_integer ... 120
@@version_number ... 120

A

abort tran on log full (DB option) ... 59
abs() ... 18
abstract plan (show) ... 55
abstract plan cache (config) ... 105
abstract plan dump (config) ... 105
abstract plan load (config) ... 105
abstract plan replace (config) ... 105
Abstract Query Plans ... 105
access rules ... 34, **71**
acos() ... 18
Acronyms ... 7
activeroles, sp_ ... 69
add_qpgroup, sp_ ... 106
add_resource_limit, sp_ ... 103
add_time_range, sp_ ... 103
addalias, sp_ ... 67
addauditrecord, sp_ ... 100
addaudittable, sp_ ... 100
addengine, sp_ ... 104

addexeclass, sp_ 104
addextendedproc, sp_ 99
addexternlogin, sp_ 96
addgroup, sp_ 67
additional network memory (config)73, **82**
addlanguage, sp_ 79
addlogin, sp_ 65
addmessage, sp_ 79
addobjectdef, sp_ 98
addremotelogin, sp_ 95
addsegment, sp_ 64
addserver, sp_ **94**, 96
addtempdb, dbcc 88
addthreshold, sp_ 64
addtype, sp_ 8
addumpdevice, sp_ 58
adduser, sp_ 67
Advanced Security Mechanisms 123
Aggregate functions 21
all (opposite of distinct) (operator) 22
all (subquery operator) 23
allocate max shared memory (config) 74
allocdump, dbcc 88
allow nested triggers (config), 36
allow nulls by default (DB option) 59
allow procedure grouping (config) 35
allow remote access (config) **61**, 94
allow resource limits (config) 103
allow sendmsg (config) 17
allow sql server async i/o (config) 107
allow updates to system tables (config)82
allow_dup_row 30
allpages (lock scheme) 44
allrows_dss (optgoal) 53
allrows_mix (optgoal) 53
allrows_oltp (optgoal) 53
alter database 59
alter database (CIS) 96
alter database…for proxy_update 96
alter encryption key 28
alter role 68
alter table (RI constraints) 31
alter table...add (column) 25
alter table...add constraint 31
alter table...add partition 26
alter table...decrypt 29
alter table...disable trigger 27, 36
alter table...drop 26
alter table...drop constraint 31
alter table...drop partition 27
alter table...enable trigger 27, 36
alter table...encrypt 29
alter table...lock 27, **44**
alter table...modify 26
alter table...partition 27
alter table...partition by 26
alter table...replace 31
alter table...unpartition 27
altermessage, sp_ 79
alterws, sp_dbcc_ 84
and (operator) 9
ANSI join 24
ansi_permissions, set 52
ansinull, set 52
any (subquery operator) 23
application context 71
archive databases 59, 60, 62
arithabort arith_overflow, set 52
arithabort numeric_truncation, set 52
arithignore, set 52
ascii() 12
ascinserts, dbcc tune 88
ASE environment variables 115
ASE licensing 122
ASE limits 122
ASE Replicator 108
ASE resources on the Internet 124
ASE_ASM (license) 123
ASE_CORE (license) 123
ASE_DEV (license) 123
ASE_DIRS,ASE_DIR(LDAP, license) 123
ASE_DTM (license) 123
ASE_EFTS (license) 123
ASE_EJB (license) 123
ASE_ENCRYPTION (license) **28**, 123
ASE_EXPRESS (license) 123
ASE_HA (license) 123
ASE_JAVA (license) **46**, 123
ASE_MESSAGING (license) 123
ASE_MESSAGING_IBMMQ (license)123
ASE_MESSAGING_TIBJMS(license) 123
ASE_PARTITIONS (license) **26**, 123
ASE_RLAC (license) **71**, 123
ASE_SBE (license) 123
ASE_SERVER (license) 123
ASE_WEBSERVICES (license) **50**, 123
ASE_XFS (license) **97**, 123
ASE_XML (license) **47**, 123
ASE_XRAY (DB X-Ray, license) 123
asecfg 111
asin() 18
async log service (DB option) 59
atan() 18
atn2() 18
audit queue size (config) 73, **100**
audit, sp_ 101, 102
audit_event_name() 14, **102**
Auditing 100
auditing (config) 100
auditinit 112
auto identity (DB option) **38**, 59
autoconnect, sp_ 97
autoformat, sp_ 51
avg() 21

B

background, set 56
Backup Server 61
backupserver 110
bcksrvr 110
bcp 112
bcp (fast/normal) 121
bcp (identity columns) 38
begin transaction 42
begin…end 38
between (operator) 9
biginttohex() 10
bindcache, sp_ 75
bindefault, sp_ 34
bindexeclass, sp_ 104
bindmsg, sp_ **32**, 80
bindrule, sp_ 34
bintostr() 10
Bit operators 10
bldmastr 110
break 38
Buffer Pools 74
buildmaster 110
bulk array size, set 98
bulk batch size, set 98

bypass recovery 91, 93
bytes, dbcc 88

C

cache partitions 75
cache wizard (sp_sysmon) 78
cacheconfig, sp_ 74, 75
cacheremove, dbcc 89
Caches 74
cachestrategy, sp_ 75
caching query plans 54
case 38
case-(in)sensitive identifiers 9
cast() 10
Catalog stored procedures 120
ceiling() 18
certificates, SSL 83
chained, set **43**, 114
changedbowner, sp_ 59
changegroup, sp_ 68
char() 12
char_convert, set 80
char_length() 12
Character set 80
charindex() 12
charset 112
check (constraint) 31
check option, create view…with 33
check password for digit (config) ... **65**, 69
checkalloc, dbcc 86
checkcatalog, dbcc 86
checkdb, dbcc 86
checkindex, dbcc 86
checknames, sp_ 80
checkpoint 43
checkreswords, sp_ 51
checksource, sp_ 27, 33, 35, 36, **51**
checkstorage, dbcc 86
checktable, dbcc 86
checkverify, dbcc 87
chgattribute, sp_ 21, **27**, 30, 37, 38, 44
ciphertext, set 29
CIS (Component Integration Services) 95
cis bulk insert array size (config) 98
cis bulk insert batch size (config) 98
cis idle connection timeout (config) 95
cis packet size (config) 98
cis rpc handling (config) 94, **98**
CIS RPCs 94
cis, dbcc 89
cis_rpc_handling, set 94, **98**
cleanpwdchecks, sp_ 66
cleanup, dbcc tune 88
clearpsexe, sp_ 104
clearstats, sp_ 83
client cursor 40
Client programs 112
client_addr, sp_ 51
clientapplname, set 56
clienthostname, set 56
clientname, set 56
close 41
close on endtran, set 41
clustered **30**, 31
cmdtext (auditing) 101
cmp_all_qplans, sp_ 106
cmp_qplans, sp_ 106
coalesce() 39
col_length() 14
col_name() 14
Column encryption 28
column_privileges, sp_ 120
columns, sp_ 120
combo (dbccdb exclusions) 85
command 74
command_status_reporting, set 87
Comment delimiters 9
commit 42
commonkey, sp_ 120
compare() 12
complete_xact, dbcc 87
Component Integration Services (CIS) 95
compressed dump 61
compression memory size (config) 60
compute (clause) 23
computed column **25**, 112
concurrency_opt_threshold 32
config_rep_agent, sp_ 108
configreport, sp_dbcc_ 84
configuration file (config) 72
Configuration parameters
  abstract plan cache 105
  abstract plan dump 105
  abstract plan load 105
  abstract plan replace 105
  additional network memory 73, **82**
  allocate max shared memory 74
  allow nested triggers 36
  allow procedure grouping 35
  allow remote access **61**, 94
  allow resource limits 103
  allow sendmsg 17
  allow sql server async i/o 107
  allow updates to system tables 82
  audit queue size 73, **100**
  auditing 100
  check password for digit **65**, 69
  cis bulk insert array size 98
  cis bulk insert batch size 98
  cis idle connection timeout 95
  cis packet size 98
  cis rpc handling 94, **98**
  compression memory size 60
  configuration file 72
  cpu grace time 107
  current audit table 100
  deadlock retries 44
  default character set id 80
  default database size 58
  default exp_row_size percent 33
  default fill factor percent 33
  default language id 79
  default network packet size 82
  default sortorder id 80
  disable character set conversion 80
  disable disk mirroring 58
  disk i/o structures 74, **108**
  dump on conditions 109
  dynamic allocation on demand 74
  enable cis 95
  enable encrypted columns 28
  enable enterprise java beans 108
  enable file access 97
  enable housekeeper GC 78
  enable java 46
  enable literal autoparam 54
  enable logins during recovery 82
  enable metrics capture 106
  enable rep agent threads 108
  enable row level access 71

enable semantic partitioning 26
enable sort-merge joins and JTC 54
enable webservices 50
enable xml 47
extended cache size 75
global cache partition number 75
heap memory per user 73
histogram tuning factor 76
housekeeper free write percent 82
i/o batch size 107
i/o polling process count 107
identity burning set factor 38
identity grab size 38
license information 124
lock scheme 44
lock shared memory 107
lock wait period 45
max cis remote connections 73, **95**
max concurrently recovered db 102
max memory 73, **74**
max native threads per engine 108
max network packet size 82
max number network listeners .. 73, **83**
max online engines 73, **82**, **83**
max parallel degree 81
max repartition degree 54
max resource granularity 54
max roles enabled per user 69
max scan parallel degree 81
maximum dump conditions 109
maximum failed logins **65**, 69
memory **74**
memory per worker process 73
metrics elap max 106
metrics exec max 106
metrics lio max 106
metrics pio max 106
min online engines 82
minimum password length **65**, 69
number of alarms 73
number of aux scan descriptors **32**, 73
number of checkpoint tasks 102
number of devices **57**, 73
number of dtx participants 73
number of dump threads 109
number of engines at startup 82
number of histogram steps 76
number of java sockets **46**, 74
number of large i/o buffers 74
number of locks **44**, 74
number of mailboxes 74
number of messages 73
number of open databases 73, 122
number of open indexes 73
number of open objects 73
number of open partitions 74
number of pre-allocated extents ... 121
number of remote connections 73
number of remote logins 73
number of remote sites 73
number of sort buffers 73, **82**
number of user connections 73, **82**
number of worker processes 73, **81**
optimization goal 53
optimization timeout limit 54
page lock promotion HWM 100
page lock promotion LWM 100
page lock promotion PCT 100
partition groups 73
permission cache entries 73
print deadlock information 44
procedure cache percent 74
procedure cache size 74
read committed with lock 44
remote server pre-read packets 95
row lock promotion HWM 100
row lock promotion LWM 100
row lock promotion PCT 100
rtm thread idle wait period 108
runnable process search count 107
sampling percent 76
send doneinproc tokens 88, **107**
shared memory starting address ...108
size of auto identity column (config) 38
size of global fixed heap **46**, 74
size of process object heap **46**, 74
size of shared class heap **46**, 74
size of unilib cache 73
sproc optimize timeout limit 54
sql server clock tick length **107**, 120
stack guard size 108
stack size 108
statement cache size 54
suspend audit when device full 100
syb_sendmsg port number 17
sysstatistics flush interval 77
systemwide password expiration **65**,69
tcp no delay 82
text prefetch size 21
time slice 107
total data cache size 74
total logical memory 74
total memory 74
total physical memory 74
txn to pss ratio 73
xp_cmdshell context 99
Configuration parameters, advanced .107
configure, sp_ 72
Configuring CIS 95
Configuring parallel processing 81
Configuring RPCs 94
Configuring shared memory dumps ...109
connect to 97
connection, reserved for DBA 82
Constraints 31
continue 39
convert() 10
convert(), for date/time formatting 10
copy_all_qplans, sp_ 106
copy_qplan, sp_ 106
corrupt, dbcc 89
cos() 19
cot() 19
count(),count_big() 21
count(*), count_big(*) 21
countmetadata, sp_ 73
cpu grace time (config) 107
cpuaffinity, dbcc tune 88
create access rule **34**, 71
create database 58
create database (CIS) 96
create database...for proxy_update 96
create default 33
create encryption key 28
create existing table 97
create function (Java) 46
create index 30
create plan 105
create procedure 34
create procedure (Java) 46
create procedure...as external name 99
create proxy_table 97

create role ... 68
create rule ... 34
create schema authorization ... **28**, 33, 71
create service ... 50
create table ... 25
create table (CIS) ... 97, 98
create table (encryption) ... 28
create table (RI constraints) ... 31
create temporary database ... 60
create trigger ... 35
create view ... 33
createws, sp_dbcc_ ... 84
current audit table (config) ... 100
current_date() ... 11
current_time() ... 11
cursor rows, set ... 41
cursorinfo, sp_ ... 41
Cursors ... 40
curunreservedpgs() ... 14

D

data_pages() ... 14
data_pgs() ... 14
Database devices ... 57
Database options
- abort tran on log full ... 59
- allow nulls by default ... 59
- async log service ... 59
- auto identity ... **38**, 59
- dbo use only ... 59
- ddl in tran ... 59
- delayed commit ... 60
- identity in nonunique index ... **38**, 60
- no chkpt on recovery ... 60
- no free space acctg ... 60
- read only ... 60
- select into/bulkcopy/pllsort ... 60
- single user ... 60
- trunc log on chkpt ... 60
- unique auto_identity index ... **38**, 60

Database recovery ... 102
database timestamp ... *See* timestamp
Database users ... 67
Databases ... 58
databases, sp_ ... 120
datachange() ... **14**, 77
datalength() ... 14
datapages (lock scheme) ... 44
datarows (lock scheme) ... 44
dataserver ... 110
Datatype conversion functions ... 10
datatype_info, sp_ ... 120
Datatypes ... 8
Date & Time ... 10
dateadd() ... 11
datediff() ... 11
datefirst, set ... 12
dateformat, set ... 12
datename() ... 11
datepart() ... 11
day() ... 11
DB X-Ray (ASE_XRAY) ... 123
db_id() ... 15
db_name() ... 15
DBA tasks ... 124
dbcacheremove, dbcc ... 89
dbcc addtempdb ... 88
dbcc allocdump ... 88
dbcc bytes ... 88
dbcc cacheremove ... 89
dbcc checkalloc ... 86
dbcc checkcatalog ... 86
dbcc checkdb ... 86
dbcc checkindex ... 86
dbcc checkstorage ... 86
dbcc checktable ... 86
dbcc checkverify ... 87
dbcc cis ... 89
dbcc commands
- supported ... 86
- unsupported ... 88

dbcc complete_xact ... 87
dbcc corrupt ... 89
dbcc dbcacheremove ... 89
dbcc dbinfo ... 89
dbcc dbrecover ... 89
dbcc dbrepair ... 87, 89
dbcc dbtable ... 89
dbcc delete_dol_page ... 89
dbcc des ... 89
dbcc engine ... 87
dbcc extentcheck ... 89
dbcc extentdump ... 89
dbcc extentzap ... 89
dbcc findnotfullextents ... 89
dbcc fix_al ... 89
dbcc fix_text ... 87
dbcc forget_xact ... 87
dbcc gam ... 90
dbcc help ... 88
dbcc indexalloc ... 87
dbcc istraceon ... 90
dbcc listoam ... 90
dbcc locateindexpgs ... 90
dbcc lock ... 90
dbcc log ... 90
dbcc logprint ... 90
dbcc logtransfer ... 90
dbcc memdump ... 90
dbcc memusage ... 91
dbcc monitor ... 91
dbcc object_atts ... 38, **91**
dbcc object_stats ... 91
dbcc orphantables ... 91
dbcc page ... 91
dbcc pglinkage ... 91
dbcc pravailabletempdbs ... 91
dbcc printolog ... 90
dbcc procbuf ... 91
dbcc prsqlcache ... 87
dbcc prtipage ... 91
dbcc pss ... 91
dbcc purgesqlcache ... 87
dbcc rebuild_log ... 91
dbcc rebuild_text ... 87
dbcc rebuildextents ... 91
dbcc refreshides ... 92
dbcc reindex ... 87
dbcc resource ... 92
dbcc save_rebuild_log ... 92
dbcc serverlimits ... 92
dbcc set_identity_burn_max ... 92
dbcc settrunc ... 87
dbcc showrecovery ... 92
dbcc sqltext ... 92
dbcc sqtprint ... 92
dbcc stacktrace ... 92
dbcc stackused ... 92
dbcc tablealloc ... 88
dbcc textalloc ... 88

dbcc thresholds 92
dbcc traceflags 92
dbcc traceoff 88
dbcc traceon 88
dbcc tune 88
dbcc upgrade_object 92
dbcc usedextents 92
dbcc user_stats 92
dbcc xls 92
dbcc_alterws, sp_ 84
dbcc_configreport, sp_ 84
dbcc_createws, sp_ 84
dbcc_deletedb, sp_ 85
dbcc_deletehistory, sp_ 85
dbcc_differentialreport, sp_ 85
dbcc_evaluatedb, sp_ 85
dbcc_exclusions, sp_ 85
dbcc_faultreport, sp_ 85
dbcc_fullreport, sp_ 85
dbcc_help_fault, sp_ 85
dbcc_patch_finishtime, sp_ 85
dbcc_recommendations, sp_ 85
dbcc_runcheck, sp_ 86
dbcc_statisticsreport, sp_ 86
dbcc_summaryreport, sp_ 86
dbcc_updateconfig, sp_ 86
dbccdb stored procedures 84
dbccdb, Setting up 84
dbextend, sp_ 64
dbinfo, dbcc 89
dbisql 113
dbo use only (DB option) 59
dboption, sp_ 59
dbrecover, dbcc 89
dbrecovery_order, sp_ 102
dbremap, sp_ 87
dbrepair, dbcc 89
dbtable, dbcc 89
ddl in tran (DB option) 59
ddlgen 113
deadlock retries (config) 44
deadlock, client error 1205 44
dealloc_first_txtpg **21**, 33
deallocate cursor 41
Debugger (for SQL) 115
declare 39
declare (cursors) 40
decrypt (permission) **29**, 69
default character set id (config) 80
default data cache 75
default database size (config) 58
default exp_row_size percent (config) . 33
default fill factor percent (config) 33
default language id (config) 79
default network packet size (config) 82
default sortorder id (config) 80
defaultloc, sp_ 97
Defaults 33
defncopy 113
degrees() 19
delayed commit (DB option) 60
delayed_commit, set **56**, 60
delete 24
delete (cursors) 41
delete shared statistics 77
delete statistics 77
delete where current of 41
delete_dol_page, dbcc 89
deleted (trigger table) 35
deletedb, sp_dbcc_ 85
deletehistory, sp_dbcc_ 85
depends, sp_ 27, 33, 35, 36, 46, **51**
derived table 22
derived_stat() 15
des, dbcc 89
des_bind, dbcc tune 88
des_greedyalloc, dbcc tune 88
des_unbind, dbcc tune 88
Developer's Edition 123
deviceattr, sp_ 58
deviochar, dbcc tune 88
diagserver 111
diagsrvr 111
difference() 12
differentialreport, sp_dbcc_ 85
directio **57**, 58
dirty reads 45
disable character set conversion (conf)80
disable disk mirroring (config) 58
disconnect 97
disk i/o structures (config) 74, **108**
disk init 57
disk mirror 58
disk refit 57
disk reinit 57
disk remirror 58
disk resize 57
disk unmirror 58
diskdefault, sp_ 57
displayaudit, sp_ 101
displaylevel, sp_ 72
displaylogin, sp_ 65
displayroles, sp_ 69
distinct (operator) 21, 22
Distributed Transaction Management 123
domain rule 34
done-in-proc network packets **88**, 93, 107
doneinproc, dbcc tune 88
drop database 59
drop default 34
drop encryption key 28
drop function (java) 46
drop index 30
drop procedure 35
drop procedure (java) 47
drop role 68
drop rule 34
drop service 51
drop table 27
drop table (CIS) 98
drop trigger 36
drop view 33
drop_qpgroup, sp_ 106
drop_resource_limit, sp_ 104
drop_time_range, sp_ 103
dropalias, sp_ 68
dropdevice, sp_ 58
dropengine, sp_ 104
dropexeclass, sp_ 104
dropextendedproc, sp_ 99
dropexternlogin, sp_ 96
dropglockpromote, sp_ 100
dropgroup, sp_ 68
dropkey, sp_ 120
droplanguage, sp_ 79
droplogin, sp_ 65
dropmessage, sp_ 79
dropobjectdef, sp_ 98
dropremotelogin, sp_ 95
droprowlockpromote, sp_ 100
dropsegment, sp_ 64
dropserver, sp_ **94**, 96

dropthreshold, sp_ 64
droptype, sp_ 8
dropuser, sp_ 68
dscp 110
dsedit 110
dsync **57**, 58
dtm_tm_role 68
dump database 61
Dump devices 57
dump on conditions (config) 109
dump transaction
  with no_log 62
  with no_truncate 62
  with standby_access 62
  with truncate_only 62
dump, compressed 61
dump, password-protected 61
Dumping & loading databases 61
dumpoptimize, sp_ 63
dynamic allocation on demand (config) 74
dynamic SQL (execute immediate) 39

E

EJB 108
elapsed_time (resource limit) 103
empty string 14
enable cis (config) 95
enable encrypted columns (config) 28
enable enterprise java beans (config) 108
enable file access (config) 97
enable housekeeper GC (config) 78
enable java (config) 46
enable literal autoparam (config) 54
enable logins during recovery (config) 82
enable metrics capture (config) 106
enable rep agent threads (config) 108
enable row level access (config) 71
enable semantic partitioning (config) 26
enable sort-merge joins and JTC(conf) 54
enable webservices (config) 50
enable xml (config) 47
encryption
  column encryption 28
  login passwords 95, 96, 112
  SSL 83
encryption, sp_ 29
engine, dbcc 87
engine, sp_ 82
Enterprise Edition 123
Enterprise Java Beans **108**, 123
Environment variables 115
Errata 7
Essential DBA tasks 124
estspace, sp_ 27
evaluatedb, sp_dbcc_ 85
exclusion list (dbccdb) 85
exclusions, sp_dbcc_ 85
exec(), execute() 39
exec, execute 35, **39**
execute cursor 40
execute immediate (dynamic SQL) 39
Execution Classes 104
exists (subquery operator) 23
exp() 18
exp_row_size 25, 26, **32**
export_options, set 56
export_qpgroup, sp_ 106
extended cache size (config) 75
extendsegment, sp_ 64
extengine, sp_ 108
extentcheck, dbcc 89
extentdump, dbcc 89
extentzap, dbcc 89
extractjava 47, **113**
extrapwdchecks, sp_ 66
extrjava 47, **113**

F

familylock, sp_ 44
FAQ for Sybase 124
fast bcp 121
faultreport, sp_dbcc_ 85
fetch 41
File system access (ASE_XFS) **97**, 123
fillfactor 30, **32**
findnotfullextents, dbcc 89
fine-grain access control 71
fipsflagger, set **56**, 113
fix_al, dbcc 89
fix_text, dbcc 87
fixindex, sp_ (dbcc dbrepair) 89
fkeys, sp_ 120
floor() 18
flushmessage, set 56
flushstats, sp_ 77
fmtonly, set 52
for browse 23
for read only (cursors) 23
for update (cursors) 23
for xml 23
for xml [all|schema] (select...) 47
forceonline_db, sp_ 103
forceonline_object, sp_ 103
forceonline_page, sp_ 102
forceplan, set 53
forcing an index 22
foreign key (constraint) 31
foreignkey, sp_ 120
forget_xact, dbcc 87
forsqlcreatej 49
forsqlinsertj 49
forsqlscriptj 49
forxmldtdj 49
forxmlj 49
forxmlschemaj 49
fragmentation, sp_ 83
freedll, sp_ 99
from (clause) 22
Full Text Search 123
fullreport, sp_dbcc_ 85
function index **30**, 112
futureonly 34

G

gam, dbcc 90
garbage collection (housekeeper) 78
get_appcontext() 15, **71**
getdate() 11
getmessage, sp_ 80
getutcdate() 11
global cache partition number (config). 75
Global variables
  server-wide, non-static variables 118
  server-wide, static variables 119
  session-specific variables 117
GMT time, getutcdate() 11

goto 39
grant (command permissions) 70
grant (encryption) 29
grant (object permissions) 69
grant dbcc 70
grant default permissions 70
grant role **69**, 71
grant...with grant option 69
group by (clause) 22
GUID - newid() 18

H

ha_role 68
has_role() **19**, 69
hash partitioning 26
hash_join, set 53
having (clause) 23
heap memory per user (config) 73
help, dbcc 88
help, sp_ 8, 27, 29, 32, 33, 34, 35, 36, **51**
help_fault, sp_dbcc_ 85
help_qpgroup, sp_ 106
help_rep_agent, sp_ 108
help_resource_limit, sp_ 104
helppartition, sp_ 27
helpcache, sp_ 75
helpcomputedcolumn, sp_ 27
helpconfig, sp_ 73
helpconstraint, sp_ 32
helpdb, sp_ 60
helpdevice, sp_ 58
helpextendedproc, sp_ 99
helpexternlogin, sp_ 96
helpgroup, sp_ 68
helpindex, sp_ 30
helpjava, sp_ 46
helpjoins, sp_ 120
helpkey, sp_ 120
helplanguage, sp_ 79
helplog, sp_ 59
helpmaplogin, sp_ 67
helpobjectdef, sp_ 98
helpremotelogin, sp_ 95
helprotect, sp_ 69, **71**
helpsegment, sp_ 64
helpserver, sp_ 95, 96
helpsort, sp_ 80
helptext, sp_ 27, 32, 33, 34, 35, 36, 46
helpthreshold, sp_ 64
helpuser, sp_ 68
hextobigint() 10
hextoint() 10
hidetext, sp_ 28, 33, 35, 36, **52**
High Availability (ASE_HA) 123
histogram tuning factor (config) 76
Historical Server 121
histserver 111
histsrvr 111
HK CHORES thread 82
HK GC thread **78**, 82
HK WASH thread 82
holdlock 45
host_id() 15
host_name() 15
housekeeper free write percent(config) 82
HOUSEKEEPER thread 78, **82**
hs_shutdown 122

I

i/o batch size (config) 107
i/o polling process count (config) 107
Identifiers 9
identity 26, **37**
identity burning set factor (config) 38
identity columns 37
identity grab size (config) 38
identity in nonunique index (DB option) 60
identity in nonunique index(DB opt.) **38**
identity() 15, **37**
identity_burn_max (sp_chgattribute) 38
identity_burn_max() 15, **37**
identity_gap (create table) 37
identity_gap (select...into) 37
identity_gap (sp_chgattribute) 37
identity_insert, set 37
identity_update, set 37
ignore_dup_key 30
ignore_dup_row 30
image/text functions 20
import_qpgroup, sp_ 106
in (operator) 9
in (subquery operator) 23
in row (Java) **26**, 46
index, forcing 22
index, function 30
index_col() **15**, 30
index_colorder() **15**, 31
indexalloc, dbcc 87
Indexes 30
indsuspect, sp_ 80
ins_syn_sql 80
insert...select 24
insert...values 24
inserted (trigger table) 35
install java (command) 47
installdbextend 64
installjava (tool) 47, **114**
installjsdb 108
installmaster, instmstr 81
installmontables 107
installpubs3, intpbs3 81
installsecurity, instsecu 100
installws 50
instjava (tool) 47, 114
interfaces file 110
International Sybase User Group 124
inttohex() 10
io_cost (resource limit) 103
IP address of a client 51
is_quiesced() **15**, 63
is_sec_service_on() 15
isdate() 12
isnull() 20
isnumeric() 12
isolation level (transactions) 45
isql 113
isql subcommands 114
istraceon, dbcc 90
ISUG 124

J

Java in ASE **46**, 123
jisql 114
job scheduler 108
join transitive closure (jtc) 54
join, ANSI 24

join, outer 25
Joins 24
js_admin_role 68
js_client_role 68
js_user_role 68
jsagent 108
jtc, set 54

K

keep count 89
kill 82

L

langinst 114
langinstall 114
language cursor 40
language, set 79
Languages & Messages 78
lct_admin() 15
LDAP (ASE_DIRS, license) 123
left() 12
len() 13
license information(config) 124
License options/keys, ASE 122
license_enabled() 16, **123**
like (operator) 9
Limits (of ASE) 122
line continuation character (\) 9
list partitioning 26
list_appcontext() 16, **71**
listener, sp_ 83
listoam, dbcc 90
listsuspect_db, sp_ 102
listsuspect_object, sp_ 102
listsuspect_page, sp_ 102
literal_autoparam, set 54
lmconfig,sp_ 123
lmutil (license manager) 123
load database 62
load transaction 62
local index 30
locateindexpgs, dbcc 90
lock nowait 45
lock nowait, set 45
Lock promotion 99
lock scheme (config) 44
lock shared memory (config) 107
lock table 45
lock wait period (config) 45
lock wait, set 45
lock, dbcc 90
lock, sp_ 44
Locking 44
locklogin, sp_ 67
lockscheme() 16
log() 18
log, dbcc 90
log10() 18
logarithm 18
logdevice, sp_ 59
Logical keys 120
Logical operators 9
Logical Process Manager 104
login 96
login password encryption 95, 96, 112
login script .... *See* login trigger
login trigger
  global 66
  login-specific 66
login, locking 67
login, unlocking 67
Logins 64
logintrigger, sp_ 66
logiosize, sp_ 59
logprint, dbcc 90
logtransfer, dbcc 90
long strings (multiple lines) 9
lower() 13
lru 22
ltrim() 13

M

makesuspect_obj, sp_ 103
manifest file 63
manuals, ASE 124
maplogin, sp_ 67
Mathematical functions 18
max cis remote connections (conf.) 73, **95**
max concurrently recovered db(conf.) 102
max memory (config) 73, **74**
max native threads per engine (conf.) 108
max network packet size (config) 82
max number network listeners (conf.) .. 73
max number network listeners (config) **83**
max online engines (config) 73, **82**, **83**
max parallel degree (config) 81
max repartition degree (config) 54
max resource granularity (config) 54
max roles enabled per user (config) 69
max scan parallel degree (config) 81
max() 21
max_rows_per_page 30, **32**
maximum dump conditions (config) ... 109
maximum failed logins (config) **65**, 69
maxwritedes, dbcc tune 88
MDA tables 107
memdump, dbcc 90
memory (config) 74
Memory allocation (12.0) 74
Memory allocation (12.5) 74
memory per worker process (config) ... 73
memusage, dbcc 91
merge_join, set 53
messaging_role 68
metrics elap max (config) 106
metrics exec max (config) 106
metrics lio max (config) 106
metrics pio max (config) 106
metrics, sp_ 107
metrics_capture, set 106
Migration tool (sybmigrate) 115
min online engines (config) 82
min() 21
Minimally logged operations 121
minimum password length (config) **65**, 69
mirroring, devices 58
modify_resource_limit, sp_ 104
modify_time_range, sp_ 103
modifylogin, sp_ **66**, 69, 79
modifystats, sp_ 77
modifythreshold, sp_ 64
modulo, % (operator) 9
mon_role 68
Monitor Server 121
monitor, dbcc 91

monitor, sp_ ... 52
monitorconfig, sp_ ... 73
monitoring tables ... 107
monserver ... 111
monsrvr ... 111
month() ... 11
mount database ... 63
mru ... 22
mut_excl_roles() ... **19**, 69

N

Named Caches ... 74
navigator_role ... 68
net password encryption(server opt)95,96
NETWORK HANDLER thread ... 83
newid() ... 18
newline character ... 9, **12**
newsgroups, ASE ... 124
next_identity() ... 16, **37**
nl_join, set ... 53
no chkpt on recovery (DB option) ... 60
no free space acctg (DB option) ... 60
nocount, set ... 56
nodata, set ... 53
noexec, set ... 53
noholdlock ... 45
nonclustered ... **30**, 31
not (operator) ... 9
NT services ... 116
nullif() ... 39
number of alarms (config) ... 73
number of aux scan descrip. (conf.) ... **32**
number of aux scan descriptors (conf.) 73
number of checkpoint tasks (config) .. 102
number of devices (config) ... **57**, 73
number of dtx participants (config) ... 73
number of dump threads (config) ... 109
number of engines at startup (config) .. 82
number of histogram steps (config) ... 76
number of java sockets (config) ... **46**, 74
number of large i/o buffers (config) ... 74
number of locks (config) ... **44**, 74
number of mailboxes (config) ... 74
number of messages (config) ... 73
number of open databases (conf.)73, 122
number of open indexes (config) ... 73
number of open objects (config) ... 73
number of open partitions (config) ... 74
number of pre-allocated ext. (config) . 121
number of remote connections (config)73
number of remote logins (config) ... 73
number of remote sites (config) ... 73
number of sort buffers (config) ... 73, **82**
number of user connections (conf.)73, **82**
number of worker processes(conf.)73, **81**
Numeric operators ... 9

O

Object storage properties ... 32
object_atts, dbcc ... 38, **91**
object_id() ... 16
object_name() ... 16
object_stats, dbcc ... 91
object_stats, sp_ ... 44
off row (Java) ... **26**, 46
on (clause) ... 22
online database ... 62
open ... 41
oper_role ... 68
Operators ... 9
optdiag ... 76, **114**
optdiag, sp__ ... 114
optimistic locking, with timestamp ... 20
optimistic_index_lock ... 44
optimization goal (config) ... 53
optimization timeout limit (config) ... 54
option show..., set ... 55
or (operator) ... 9
order by (clause) ... 23
orphantables, dbcc ... 91
outer join ... 25

P

page lock promotion HWM (config) ... 100
page lock promotion LWM (config) ... 100
page lock promotion PCT (config) ... 100
page size, server ... 5
page, dbcc ... 91
pageinfo() ... 16
pagesize() ... 16
Parallel index creation ... 81
Parallel query processing ... 81
parallel_degree, set ... 81
parallel_query, set ... 53
parseonly, set ... 53
partition groups (config) ... 73
partition_id() ... 16
partition_name() ... 16
partition_object_id() ... 16
partitioning, table ... 26
passthru, sp_ ... 97
password encryption ... 95, 96, 112
password, sp_ ... 65
passwordpolicy, sp_ ... 65
patch_finishtime, sp_dbcc_ ... 85
patindex() ... **13**, 20
Pattern matching operators ... 9
permission cache entries (config) ... 73
Permissions ... 69
pglinkage, dbcc ... 91
pi() ... 18
pkeys, sp_ ... 120
placeobject, sp_ ... 28, 30, **64**
plan dump, set ... 105
plan exists check, set ... 105
plan for, set (XML) ... 55
plan load, set ... 105
plan optgoal, set ... 53
plan opttimeoutlimit, set ... 54
plan replace, set ... 105
plan_dbccdb, sp_ ... 84
pointer_size() ... 16
poolconfig, sp_ ... 75
Pools ... 74
post_xpload, sp_ ... 63
power() ... 18
pravailabletempdbs, dbcc ... 91
prefetch ... 22
prefetch, set ... 53
prepare transaction ... 43
preupgrade ... 114
preupgrd ... 114
primary key (constraint) ... 31
primarykey, sp_ ... 120
print ... 39
print deadlock information (config) ... 44

printolog, dbcc 90
proc_output_params, set 56
proc_return_status, set 56
proc_role() **19**, 69
procbuf, dbcc 91
procedure cache percent (config) 74
procedure cache size (config) 74
process_limit_action, set 81
procqmode, sp_ 35
procxmode, sp_ **35**, 43
Programming 38
Proxy tables (CIS) 97, 98
proxy, set 67
prsqlcache, dbcc 87
prtipage, dbcc 91
pss, dbcc 91
pssinfo() 16
ptn_data_pgs() 16
pubs2/pubs3 80
purgesqlcache, dbcc 87

Q

Query metrics 106
query plans, caching 54
query plans, settings 53, 55
query plans, sp_showplan 52
quiesce database 63
quoted_identifier, set 9, **56**
quotes (string delimiters) 9

R

radians() 19
raiserror **40**, 80
rand() 18
range partitioning 26
raw_object_serialization, set 99
read committed 45
read committed with lock (config) 44
read only (DB option) 60
read uncommitted 45
readpast 45
readtext 20
rebuild master device (buildmaster) 110
rebuild_log, dbcc 91
rebuild_text, dbcc 87
rebuild_text, sp_ 87
rebuildextents, dbcc 91
recommendations, sp_dbcc_ 85
recompile, create procedure…with 34
recompile, execute with 39
recompile, sp_ 28, **77**
reconfigure 74
recovery bypass ..... *See* bypass recovery
recovery of databases 102
references (constraint) 31
Referential Integrity Constraints 31
refreshides, dbcc 92
reindex, dbcc 87
Remote access with RPCs 94
remote server pre-read packets (conf.) 95
remote_indexes, set 99
remoteoption, sp_ 95
remotesql, sp_ 97
remove java 47
rename, sp_ 28, 32, 33, 34, 35, 36, **52**
rename_qpgroup, sp_ 106
renamedb, sp_ 60
reorg 78
repartition_degree, set 54
repeatable read 45
replicate() 13
Replication Server 108
replication, set 108
replication_role 36, **68**
Replicator, ASE 108
reportstats, sp_ 83
reserved connection 82
reserved words 51
reserved_pages() 17
reserved_pgs() 16
reservepagegap 30, **32**
Resource Governor 103
Resource limits 103
resource, dbcc 92
resource_granularity, set 54
reverse() 13
revoke (command permissions) 70
revoke (encryption) 29
revoke (object permissions) 70
revoke dbcc 70
revoke default permissions 70
revoke role **69**, 71
revoke...grant option for 70
ribo 115
right() 13
rm_appcontext() 17, **71**
role, set 69
role, sp_ **69**, 71
role_contain() **19**, 69
role_id() **19**, 69
role_name() **19**, 69
Roles 68
rollback transaction 42
rollback trigger 36, **42**
round() 18
roundrobin partitioning 27
row lock promotion HWM (config) 100
row lock promotion LWM (config) 100
row lock promotion PCT (config) 100
row_count (resource limit) 103
row_count() 17
rowcnt() 17
rowcount, set 53
row-level access control 71
row-level locking 44
RPCs 94
rtm thread idle wait period (config) 108
rtrim() 13
Rules 33
runcheck, sp_dbcc_ 86
runnable process search count(conf.) 107
runws 50

S

sa_role 68
sampling percent (config) 76
save transaction 43
save_rebuild_log, dbcc 92
scan_parallel_degree, set 81
scratch database (DB option) 60
Segments 63
select 22
select @variable 22
select into/bulkcopy/pllsort (DB option) 60
select...into 22
select...into (CIS) 97

select...into (encryption) 29
select...into existing table 22, **97**
self_recursion, set 36
semantic partitioning 26
semi-dynamic config options 6
send doneinproc tokens (config).. 88, **107**
server cursor 40
server page size 5
Server programs................................ 110
server_info, sp_ 120
serverlimits, dbcc................................ 92
serveroption, sp_ (CIS)........................ 96
serveroption, sp_ (EJB) 109
serveroption, sp_ (RPCs) 95
session authorization, set 67
set ansi_permissions 52
set ansinull 52
set arithabort arith_overflow 52
set arithabort numeric_truncation 52
set arithignore...................................... 52
set background.................................... 56
set bulk array size 98
set bulk batch size............................... 98
set chained **43**, 114
set char_convert.................................. 80
set ciphertext 29
set cis_rpc_handling...................... 94, **98**
set clientapplname 56
set clienthostname 56
set clientname 56
set close on endtran 41
set command_status_reporting 87
set cursor rows 41
set datefirst.. 12
set dateformat 12
set delayed_commit **56**, 60
set export_options 56
set fipsflagger **56**, 113
set flushmessage 56
set fmtonly.. 52
set forceplan... 53
set hash_join 53
set identity_insert 37
set identity_update 37
set index... 53
set jtc.. 54
set language... 79
set literal_autoparam 54
set lock nowait...................................... 45
set lock wait.. 45
set merge_join...................................... 53
set metrics_capture 106
set nl_join 53
set nocount... 56
set nodata 53
set noexec... 53
set option show... 55
set parallel_degree 81
set parallel_query 53
set parseonly 53
set plan dump...................................... 105
set plan exists check 105
set plan for (XML).................................. 55
set plan load 105
set plan optgoal 53
set plan opttimeoutlimit......................... 54
set plan replace 105
set prefetch 53
set proc_output_params........................ 56
set proc_return_status........................... 56
set process_limit_action 81
set proxy 67
set quoted_identifier.........................9, **56**
set raw_object_serialization 99
set remote_indexes...............................99
set repartition_degree 54
set replication.....................................108
set resource_granularity.......................54
set role..69
set rowcount 53
set scan_parallel_degree 81
set self_recursion..................................36
set session authorization.......................67
set showplan 55
set sort_merge.......................................55
set sort_resources 82
set statement_cache **54**
set statistics io 55
set statistics plancost 55
set statistics simulate 55
set statistics subquerycache 55
set statistics time...................................55
set string_rtruncation 53
set stringsize...47
set switch 93
set table count 54
set textptr_parameters **21**, 99
set textsize..20
set transaction isolation level 45
set transactional_rpc.............................98
set triggers 36
set_appcontext() 17, **71**
set_identity_burn_max, dbcc 92
set_qplan, sp_ 106
setlangalias, sp_ 79
setpglockpromote, sp_........................100
setpsexe, sp_......................................104
setrowlockpromote, sp_ 100
setsuspect_granularity, sp_ 103
setsuspect_threshold, sp_ 103
settrunc, dbcc 87
setuser...67
shared..45
Shared memory dumps.......................109
shared memory starting address(conf)108
shmdumpconfig, sp_...........................109
shmdumpsize, sp_..............................109
show switch 93
show_options, sp_ 117
show_role() **19**, 69
show_sec_services() 17
showcontrolinfo, sp_ 105
showexeclass, sp_..............................104
showplan, set..55
showplan, sp_.......................................52
showplan_in_xml() 17, **55**
showpsexe, sp_ 104
showrecovery, dbcc 92
shutdown 82
sign()...18
simulated statistics.................**55**, 77, 114
sin()..19
single user (DB option) 60
site handler RPCs 94
size of auto identity column..................38
size of global fixed heap (config)....**46**, 74
size of process object heap (conf.).**46**, 74
size of shared class heap (config)..**46**, 74
size of unilib cache (config)..................73
Small Business Edition 123
sms_shutdown 121
sms_status..121

Sort order ... 80
sort_merge, set ... 55
sort_resources, set ... 82
sorted_data ... 30
sortkey() ... 13
soundex() ... 13
sp__optdiag ... 114
sp_activeroles ... 69
sp_add_qpgroup ... 106
sp_add_resource_limit ... 103
sp_add_time_range ... 103
sp_addalias ... 67
sp_addauditrecord ... 100
sp_addaudittable ... 100
sp_addengine ... 104
sp_addexeclass ... 104
sp_addextendedproc ... 99
sp_addexternlogin ... 96
sp_addgroup ... 67
sp_addlanguage ... 79
sp_addlogin ... 65
sp_addmessage ... 79
sp_addobjectdef ... 98
sp_addremotelogin ... 95
sp_addsegment ... 64
sp_addserver ... **94**, 96
sp_addthreshold ... 64
sp_addtype ... 8
sp_addumpdevice ... 58
sp_adduser ... 67
sp_altermessage ... 79
sp_audit ... 101, 102
sp_autoconnect ... 97
sp_autoformat ... 51
sp_bindcache ... 75
sp_bindefault ... 34
sp_bindexeclass ... 104
sp_bindmsg ... **32**, 80
sp_bindrule ... 34
sp_cacheconfig ... 74, 75
sp_cachestrategy ... 75
sp_changedbowner ... 59
sp_changegroup ... 68
sp_checknames ... 80
sp_checkreswords ... 51
sp_checksource ... 27, 33, 35, 36, **51**
sp_chgattribute ... 21, **27**, 30, 37, 38, 44
sp_cleanpwdchecks ... 66
sp_clearpsexe ... 104
sp_clearstats ... 83
sp_client_addr ... 51
sp_cmp_all_qplans ... 106
sp_cmp_qplans ... 106
sp_column_privileges ... 120
sp_columns ... 120
sp_commonkey ... 120
sp_config_rep_agent ... 108
sp_configure ... 72
sp_copy_all_qplans ... 106
sp_copy_qplan ... 106
sp_countmetadata ... 73
sp_cursorinfo ... 41
sp_databases ... 120
sp_datatype_info ... 120
sp_dbcc_alterws ... 84
sp_dbcc_configreport ... 84
sp_dbcc_createws ... 84
sp_dbcc_deletedb ... 85
sp_dbcc_deletehistory ... 85
sp_dbcc_differentialreport ... 85
sp_dbcc_evaluatedb ... 85
sp_dbcc_exclusions ... 85
sp_dbcc_faultreport ... 85
sp_dbcc_fullreport ... 85
sp_dbcc_help_fault ... 85
sp_dbcc_patch_finishtime ... 85
sp_dbcc_recommendations ... 85
sp_dbcc_runcheck ... 86
sp_dbcc_statisticsreport ... 86
sp_dbcc_summaryreport ... 86
sp_dbcc_updateconfig ... 86
sp_dbextend ... 64
sp_dboption ... 59
sp_dbrecovery_order ... 102
sp_dbremap ... 87
sp_defaultloc ... 97
sp_depends ... 27, 33, 35, 36, 46, **51**
sp_deviceattr ... 58
sp_diskdefault ... 57
sp_displayaudit ... 101
sp_displaylevel ... 72
sp_displaylogin ... 65
sp_displayroles ... 69
sp_drop_all_qplans ... 106
sp_drop_qpgroup ... 106
sp_drop_qplan ... 105
sp_drop_resource_limit ... 104
sp_drop_time_range ... 103
sp_dropalias ... 68
sp_dropdevice ... 58
sp_dropengine ... 104
sp_dropexeclass ... 104
sp_dropextendedproc ... 99
sp_dropexternlogin ... 96
sp_dropglockpromote ... 100
sp_dropgroup ... 68
sp_dropkey ... 120
sp_droplanguage ... 79
sp_droplogin ... 65
sp_dropmessage ... 79
sp_dropobjectdef ... 98
sp_dropremotelogin ... 95
sp_droprowlockpromote ... 100
sp_dropsegment ... 64
sp_dropserver ... **94**, 96
sp_dropthreshold ... 64
sp_droptype ... 8
sp_dropuser ... 68
sp_dumpoptimize ... 63
sp_encryption ... 29
sp_engine ... 82
sp_estspace ... 27
sp_export_qpgroup ... 106
sp_extendsegment ... 64
sp_extengine ... 108
sp_extrapwdchecks ... 66
sp_familylock ... 44
sp_find_qplan ... 106
sp_fixindex (dbcc dbrepair) ... 89
sp_fkeys ... 120
sp_flushstats ... 77
sp_forceonline_db ... 103
sp_forceonline_object ... 103
sp_forceonline_page ... 102
sp_foreignkey ... 120
sp_fragmentation ... 83
sp_freedll ... 99
sp_getmessage ... 80
sp_help .. 8, 27, 29, 32, 33, 34, 35, 36, **51**
sp_help_qpgroup ... 106
sp_help_qplan ... 105
sp_help_rep_agent ... 108

sp_help_resource_limit.................... 104
sp_helppartition.................... 27
sp_helpcache.................... 75
sp_helpcomputedcolumn.................... 27
sp_helpconfig.................... 73
sp_helpconstraint.................... 32
sp_helpdb.................... 60
sp_helpdevice.................... 58
sp_helpextendedproc.................... 99
sp_helpexternlogin.................... 96
sp_helpgroup.................... 68
sp_helpindex.................... 30
sp_helpjava.................... 46
sp_helpjoins.................... 120
sp_helpkey.................... 120
sp_helplanguage.................... 79
sp_helplog.................... 59
sp_helpmaplogin.................... 67
sp_helpobjectdef.................... 98
sp_helpremotelogin.................... 95
sp_helprotect.................... 69, **71**
sp_helpsegment.................... 64
sp_helpserver.................... 95, 96
sp_helpsort.................... 80
sp_helptext.......27, 32, 33, 34, 35, 36, 46
sp_helpthreshold.................... 64
sp_helpuser.................... 68
sp_hidetext.................... 28, 33, 35, 36, **52**
sp_import_qpgroup.................... 106
sp_indsuspect.................... 80
sp_listener.................... 83
sp_listsuspect_db.................... 102
sp_listsuspect_object.................... 102
sp_listsuspect_page.................... 102
sp_lmconfig.................... 123
sp_lock.................... 44
sp_locklogin.................... 67
sp_logdevice.................... 59
sp_logintrigger.................... 66
sp_logiosize.................... 59
sp_makesuspect_obj.................... 103
sp_maplogin.................... 67
sp_metrics.................... 107
sp_modify_resource_limit.................... 104
sp_modify_time_range.................... 103
sp_modifylogin.................... **66**, 69, 79
sp_modifystats.................... 77
sp_modifythreshold.................... 64
sp_monitor.................... 52
sp_monitorconfig.................... 73
sp_object_stats.................... 44
sp_passthru.................... 97
sp_password.................... 65
sp_passwordpolicy.................... 65
sp_pkeys.................... 120
sp_placeobject.................... 28, 30, **64**
sp_plan_dbccdb.................... 84
sp_poolconfig.................... 75
sp_post_xpload.................... 63
sp_primarykey.................... 120
sp_procqmode.................... 35
sp_procxmode.................... **35**, 43
sp_rebuild_text.................... 87
sp_recompile.................... 28, **77**
sp_remoteoption.................... 95
sp_remotesql.................... 97
sp_rename.......28, 32, 33, 34, 35, 36, **52**
sp_rename_qpgroup.................... 106
sp_renamedb.................... 60
sp_reportstats.................... 83
sp_role.................... **69**, 71
sp_server_info.................... 120
sp_serveroption (CIS).................... 96
sp_serveroption (EJB).................... 109
sp_serveroption (RPCs).................... 95
sp_set_qplan.................... 106
sp_setlangalias.................... 79
sp_setpglockpromote.................... 100
sp_setpsexe.................... 104
sp_setrowlockpromote.................... 100
sp_setsuspect_granularity.................... 103
sp_setsuspect_threshold.................... 103
sp_shmdumpconfig.................... 109
sp_shmdumpsize.................... 109
sp_show_options.................... 117
sp_showcontrolinfo.................... 105
sp_showexeclass.................... 104
sp_showplan.................... 52
sp_showpsexe.................... 104
sp_spaceused.................... **28**, 60
sp_special_columns.................... 120
sp_sproc_columns.................... 120
sp_ssladmin.................... 83
sp_start_rep_agent.................... 108
sp_statistics.................... 120
sp_stop_rep_agent.................... 108
sp_stored_procedures.................... 120
sp_syntax.................... 52, **80**
sp_sysmon.................... 77
sp_table_privileges.................... 121
sp_tables.................... 121
sp_tempdb.................... 60
sp_thresholdaction.................... 64
sp_transactions.................... 43
sp_unbindcache.................... 75
sp_unbindcache_all.................... 75
sp_unbindexeclass.................... 104
sp_unbindmsg.................... **32**, 80
sp_unbindrule.................... 34
sp_version.................... 81
sp_volchanged.................... 63
sp_webservices.................... 50
sp_who.................... 52
space().................... 13
spaceused, sp_.................... **28**, 60
special_columns, sp_.................... 120
sproc optimize timeout limit (config).....54
sproc_columns, sp_.................... 120
SQL Advantage.................... 115
SQL debugger.................... 115
sql server clock tick length(conf.)**107**, 120
SQL.INI file.................... 110
sqladv.exe.................... 115
sqldbgr.................... 115
SQLJ.................... 46
sqlsrvr.................... 110
sqltext, dbcc.................... 92
sqlupgrade.................... 115
sqlupgraderes.................... 115
SQLX.................... 47
sqrt().................... 18
sqsh.................... 113, **124**
sqtprint, dbcc.................... 92
square().................... 18
srvbuild.................... 111
srvbuildres.................... 111
SSL certificates.................... 83
ssladmin, sp_.................... 83
sso_role.................... **68**, 101
stack guard size (config).................... 108
stack size (config).................... 108
stacktrace, dbcc.................... 92

stackused, dbcc....92
standby_access (dump tran)....62
standby_access (online database)....62
start_rep_agent, sp_....108
starting ASE (NT)....116
starting ASE (Unix)....111
startsterver....111
statement cache size (config)....54
statement_cache, set....**54**
statistics io, set....55
statistics plancost, set....55
statistics simulate, set....55
statistics subquerycache, set....55
statistics time, set....55
statistics, sp_....120
statisticsreport, sp_dbcc_....86
stop_rep_agent, sp_....108
stopping ASE (shutdown)....82
stopws....50
storage, required for datatypes....8
store_index, set....53
Stored Procedures....34
stored_procedures, sp_....120
str()....13
str_replace()....13
string delimiters (quotes)....9
String functions....12
String operators....9
string, empty....14
string_rtruncation, set....53
strings spanning multiple lines....9
stringsize, set....47
stripe on....**61**, 62
strtobin()....10
stuff()....13
subqueries....23
subquerycache, set statistics....55
substring()....14
sum()....21
summaryreport, sp_dbcc_....86
Supported DBCC commands....86
suser_id()....**19**, 66
suser_name()....**19**, 66
suspend audit when device full (conf.)100
switch, set....93
switch, show....93
SYB_BACKUP....61
syb_identity....37
SYB_IDENTITY_COL....38
syb_quit()....17
syb_sendmsg port number (config)....17
syb_sendmsg()....17
Sybase FAQ....124
sybase_ts_role....**68**, 88
sybatch....111
sybinit4ever....111
syblicenseslog....124
sybmgmtdb....108
sybmigrate....115
SybPerl....124
sybsyntax....80
sybsystemprocs....80
syconfig....111
syntax conventions....6
syntax, sp_....52, **80**
SYS_SESSION....72
syslogshold....43
sysmon, sp_....77
sysquerymetrics....106
sysqueryplans....105
sysstatistics flush interval (config)....77
System functions....14
System roles....68
systemwide password expir.(conf.) **65**, 69

T

table count, set....54
table partitioning....26
table_privileges, sp_....121
tablealloc, dbcc....88
Tables....25
tables, sp_....121
tan()....19
tcp no delay (config)....82
TCP/IP address of a client....51
tempdb, sp_....60
tempdb_id()....17, **60**
tempdb_space (resource limit)....103
Temporary databases....60
text prefetch size (config)....21
text/image functions....20
textalloc, dbcc....88
textptr()....20
textptr_parameters, set....**21**, 99
textsize, set....20
textvalid()....20
thresholdaction, sp_....64
Thresholds....64
thresholds, dbcc....92
Time & Date....10
time range....103
time slice (config)....107
time zone information....11
timeslice error....107
timestamp....**8**, 20, 119
to_unichar()....14
total data cache size (config)....74
total logical memory (config)....74
total memory (config)....74
total physical memory (config)....74
Traceflags....93
traceflags, dbcc....92
traceoff, dbcc....88
traceon, dbcc....88
tran_dumpable_status()....**17**, 62
transaction isolation level....45
transaction isolation level, set....45
transactional_rpc, set....98
Transactions....42
transactions, sp_....43
Triggers....35
triggers, set....36
Trigonometric functions....18
trunc log on chkpt (DB option)....60
truncate table....24
tsequal()....20
tune, dbcc....88
txn to pss ratio (config)....73

U

uhighsurr()....14
ulowsurr()....14
unbindcache, sp_....75
unbindcache_all, sp_....75
unbindexeclass, sp_....104
unbindmsg, sp_....**32**, 80
unbindrule, sp_....34

Undocumented commands, warning & disclaimer ... 7
union ... 24
Unions in views ... 33
unique (constraint) ... 31
unique (index) ... 30
unique auto_identity index(DB opt.) **38**, 60
unlocking a login
(or a role) with dataserver -u ... 111
'sa', with traceflag 4044 ... 94
with sp_locklogin ... 67
unlogged operations ... 121
unmount database ... 63
unsigned datatypes ... 8
Unsupported DBCC commands ... 88
update ... 24
update (cursors) ... 41
update all statistics ... 76
update index statistics ... 76
update partition statistics ... 76
update statistics ... 76
update table statistics ... 76
update where current of ... 41
update() ... 36
updateconfig, sp_dbcc_ ... 86
upgrade_object, dbcc ... 92
upper() ... 14
uscalar() ... 14
use ... 40
used_pages() ... 17
used_pgs() ... 17
usedextents, dbcc ... 92
user ... **19**, 67
user_id() ... **19**, 67
user_name() ... **19**, 67
user_stats, dbcc ... 92
User-defined roles ... 68
Users ... 67
UTC time, getutcdate() ... 11
UUID - newid() ... 18

V

valid_name() ... 17
valid_user() ... 19
variable assignment ... 22
version ID of ASE (@@version) ... 120
version, sp_ ... 81
Views ... 33
volchanged, sp_ ... 63

W

waitfor delay ... 40
waitfor errorexit ... 40
waitfor mirrorexit ... **40**, 58
waitfor processexit ... 40
waitfor time ... 40
Web Services ... **49**, 123
webservices, sp_ ... 50
webservices_role ... **50**, 68
where (clause) ... 22
who, sp_ ... 52
writetext ... 20

X

xa_bqual() ... 17
xa_gtrid() ... 17
xls, dbcc ... 92
XML ... 47
xml (select…for xml) ... 23
xmlextract() ... 47
xmlparse() ... 47
xmlrepresentation() ... 48
xmltest (predicate) ... 48
xmlvalidate() ... 48
XP Server ... 99
xp_cmdshell ... 99
xp_cmdshell context (config) ... 99
xp_deletemail ... 99
xp_enumgroups ... 99
xp_findnextmsg ... 99
xp_logevent ... 99
xp_readmail ... 99
xp_sendmail ... 99
xp_startmail ... 99
xp_stopmail ... 99
XPath ... 47, **49**
xpserver ... 111
XQL ... 49
XQuery ... 49

Y

year() ... 11

Z

zero, divide by
nullif() ... 39
traceflag 3610 ... 93
zeroes, padding with leading ... 14